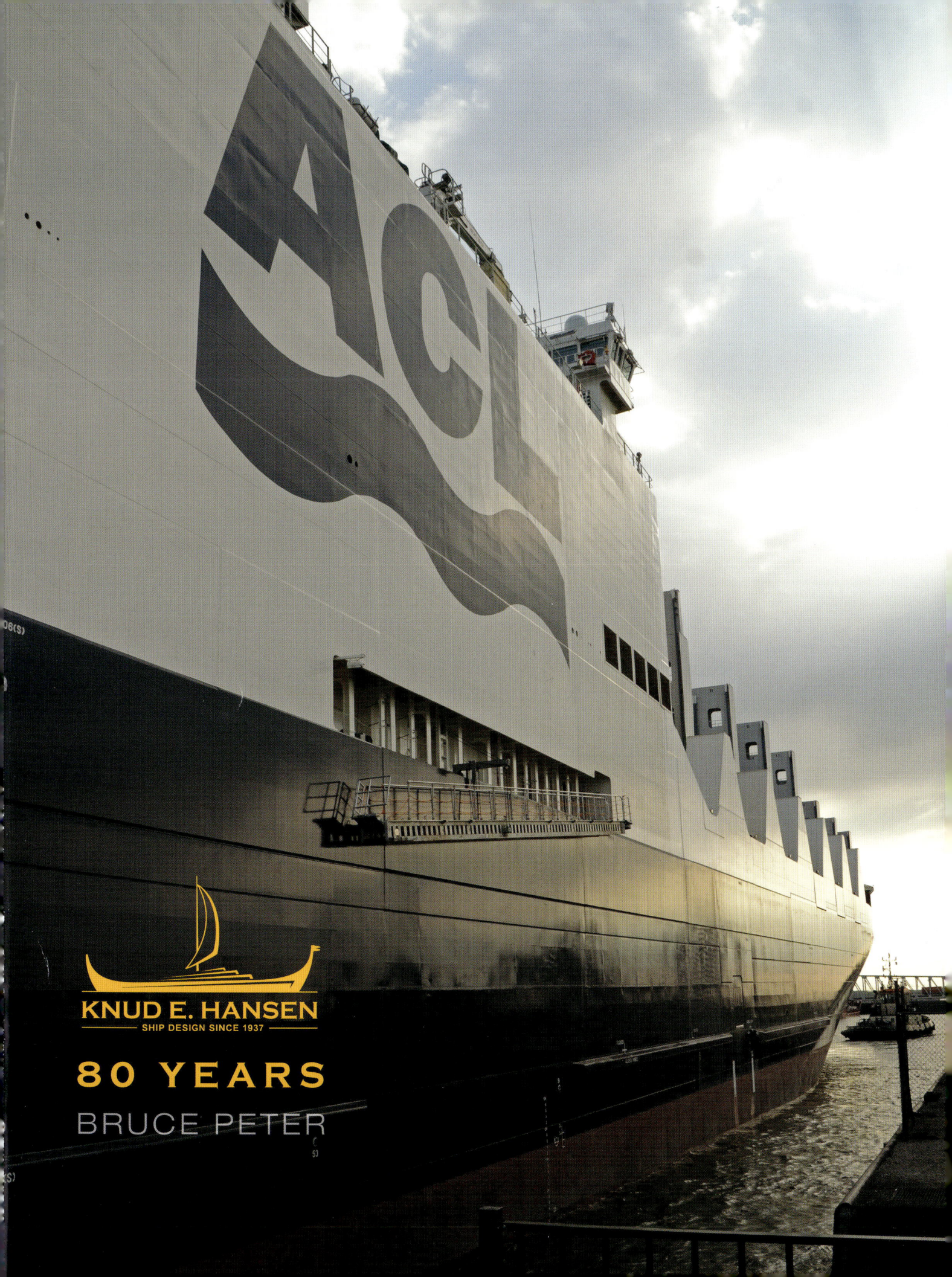

KNUD E. HANSEN
SHIP DESIGN SINCE 1937

80 YEARS
BRUCE PETER

First published in the
Isle of Man in 2017 by
Ferry Publications
PO Box 33
Ramsey
Isle of Man
IM99 4LP

Copyright © 2017 Ferry Publications. All rights reserved.

ISBN 978-1-911268-16-1

The rights of Bruce Peter to be identified as the author of this work have been asserted in accordance with the Copyright Act 1991.

No part of this publication may be reproduced, stored in a retrieval system or transmitted in any form or by any means, electronic, mechanical, photocopying, recording or otherwise, without prior permission in writing from the publisher.

Produced in the Isle of Man by Lily Publications Ltd. Ferry Publications is a trading name of Lily Publications Ltd.

contents

Foreword 5

Introduction 7

Knud E. Hansen's early career 10

Post-war rebuilding 26

The Bertelsen era 56

The Scandinavian second generation of ferries 100

The new cruise ships 116

Ro-ro freight ferries 132

Cruise ship conversions 146

The jumbo ferry era 164

The turbulent nineties 192

The Wollesen era 230

Bibliography 252

Index 254

4 KNUD E. HANSEN • 80 YEARS

Foreword

To have reached the age of eighty is a remarkable achievement – but at KNUD E. HANSEN we know that the only way ahead is to keep innovating. During the past five years, ships designed by KNUD E. HANSEN have won three ShipPax awards and, at the time of going to press, we have been shortlisted for other commendations.
While the sea can be a very hostile environment, as the situation in the past decade has demonstrated, the shipping market can be equally unforgiving of those whose vessels are insufficiently competitive. In naval architecture – just as in shipping operations – there is no room for complacency. KNUD E. HANSEN's fresh thinking permeates our organisation and is applied not only to projects commissioned by our customers but also to the many varied and imaginative concept ships our designers have produced in recent years. We have also devised a new immersive virtual reality tool, known as 'ShipSpace', enabling our clients to experience our unbuilt designs from within.
Shipping always has been a global business and, nowadays, thanks to instant digital communication, that is even more so the case. Design drawings can be produces in any of our offices around the world and sent instantly to shipping companies for approval and to shipyards, enabling steel to be cut and blocks to be fabricated with unprecedented speed. Such technologies are only as good as the people operating them, however, and, as Managing Director, I feel especially proud of our approximately eighty talented employees, recruited from around the world; their expertise and dedication reflect the true spirit of KNUD E. HANSEN.
I would also like to express my thanks to Bruce Peter for continuing his enthusiastic interest in our design work and for assembling this book; I am also grateful to Miles Cowsill of Ferry Publications for producing it. Above all, I wish to thank our many clients around the world who have sustained our company over its long existence; without them, there would be no KNUD E. HANSEN.
I hope you will enjoy this book which records a great adventure on ship design, spanning eighty turbulent years.

Finn Wollesen Petersen
Managing Director
KNUD E. HANSEN
Helsingør
October 2017

6 KNUD E. HANSEN A/S • 75 YEARS OF SHIP DESIGN

Introduction

On 1 November 1937, a 37-year-old Danish naval architect called Knud E. Hansen gave up his job in the drawing office of the Helsingør Jernskibs og Maskinbyggeri shipyard to establish his own ship design consultancy. In the 80 years since then, the company he founded, Knud E. Hansen A/S (nowadays known as KNUD E. HANSEN), has become famed throughout the global shipping community for its innovative and prolific output of vessels of all sizes and types. In the past five years it has, among other projects, designed and supervised: the construction in China of five very large and highly complex container/roll-on, roll-off (con-ro) ships for Atlantic Container Line's trans-Atlantic service; six large con-ros built in South Korea for the National Shipping Company of Saudi Arabia (now known as BAHRI); two ice-strengthened passenger and car ferries built in Romania to serve Fogo and Change Island in Labrador in Canada; a cruise ferry built in China for Chinese domestic service; an ice-strengthed bitumen tanker built in Turkey for the Canadian Great Lakes; four very large roll-on, roll-off freight ferries built in China for North Sea and Baltic routes; a sophisticated icebreaker and research ship built in Romania for the Australian government's use in Antarctica; two conversions of container ships into a high-capacity livestock carriers in Batam in Indonesia, Poland and Denmark for operation between Australia and Indonesia; two superyachts with low energy consumption built in the Netherlands for private owners in Denmark and a conversion of a Portuguese ferry into a cruise ship in Norway for coastal service on the Norwegian West Coast and to Spitzbergen. Numerous Heating, Ventilation and Air Conditioning (HVAC) installations have also been designed and installed on cruise ships and naval vessels as well as on other types of tonnage and, in addition, a wide diversity of innovative concept ships have been proposed, ranging from roll-on, roll-off refrigerated food carriers to expedition cruise vessels.

In 2010, KNUD E. HANSEN opened a new office in Fort Lauderdale in the USA, primarily to serve the Caribbean cruise industry, handling major refit projects for all of the major cruise operators. The company is now truly 'globalised', employing more than 80 people in seven offices around the world (two in Denmark and one each in the UK, Australia, Greece, the Faroe Islands and the USA). To enable information and design work to be shared between them, major investments have been made in state-of-the-art information technology and in CFD and 3D capabilities.

KNUD E. HANSEN is perpetuating a great tradition of advanced ship design, dating back to the Victorian era. The company's founder was born and grew up in an era dominated by steam power yet, in Denmark's smaller provincial harbours, sailing ships were still commonplace. In 1912, the first diesel ship for deep sea service appeared – the Danish-designed, built and owned *Selandia*, completed by Burmeister & Wain in 1912 for the East Asiatic Company's Copenhagen–Bangkok route. By the early 1930s, motor ship development had progressed considerably and it was possible to achieve remarkable power outputs from the latest compact two-stroke double-acting engines. The design of merchant ships progressed equally in terms of layout, construction, servicing, safety and style. Whereas in the twentieth century's first years a sea voyage was often to be dreaded, by the thirties, taking a ship had become a glamorous thing to aspire to, the grimness of 'the steerage' having been replaced by the relative comfort of Tourist Class. In this period, verticality, which had dominated ship aesthetics from the days of sail and early steam, was replaced by the horizontal expression of the latest generation of motor ship, with short, broad funnels, rounded stems and curving forward superstructures.

Hansen would have been keenly aware of these developments, doubtless firing his own passion for ship design. Naval architecture has continued to progress in leaps and bounds since his lifetime, but the invisibility of modern ships behind vast secured compounds in out-of-town ports, coupled with the nostalgia and conservatism of many amateur observers of the shipping scene, means that they are often misunderstood, if they are appreciated at all. Notwithstanding the vital roles of modern merchant ships in our contemporary world of mass production, globally distributed value chains, consumerism and leisure, so far as most of the general public is concerned, ship design remains mysterious. Those who experience a ferry crossing or a cruise holiday probably have no conception of why the vessel they are on board looks and feels the way it does. In contrast, during recent decades, architects and product designers working on *terra firma* have become well-known celebrities with high media profiles and most informed cultural observers recognise their names and key works. Naval architects, in contrast, work discreetly and so are not widely recognised for their important contribution to the creation of integrated seaborne transport logistics and leisure systems which stretch throughout the world's sea lanes. Yet, naval architecture is a long-established profession, tracing its origins to the ancient Phoenician and Greek civilisations and the design of the ships they used for their explorations and conquests throughout the known world of their times. There have been sea-going vessels ever since and so the skills of the modern naval architect have evolved with a healthy respect for the past.

The oceans, which cover 70% of the surface of our world, are incomprehensibly vast and hostile expanses which are persistent and unchangeable. For architects and designers working ashore, water is an irritation to be repelled, or a decorative substance to be played with, but for a ship it is the life element. The ocean offers naval architects a stormy challenge and each vessel must be methodically designed and constructed to survive it. Beneath their smooth skins of neatly welded shell plating, modern merchant ships are intensely complex mechanical organisms with circulatory systems of plumbing, lighting, smoke detectors, oil pipes, air conditioning and waste disposal systems, all activated by an immensely powerful group of mighty engines. Designed to expand, contract and flex in a controlled manner, ships represent structure at its most alive and animated.

The story of modern shipping is of technology, visible and invisible, going to sea. Ships blur the distinction between what has traditionally been thought of as architectural – permanent structures, enshrined and located – and the engineered, glimpsed in motion, passing at speed. Notwithstanding their complexity and scale, ships are also transient structures, built to move and work efficiently; those that avoid natural disasters are inevitably scrapped and recycled, or, as we shall see, occasionally radically rebuilt to fit new roles. Such considerations bear upon our understanding of modern naval architecture in wider contexts.

So what, then, does a naval architecture consultancy, such as KNUD E. HANSEN actually do and why is its work so vital to the design of modern merchant ships?

Traditionally, any ship owner or entrepreneur wishing to acquire new tonnage would typically have invited bids from a range of shipyards capable of building it, with each yard's drawing office submitting a design based on its own interpretation of the owner's wishes. The larger and longer-established lines had their own technical departments to carry out much of this work and some even owned shipbuilding subsidiaries. For smaller companies, however, the final selection was inevitably a compromise between the quality and appropriateness of the design submissions and their respective costs. As Knud E. Hansen's consultancy was, in contrast, independent, it could work closely with each ship owner to develop designs precisely tailored to their needs, before going out to tender for construction. Hansen thereby found a lucrative niche which greatly benefited emergent shipping companies and often gave their ships a vital competitive advantage.

Every modern sea-going vessel begins as a concept derived from a requirement to carry a given amount of cargo or a particular number of passengers from one place to another. A speed must be determined, based on the number of voyages to be made over a day, week, month or year or the optimal number of days for particular demographics of holidaymakers taking cruises. How often the vessel will be bunkered and provisioned, and the navigating constraints of the waterways and harbours to be used are other issues to be resolved during the earliest planning stages.

A project's development will be based upon a finely balanced mix of existing knowledge and careful predictions of future conditions – after all, every ship represents a considerable financial risk and may take years to design and build. While there may be some image in the owner's mind, for the consultant naval architect, a ship starts as a featureless block so that preconceptions do not cloud finding the most effective design solution. Experience and precedent will determine its overall dimensions, based on carrying capacity, speed and the size of ports of call. Only after these primary concerns have been defined and clearly laid out in the design brief can anyone start to

Managing Director, Finn Wollesen, and two of his colleagues, Niels Georg Larsen and Christian G. Damsgaard, discuss the details of a general arrangement drawing in the KEH offices in Helsingør. (Philippe Holthof)

consider the details of what the ship will actually look like when built and how it will be laid out internally.

The cargo holds, trailer decks, passenger accommodation, machinery spaces, auxiliary services, fuel and ballast tanks, crew accommodation, stores areas, safety equipment such as lifeboats, deck areas and deck machinery all make up what is collectively known as the general arrangement or GA drawing. This, along with the lines plan and transverse sectional drawings, provide the 'recipe' for building a ship and therefore form the centrepiece of the design output of the consulting naval architect. Usually, the detailed construction drawings which show how individual aspects will be built are the responsibility of the shipyard, but the consultant naval architect will often be retained by a ship owner to supervise the translation of the GA into the building process through the production of steel fabrication drawings and other details. Depending on the level of experience and competence of the shipyard, sometimes consultant naval architects will be involved until the ship has been completed, tested, accepted and delivered.

Apart from the conceptualisation of new ships, the role of naval architecture is to apply the science and technology of ship design so that the vessel remains secure and upright and the spaces inside it stay dry, safe and comfortable. In designing the hull lines, the principles of hydrodynamics are applied to minimise resistance and drag. The aim is to achieve a satisfactory compromise between the optimum sea-keeping characteristics and the restrictions of size, payload and fuel economy. Detailed stability calculations are needed, and the international safety regulations and conventions governing shipping must be interpreted and applied for the ship to be registered by the classification societies. The design of a ship must take into account its precise performance when damaged by fire, collision or other mishap, such as sinking. The naval architect's work includes detailed planning to meet specific criteria for the ship's safe and timely evacuation. The sea can be harsh and the marine environment needs to be treated with respect. This means designing ships with significant safety margins while also minimising their environmental impact – and KNUD E. HANSEN's staff are highly attentive to these concerns.

On the one hand, as design briefs have become more complex due to increasing specialisation and ever more demanding regulatory frameworks – for example, governing energy efficiency and the need for passenger vessels to be capable of safely to return to port in the event of accidents – the development of new ships has become commensurately more involved and often highly collaborative. On the other hand, up-to-date computer software for carrying out finite element analysis of steel and aluminium structures and the optimisation of hull lines has transformed practices and enabled great leaps forward in efficiency and predictive accuracy to be achieved. Nowadays, it is quite commonplace for different naval architecture firms to be involved in developing a new ship design – one producing an outline concept (the so-called 'initial design'), another producing the resolved 'basic design' and a third carrying out independent verification or working on behalf of the shipyard to further develop the concept and oversee construction. While the necessary design documentation can nowadays be sent around the world at the touch of a button, senior naval architects still spend a lot of their time visiting shipyards where construction and conversions are taking place, their informal office wear of tea-shirts and jeans, or business suits for formal meetings, replaced by the boiler suits and hard-hats of the shop floor.

A small part of the vast KNUD E. HANSEN archive, housed in the company's basement and stretching from the present back to the 1930s.
(Bruce Peter)

Today, many of the large ships designed by KNUD E. HANSEN are built in China – a country whose shipbuilding sector dates mainly from the 1990s and since but which has in a very short time built up world-beating steel fabrication skills. KNUD E. HANSEN – and many other firms in the large and successful Danish Maritime Cluster – contribute their advanced knowledge and specialist skills, which underpin and complement Chinese productivity. Today, ship design and shipbuilding are truly international and cosmopolitan enterprises. The naval architect is, in fact, a key team player in the design process, along with a brace of engineers, other design consultants dealing with interiors and onboard servicing, and the owner's and builder's own technical departments. With many of these additional services available 'in-house', KNUD E. HANSEN can provide a 'one-stop shop' for even the most demanding of ship owners.

Since 1937, KNUD E. HANSEN has designed vessels of all kinds. Indeed, to look through the company's vast archive of general arrangement drawings and design details, which stretches back the full 80 years of its existence, is to see the cutting edge of ship design development during more than half a century. The author and publisher wish KNUD E. HANSEN every success in the future and we hope that readers will enjoy this overview of 80 years of ship design, 'made in Denmark'.

Bruce Peter
Glasgow – September 2017

Knud E. Hansen's early career

KNUD E. HANSEN • 80 YEARS **11**

With the sailing ship *Statsraad Lehmkuhl* in the foreground, the recently introduced *Venus* leaves Bergen on one of her regular North Sea crossings to Newcastle. (Bruce Peter collection)

A stern-quarter view of the *Venus* at her berth in Bergen, showing her cruiser stern, a form which Hansen favoured for hull aft-bodies. (Bruce Peter collection)

Knud E. Hansen in the late-1930s at around the time of the establishment of Knud E. Hansen A/S. (KNUD E. HANSEN Archive)

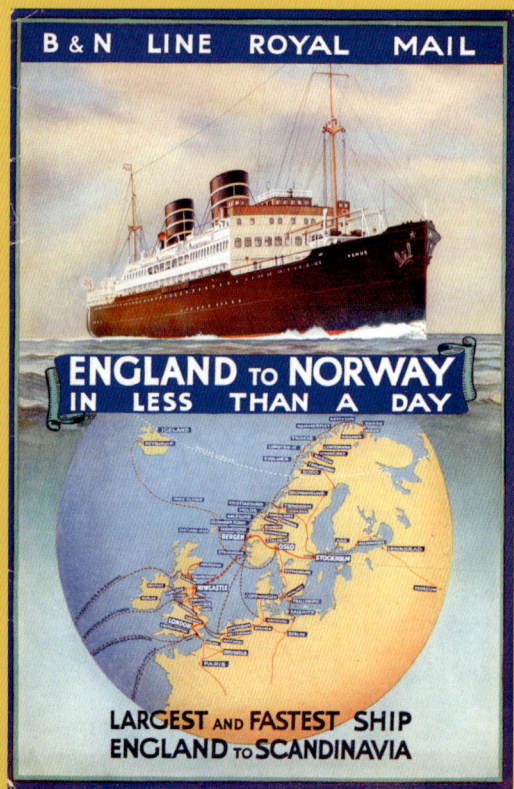

The cover from an early-1930s brochure, promoting the service by the *Venus* between Newcastle, Stavanger and Bergen; as was typical of such imagery, the size of the funnels has been greatly exaggerated. (Bruce Peter collection)

The newly-completed *Venus* is seen off Helsingør during her builder's trials. (Bruce Peter collection)

Knud Emil Thorvald Henning Hansen was, by all accounts, an energetic and refined gentleman with an inquisitive mind. Born in Espergærde, near Helsingør, in 1900, he was the son of Eduard Hansen, a skipper of coastal sailing ships, and so the sea was in his blood from the outset. Hansen junior studied naval architecture at the Polyteknisk Læreanstalt in Copenhagen (nowadays Danmark's Tekniske Universitet or DTU). Upon graduation in 1925, he gained experience in shipbuilding by working in a number of yards in Denmark and abroad, initially at Københavns Flydedok & Skibsværft. Thereafter, he travelled to Britain – at that time widely regarded as being the world's leading shipbuilding nation with the largest merchant fleet – and to the Netherlands to find out about ship design practices in these countries. From 1927 until 1929, he worked in the drawing office of Burmeister & Wain, the famous Copenhagen shipyard and marine engine builder, before he joined the staff of the Helsingør Jernskibs og Maskinbyggeri, where he remained until 1937.

Since boyhood, Hansen had been particularly interested in traditional Nordic craft – such as Baltic schooners, fishing cutters and Viking longships – and he thought that their designs embodied lessons for latter day naval architects. One of his beliefs was that beauty and utility were inextricably connected, as demonstrated by Scandinavian vernacular ship types that had withstood the test of time; this position was in line with the era's emerging modernist belief system, which emphasised rationality in many areas of cultural production, not least architecture and engineering ashore. Indeed, for would-be modernists, passenger ships appeared to embody an ideal type-form for human habitation and the largest and most glamorous-looking examples were held as icons of human ingenuity in the conquest of nature. For Hansen, naval architecture was not simply an engineering discipline but, rather, to design a ship was to take part in the furtherance of a Nordic cultural inheritance dating back many centuries. This position relates to an inter-war Scandinavian conception of there being a 'functional tradition' in design, an idea propounded in particular by the architect Kay Fisker, who, as Professor of Architecture at the Royal Academy, was regarded as being a 'father figure' of Sanish modernism and who subsequently became a friend and colleague of Hansen's. Reflecting this stance, the Knud E. Hansen A/S logo was (and remains) a Viking longship.

On being appointed to the Helsingør Jernskibs og Maskinbyggeri, the first significant passenger ship design in which Knud E. Hansen was involved was the Det Bergenske Dampskipsselskap's *Venus*, a sturdy 6,269 gt motor ship intended for North Sea service between Bergen and Newcastle. Upon completion in 1931, she was the largest passenger vessel trading on the North Sea and her two Burmeister & Wain diesels gave her a service speed of 19 knots. With intense competition from Fred. Olsen Line's Oslo and Kristiansand to Newcastle route, speed was very important and the *Venus* was one of the fastest motor ships of her era. Her performance reduced the passage time from 27 hours to 21 hours. The text in an inaugural brochure reflects the forward-looking characteristics of the Venus' design:

'From a naval architect's standpoint, the new ship is remarkable, inasmuch as she embodies a

The excursion ship *Sankt Ibb* at Mölle, dressed with signal flags. (Anders Bergenek collection)

series of progressive improvements. The dimensions of the hull, combined with the large quantity of water ballast will, it is claimed, ensure easy movement when at sea. The double bottom is exceptionally strong, being carried unusually high. The life-saving equipment is the latest in efficiency. All the lifeboats are lowered by 'Welin' davits. The ventilation and heating of the cabins and public rooms is by the low-pressure system of Thermotanks, which ensures silent working. Punkah Louvres, fitted in each cabin, can be regulated by the passenger, for the desired volume of fresh air, cold or warm.'

While the *Venus* enjoyed a lengthy and distinguished career which lasted until the latter 1960s, unfortunately, she became notorious for her rolling motion; possibly, this resulted from her hull being rather fine-lined in the interest of maintaining a high service speed – and this led to her gaining the unattractive epithet of 'Vomiting Venus.' Fortunately for passengers, since the 1930s, a great deal of research has been carried out into ships' hydrodynamics and motion, not least by the naval architects of Knud E. Hansen A/S, and so subsequent generations have become increasingly stable.

Almost from the outset of his career, Knud E. Hansen was involved in short-sea ferry design. As we shall see, this specialised area of naval architectural practice subsequently became a very important and lucrative aspect of Knud E. Hansen A/S's activities. When Hansen designed his first ferries in the mid-1930s, the genre already had a fairly lengthy heritage, dating back to the mid-nineteenth century. In 1850, the Edinburgh, Perth and Dundee Railway introduced the *Leviathan*, the first roll-on, roll-off train ferry, which traversed the River Forth between Granton, near Edinburgh, and Burntisland (the Forth Railway Bridge had yet to be constructed). These provided the inspiration for early Danish train ferry designs. Essentially, they were paddle-propelled barges with tracks built into a flat train deck and their navigation bridges above amidships. Although these vessels appeared to be double-ended, their paddles actually worked much more effectively ahead than astern.

A 'second generation' of Danish rail ferry was introduced in the early twentieth century with screw propellers, rather than paddles, and much more substantial superstructures filling the entire hull width above their train decks. Thus, they first introduced the typical general arrangement and aesthetic elements of the modern Scandinavian ferry. This approach was perpetuated into the 1930s and, by then, several of the larger examples for the important Nyborg–Korsør crossing were built in Helsingør – for example, the *Korsør* (1927), *Nyborg* (1931) and *Sjælland* (1933). However, much of the design work was carried out at the Orlogsværftet (the Danish Naval Shipyard). In the Helsingør yard's Drawing Office, Knud E. Hansen was involved in translating the general arrangements into detailed construction drawings – and, in so doing, he learned a great deal about designing ferries.

Hansen was a prodigious worker who even began to take on private commissions to design vessels on a freelance basis outwith office hours. His first such project was in 1935, when he produced plans for a small excursion motor vessel, the 527 grt *Sankt Ibb*, which was built at

Two DSB ferries of different vintages cross the Great Belt in this mid-1960s scene; in the foreground is the 1939-built train ferry *Storebælt* and behind is the then-new car ferry *Arveprins Knud*. Through his work at Helsingør Jernskibs- og Maskinbyggeri, Knud E. Hansen learned a great deal about ferry design. The vessels pictured show the development of the streamlining of superstructures and funnels in the 1930s-60s period, aesthetic developments of which Knud E. Hansen was at the forefront. (Bruce Peter collection)

Above: The car and train ferry *Freia* crosses the Great belt in the latter-1930s. (Bruce Peter collection)
Below: The *Freia* is seen leaving Korsør. (Bruce Peter collection)

The innovative Larvik-Frederikshavn car ferry *Peter Wessel* is seen dressed overall for delivery in the Limfjord at Aalborg and is also viewed at sea from the stern quarter, showing the arrangement of her aft car deck access. (Bruce Peter collection)

16 KNUD E. HANSEN • 80 YEARS

The *Kronprins Olav* is seen nearing completion at Helsingør in 1937; note her curved and slanted forward superstructure with the funnel shaped to match – the height of 1930s modernity and elegance. (Museet for Søfart)

Below: The *Kronprins Olav*'s forward hold had side-hatches so that cars could be driven directly on board. Within, there was an elevator, allowing them to be moved from deck to deck for stowage. (Bruce Peter collection)

Right and below: The vessel's interiors, designed by Kay Fisker, were widely praised for their sense of spaciousness and well-resolved details; here we see the First Class dining saloon, the hallway (with Poul Henningsen wall lights) and a group of chairs in the First Class smoking saloon.
(Bruce Peter collection)

Frederikshavn Værft & Flydedok A/S for the Dampskibsselskabet Øresund's passenger-only service across the Øresund between Copenhagen, Helsingborg and Mölle in Sweden.

The first Danish car ferries

In Denmark, ferry traffic was dominated by railway-owned vessels dedicated to carrying trains, much to the growing frustration of the gradually increasing numbers of motorists. When various private entrepreneurs began introducing car ferries – and even ones able to transport commercial road vehicles – DSB belatedly came to the realisation that road traffic should be accommodated after all. The most acceptable solution from their perspective was to build a new multi-purpose Great Belt ferry, able to carry both road and rail vehicles, even if the train capacity was largely symbolic. Although DSB usually built their ferries in Helsingør, due to a lack of capacity there, the project was subcontracted to Aalborg Maskin- og Skibsbyggeri.

The 997 gt *Freia*'s design was a joint effort by DSB's own technical staff and the drawing offices at the Helsingør and Aalborg shipyards. In the Helsingør office, Knud E. Hansen was given overall responsibility for coordinating the design work. The vessel's hull form was typical of DSB train ferries, rather than other operators' car ferry designs as it tapered inwards from one-third forward and one-third aft in order to fit DSB's port facilities. Typically, DSB ferry berths had V-shaped inlets and the ships' hulls were formed to sail into these with a snug fit. This solution dated from an earlier era when vessels tended to be less manoeuvrable and from a mindset geared to railway, rather than car, traffic (obviously, cars can turn to be parked much more tightly than railway vehicles, which often have long overhangs at each end).

The *Freia*'s vehicle deck, accommodating 55 cars, was arranged on the drive-through principle, meaning that a lifting bow visor was installed as well as folding doors in the bow quarters for use when operating as a relief vessel between Århus and Kalundborg. At the upper level, wide casings containing sitting saloons flanked a double-height space along the centreline. There, a single railway track was installed so that a three-coach diesel 'Lyntog' express train could be loaded via the stern. To protect against fire, the vehicle deck was fitted with a sprinkler system, split into 14 loops, each of which would activate separately in the event of cars igniting below. Installations of this kind became standard features of most subsequent ro-ro ferries, representing a major safety enhancement.

Having been launched in Aalborg, the *Freia* was then towed to Helsingør to be fitted out prior to being introduced between Nyborg and Korsør in 1936. Thereafter, she went on to enjoy a very long and lucrative career in the DSB fleet, serving on a variety of Danish domestic routes. Indeed, little altered, she continued in DSB service until 1975. She then passed to Italian owners to operate across the Bay of Naples as the *Ischia Express*, only being withdrawn in 2007 by which time her hull was over 70 years old.

Meanwhile, attention turned to the establishment of an international ferry route from Denmark to

The little passenger and car ferry *Nordbornholm* was another product of Aalborg Værft. (Museet for Søfart)

A stern-quarter view of the *Nordbornholm*. (Museet for Søfart)

Norway. To achieve this aim, various Danish and Norwegian bus-operators formed a consortium, Larvik-Frederikshavnferjen A/S to begin a ferry route from Frederikshavn to Larvik, a small port near to the mouth of the Oslofjord.

Given Knud E. Hansen's recent involvement in ferry design at Helsingør and his obvious great interest in the type, he was asked personally to design the new Larvik–Frederikshavn ferry, working on a freelance basis. This meant that the task was carried out during evenings and weekends. The new ferry, measuring 1,415 gt and named the *Peter Wessel*, was ordered from Aalborg Maskin- og Skibsbyggeri, building on the yard's expertise from the *Freia* project.

The *Peter Wessel* was, however, more than twice as big – indeed, she was the largest car ferry yet seen. On board, there was accommodation for 60 cars and 500 passengers, including 141 berthed in cabins, mainly squeezed in below the car deck forward and aft of the engine room. In addition, there were a small number of superior cabins on boat deck. Powered by two Atlas-Polar diesels, she was capable of 16 knots. A casing – containing machinery, pipework and stairways – ran along her centreline, splitting the vehicle deck into two areas. Above, her passenger accommodation consisted of a smoking saloon and cocktail bar forward, and a dining saloon with a buffet counter aft of amidships where passengers would be slightly less likely to feel sea motion.

For open-sea service, the *Peter Wessel*'s bow had a more pronounced rake than the *Freia*, and this meant that the bow visor was also required to have flare, rather than flat sides, as used on existing drive-through ferries. The configuration of her hull – and those of subsequent ferries designed by Knud E. Hansen – featured a knuckle joint at vehicle deck height. Although this was less pronounced than on examples for use in sheltered waters, the solution showed the need to compromise between fine

The Grenaa-Hundested ferry *Marsk Stig*. (Bruce Peter collection)

The refrigerated cargo ship *Australian Reefer*. (Museet for Søfart)

The J. Lauritzen-owned refrigerated cargo vessel *American Reefer* is seen undergoing builder's trials. (Museet for Søfart)

Right: The launch of the J. Lauritzen cargo liner *Nora* at Aalborg Værft on 14 October 1939. (Museet for Søfart)

The *Argentinean Reefer*. (Museet for Søfart)

The cargo steamer *Angamos*, ordered by the Chilean Government, is seen during wartime lay-up with neutrality markings painted on her hull. Finally, she was handed over to her owner after Germany's surrender. (Museet for Søfart)

The *Nora* at anchor with wartime neutrality markings painted on her hull topsides. (Museet for Søfart)

lines at water level and a relatively broad and regular vehicle deck above to optimise capacity. Such designs were very effective in relatively calm conditions but, above a certain wave height, the knuckle joint tended to cause 'slamming' motion. The vehicle deck's aft end was enclosed by a set of watertight folding doors, located beneath the rear of her superstructure, ensuring complete protection from following seas. In this respect, she established the preferred Scandinavian means of avoiding free surface effect – whereby water sloshing around on the deck's surface causes a rapid loss of stability – through total enclosure of the garage space. To remove small amounts, drains with non-return valves, known as scuppers, were fitted, piping the water overboard above the load waterline. In contrast, on British Channel ferries of the same era, partially-open stern designs were used in conjunction with freeing ports, cut into the shell plating immediately above the belting to drain excess water away. Each solution had advantages and disadvantages. In the event of flooding through collision or hatches breaking open, ferries without freeing ports were liable quickly to become unstable, whereas in rough weather, freeing ports could also let water in and this too was potentially dangerous.

The *Peter Wessel*'s drive-through ability and her opening bow visor enabled very rapid loading and discharge of cars, but, for safety reasons, these features also made her only suitable for use in summer conditions when the sea was relatively calm. Consequently, she operated between late-May and mid-September, which was, in any event, the period during which there was the most vehicle traffic. (At that time, car ownership in Denmark stood at just under 100,000.) The remainder of the year, she was laid up. Economically, she was not a success in pre-war days and in the late-1930s attempts were made to sell her. When Germany's invaded Denmark and Norway in April 1940, she was seized for military usage but survived largely unscathed to re-enter civilian service and find great success in the post-war era when car ownership grew greatly.

Back in 1936, when Hansen was designing the *Peter Wessel* during his evenings and travelling regularly to Aalborg at weekends during her construction phase, during weekdays in the Helsingør drawing office, he was entrusted with leading the design process for what was to be Denmark's most prestigious passenger ship to operate DFDS's overnight service between Copenhagen and Oslo.

In the mid-1930s, modern Danish architecture and interior design began to attract international admiration and so DFDS' forward-thinking technical director, J.A. Kørbing, resolved that their new ship should be a floating showcase for the latest technical and aesthetic developments. They did not have to look far for design inspiration as, in June 1936, the Dampskibs-Selskabet paa Bornholm af 1866 (popularly known as the '66' Company), which traded between Copenhagen and the island of Bornholm in the Southern Baltic, had taken delivery from Burmeister & Wain of a new passenger motor ship, the 1,726 gt *Hammershus*. Dissatisfied with B&W's own interior design proposals, one of the '66' Company's directors, Thorkil Lund, had contacted the progressive Copenhagen-based architect and academic Kay Fisker for assistance. Although the vessel was only small, she provoked considerable interest on account of the strikingly modern interiors Fisker designed. Indeed, the Copenhagen newspapers hailed her as being 'a proper little *Queen Mary*'.

For DFDS' *Kronprins Olav* project, Hansen and Fisker collaborated to produce an impressively coherent design solution. Delivered in December 1937, the 3,038 grt vessel not only appeared strikingly modern – having a curved stem, a high forecastle, semi-circular forward superstructure, a broad, tapering funnel and a sharply raked cruiser stern, which together created a sense of urgent forward movement – but also was technically advanced. Her twin 7-cylinder B&W diesels gave an 18.5-knot service speed, the fastest in the DFDS fleet. Inboard, Fisker emphasised her curved superstructure in the First Class smoking saloon's furniture and lighting arrangement. In each class, the saloons were separated by plate glass doors and, thanks to their lightness and avoidance of clutter, they gave an impression of being far more spacious than was the case.

To load cars, the *Kronprins Olav*'s bow quarters had side hatches and, inboard, a hydraulic elevator was fitted so that some could be parked the deck above. A sprinkler system was installed in the deckheads to deal with fires resulting from petrol spillage. Although commercial vehicles could not be carried, the arrangement was much more resilient than the drive-through solution used on the *Peter Wessel*. Over time, however, the design of vehicle deck access equipment improved meaning that bow- and stern-loading eventually became favoured over side-loading.

In service, the *Kronprins Olav* was a great success, nearly doubling the Copenhagen–Oslo route's profitability. Passengers and architectural critics alike acclaimed her elegance and modernity, leading a prominent Norwegian ship owner, Knut Knutsen, to propose building a sister ship to enable the Copenhagen–Oslo route to offer daily departures, while also breaking DFDS' monopoly. Although Knutsen's idea received political support in Norway, the unstable political situation in Europe ensured that nothing came of it, much to DFDS' relief.

Once the *Kronprins Olav* project was completed, in November 1937, Knud E. Hansen resigned from the Helsingør shipyard to found his own naval architecture consultancy, Knud E. Hansen A/S, initially

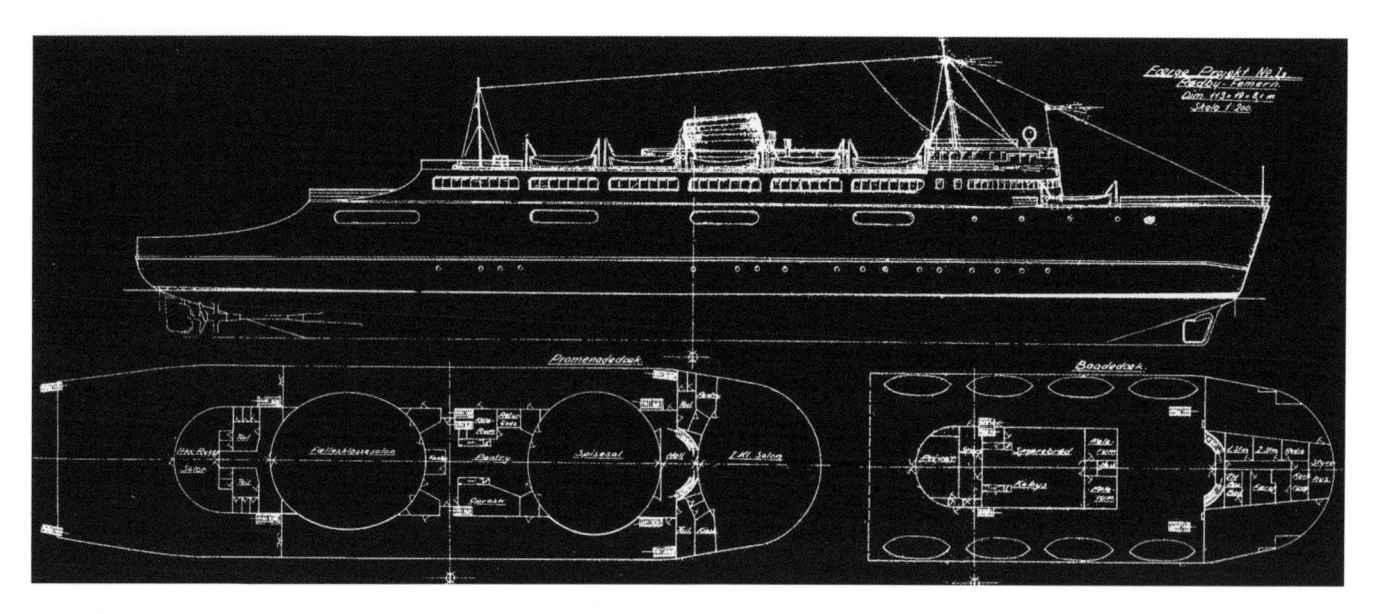

A 1942 proposal by Knud E. Hansen for a new DSB train ferry for a projected service between Rødby and Femern, labelled 'Project no. 1.1'.
(Bruce Peter collection)

employing three assistants. His unique expertise in designing car-carrying short-sea ferries and passenger ships meant that his services increasingly came to be in considerable demand during the latter 1930s. Not only was his design output held in high esteem, but also, as he had an equal knowledge of Scandinavian historic ship types, he was retained as a consultant by the Danish National Maritime Museum at Kronborg Castle.

Hansen subsequently collaborated with the Helsingør drawing office to produce designs for a new Great Belt train ferry for DSB, the 2,941 gt *Storebælt*, which was delivered in 1939. Her design was similar to the ferries built for DSB during his earlier tenure there. Thereafter, he provided designs for a pair of small Aalborg-built passenger and cargo motor ships, the *Nordbornholm* and the *Østbornholm*, for the Østbornholm Dampskibsselskab. Compact vessels of short length relative to their breadth and height, they too entered service in 1939. As on the *Kronprins Olav*, cars were side-loaded through hatches in the shell plating.

Hansen's next ferry project was another drive-through vessel, the 1,217 gt *Marsk Stig*, for Grenaa-Hundested Færgefart, a successful Danish domestic ferry operator. In many respects similar to the *Peter Wessel*, she too was built in Aalborg but, upon delivery in May 1940 she was laid up on account of Denmark's recent invasion by Germany.

Cargo ship designs

In addition to ferries, Hansen produced innovative designs for a range of freight vessel types. Among his early clients were the Copenhagen-based ship owners, Ivar and Knud Lauritzen, of J. Lauritzen, a rapidly-expanding shipping company which in 1938 purchased the Aalborg Maskin- og Skibsbyggeri,

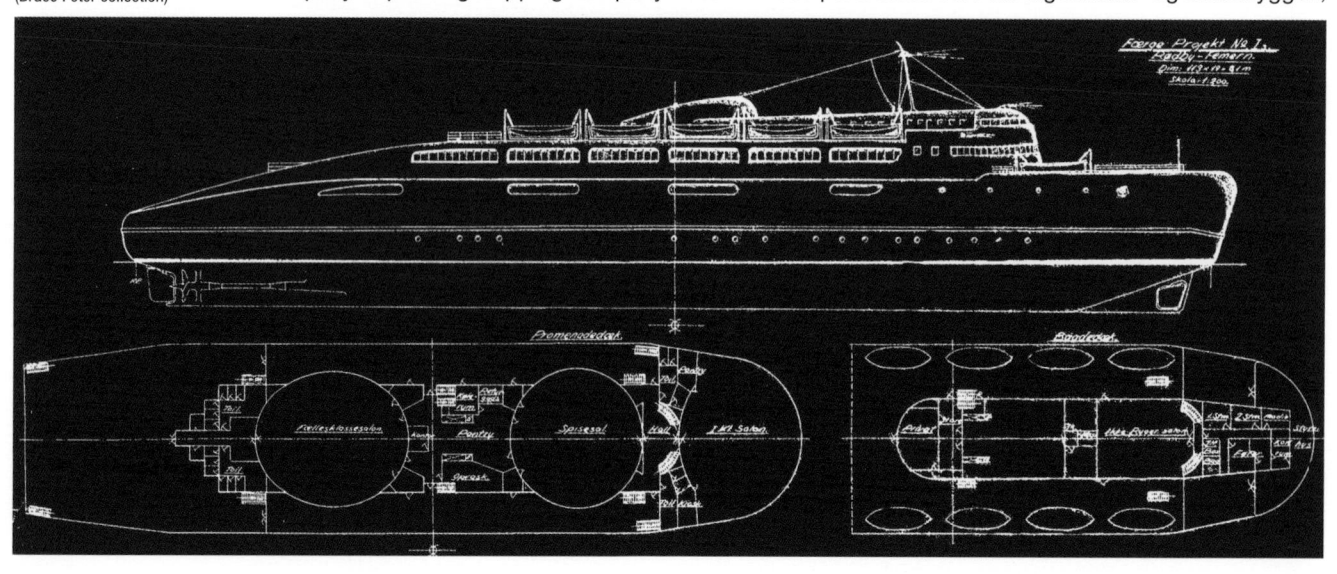

Knud E. Hansen's 'Project no. 1.2' proposal for the Rødby-Femern ferry; note the circular design of the saloons.
(Bruce Peter collection)

KNUD E. HANSEN • 80 YEARS 23

The launching of the Greenland coastal vessel *Tikerak* in Holbæk. (Museet for Søfart)

The *Tikerak* is seen amid ice floes. (Museet for Søfart)

A small wooden-hulled vessel, similar to a fishing boat, for feeder service on the Greenland coast. (Museet for Søfart)

The coastal ship *G.C. Amdrup*, another Knud E. Hansen A/S design for Greenland service. (Museet for Søfart)

The cargo steamer *Linda Clausen*, built in Svendborg during the Second World War. (Museet for Søfart)

where the *Freia* and *Peter Wessel* had been built, renaming the yard Aalborg Værft. It was probably through the Aalborg connection that Hansen's firm encountered the Lauritzens. Not only did their company run general cargo vessels in both tramping and liner service, but also had begun to specialise in the operation of refrigerated cargo ships (known as 'reefers'). Such vessels, which carry chilled fruit and deep-frozen meat cargoes, are relatively sophisticated as, apart from their main engines, they require auxiliary units to power their refrigeration plants and, in terms of construction, they are also more complex due to the need for thick insulation surrounding their cargo holds.

In the 1934–35 period, J. Lauritzen had taken delivery from Burmeister & Wain of two motor reefers of a very progressive design, the *Asta* and *Dora*, devised by the shipyard's own technical department. Following their success, Knud E. Hansen's firm was contacted to design larger examples – the 2,308 grt *American Reefer* and *Australian Reefer*, which were built by Nakskov Skibsværft and entered service in 1937, the 2,815 gt *Indian Reefer*, delivered from Helsingør Jernskibs og Maskinbyggeri in 1939, and the *Argentinean Reefer*, completed by Aalborg Værft in 1941. As with the similarly dimensioned *Kronprins Olav*, they had very sleek hull lines with pronounced cruiser sterns, powered by twin Burmeister & Wain diesels, giving a 15.5-knot service speed. In 1940, a non-refrigerated example, the 2,937 grt *Nora*, was also delivered by Aalborg Værft to J. Lauritzen for use on their West Coast Line service, a cross-trading operation linking New York via the Panama Canal with ports on the Pacific seaboard of South America. Hansen additionally designed the Aalborg-built 3,800 grt *Angamos*, a Chilean government military supply ship, the layout of which was derived from that of the *Nora*; the contract was won through J. Lauritzen, whose fleet were regular callers at Chilean ports. The vessel was fitted with a triple-expansion steam engine and was therefore capable of only 12 knots.

The Second World War

When Denmark was invaded by Germany, its Danish merchant fleet was cut in two. Vessels in Scandinavian waters could only trade in this area for the war's five-year duration and became known as the 'home fleet'. The remainder, in neutral or Allied ports outside the German blockade or seized by the Allies, formed the so-called 'overseas fleet'.

At first, the Germans ambitiously planned to build new transport infrastructure to improve links in the new empire they had created by annexing their neighbours. One such project was a joint initiative between Deutsche Reichsbahn and DSB to develop a new direct train ferry service across the Southern Baltic between Rødby and the island of Femern, off the North German coast. From Femern, a bridge would connect to the mainland, making the route the shortest transport link between Denmark and Germany. The project, known as 'Fugleflugtslinien', required heavy investment from both sides, but nonetheless, a planned completion date was set for 1945.

In 1942, DSB approached Knud E. Hansen A/S to request conceptual general arrangement drawings for a new class of train ferry for the route. This resulted in three different ferry design proposals being devised, known as 'Project no. 1.1', 'Project no. 1.2' and 'Project no. 1.3'. Each scheme was for a vessel 113 metres long and 19 metres broad, capable of transporting five-coach 'Lyntog' express diesel trains. Above the train deck, three elliptically shaped saloons were proposed with hallways, promenades, and service facilities such as the galley in the 'negative' spaces between. The forward ellipse was to have contained a First Class saloon, with the restaurant amidships and a Second Class saloon aft.

Of the three versions, Project no. 1.3 was the most conservative and, in terms of external appearance and was clearly derived from DSB's existing Great Belt ferry designs. 'Project no 1.2', however, had a bull-nosed bow visor and a highly curvaceous streamformed superstructure and funnel in the manner of recent American ships styled by the industrial designers Raymond Loewy and Norman Bel Geddes. In particular, the design resembled Loewy's styling of the Virginia Ferry Corporation's *Princess Anne* of 1936. 'Project no. 1.1' was an intermediate option with less flamboyant streamlining and this was probably the design Knud E. Hansen himself most liked. Because of the war, these proposals were stillborn, but their influence was evident in numerous Danish car and train ferries introduced in the post-war era, not least those devised by Hansen and his employees. Apart from working on these schemes, Knud E. Hansen A/S's business was quiet during the war years with only around a dozen minor conversion projects, designs for small fishing cutters and two wooden-hulled cargo vessels for Greenland coastal service being produced. These were the *G.C. Amdrup*, designed in 1943 and built in Frederikssund but not completed until 1947, plus the *Tikerak*, constructed in Holbæk and delivered in 1949.

So far as can be ascertained, the only vessel of any size to be designed by Knud E. Hansen A/S and actually built in the war years was the 1,082 grt general cargo steamer *Linda Clausen* for the C. Clausen Dampskibsrederi of Svendborg, a smallish operator of tramp steamers. Construction began at A/S Svendborg Skibsværft in 1943, but the vessel was not actually finished until February 1945. Apart from a lack of materials, Danish shipyard workers and managements tended to carry out their duties as slowly as possible while the nation was occupied so as not to provide capacity to build ships for Germany.

Post-war rebuilding

KNUD E. HANSEN • 80 YEARS **27**

The Great belt car and train ferry *Broen* is seen at Nyborg in the latter 1950s. (Bruce Peter collection)

Above: The Greenock-built coastal cargo vessel *Teddy*. (Bruce Peter collection)

Right: The Norwgian cargo liner *Fernwood*. (KNUD E. HANSEN Archive)

Svend A. Bertelsen at his desk. (KNUD E. HANSEN Archive)

The ending of hostilities in 1945 brought an urgent requirement to replace the many vessels lost during the conflict. The Danish merchant fleet had suffered badly with about half of the tonnage from 1939 destroyed or damaged beyond repair by war actions. In 1939, the fleet had amounted to 558 ships, whereas by 1945 it was reduced to only 226 vessels. Unfortunately for Denmark's ship owners and shipyards, a scarcity of building materials – especially steel and non-ferrous metals – caused relatively long delivery times for new tonnage. So serious was the lack of steel that when Det Bergenske Dampskipsselskap's war-damaged *Venus* was slowly rebuilt at the Helsingør and Århus shipyards, existing damaged plates were flattened and re-used. A few years later, the commissioning of a new steelworks at Frederiksværk in 1949 solved the steel shortage and for some years thereafter all the Danish shipyards struggled to cope with full order books.

From 1945, Knud E. Hansen and his assistants – who were at that time Preben Agner, Gerhard Erichs and Gunnar Toft Madsen – produced designs for wooden-hulled fishing cutters and also some small coastal cargo vessels. Erichs came from Sønderjylland, close to the German border. Having served his apprenticeship in the Helsingør Skibsværft, he studied at Helsingør Teknikum alongside Agner and Madsen. A typical KEH-designed coaster of the era was the 789 gt *Teddy*, built on the River Clyde by George Brown & Co. (Marine) Ltd of Greenock in 1947 for the Danish ship owner Hans Svenningsen, whose speciality was the transport of forestry products between Sweden and Denmark. Soon, commissions were received to design ocean-going cargo ships, mainly for Norwegian ship owners. The earliest of these was the 4,500 dwt *Fernfjord*, completed by Sarpsborg Mekaniske Verksted near Oslo in 1949, the first of a series of near-sisters for Fearnley & Eger's fleet.

To cope with growing demand, fourth employee, Svend Aage Bertelsen, joined Knud E. Hansen A/S in April 1948. He was to become one of Hansen's closest assistants and a key figure in the firm's subsequent development. Bertelsen was born in 1922 in Grindsted in Jylland. Later, his family moved to Ålsgårde, north of Helsingør. There, he learned his skills as a naval architect by working at the Helsingør Skibsværft and by attending the local Teknikum. Having started out as a youthful engineering graduate, Bertelsen was to remain with Knud E. Hansen A/S for 37 years, eventually becoming its managing director and overseeing its busiest and most successful period from 1960 until 1985.

The first post-war passenger ships

In 1948, Hansen was contacted by Thorkil Lund of the Dampskibsselskab på Bornholm af 1866, who requested his assistance in designing a new passenger and mail ship for the Copenhagen–Rønne service. This was to be an enlarged and modernised version of the route's existing *Hammershus* (1936) and *Rotna* (1940). Since the end of the Second World War, routes to Bornholm had experienced a significant upturn in passenger numbers, especially summer tourists,. It was not until 1950, however, that finance could be gathered and a building slot reserved with Burmeister & Wain to enable the new 2,314 gt *Kongedybet*, designed by Hansen, actually to be built. As with his 'Project no. 1.1' design for DSB, the vessel's superstructure and funnel were modestly streamlined. Inboard, Kay Fisker was commissioned

Top left and above: The Bornholm passenger ship *Kongedybet* during her builder's trials. (Bruce Peter collection)

Above and right: The *Kongedybet*'s smoking saloon with its abstractly-shaped, back-lit ceiling. (Bruce Peter collection)

30 KNUD E. HANSEN • 80 YEARS

The little Bornholm car ferry *Østbornholm* in as-delivered condition. (Bruce Peter collection)

The *Østbornholm*'s somewhat constricted car deck, laid in teak planking. (Bruce Peter collection)

Above: The lengthening of the *Østbornholm* at Burmeister & Wain's shipyard; having been cut amidships, a new mid-body section is built in the gap. (Anders Bergenek collection)

Right: After lengthening, the *Østbornholm* passes at sea. (Museet for Søfart)

Top: The *Nordbornholm* and the *Kongedybet*, berthed together at Kalvebod Brygge in Copenhagen. (Bruce Peter collection)

Above and right: Two views of the *Broen* crossing the Great Belt. (Bruce Peter collection) to design the interiors, the semi-circular smoking saloon having a striking abstract treatment of the ceiling illumination. Carrying mainly passengers and mail, the *Kongedybet* was, however, a vessel of a type soon to become increasingly rare on Scandinavian routes. Their future lay with drive-through car ferries and during the ensuing years many new routes were opened, often in conjunction with the expansion of the trunk road network.

Between designing the *Kongedybet* and the vessel being built, Knud E. Hansen received from DSB the first of many post-war contracts to design drive-through ferries. The 1,581 grt *Broen* was similar in width and tonnage to the pre-war *Peter Wessel*, but could accommodate up to 1,000 passengers and 60 cars but, like the *Freia*, her hull tapered inwards from one-third forward and one-third aft so as to fit DSB's standard ferry berths. Built by the Frederikshavn Værft & Flydedok A/S, she was delivered in 1952. The *Broen*'s design became a prototype for a whole series of DSB train and car ferries built throughout the latter 1950s and 1960s. After a lengthy career stretching until the early-1990s, the vessel was converted into a floating nightclub. In 2016, she was saved for preservation as a floating museum and venue for events in the town of Nyborg.

Following the *Kongedybet*'s entry into service, the '66' Company next requested that Knud E. Hansen design a new vessel to sail on the short 'back door' route to Bornholm from Simrishamn in Sweden to Alinge. Replacing an 1899-vintage screw steamer of the same name, the new 1,047 gt *Østersøen* represented a considerable improvement in terms of comfort and modernity. Ordered from the Svendborg Skibsværft in 1951, in many respects the ship was a 'baby' version of the *Kongedybet*. Within a short but beamy hull (41.10 x 10.49 metres), there was space for 500 passengers and 24 cars, loaded through side ports. Driven by a single B&W diesel, her service speed being only 13 knots. The building process was somewhat protracted, with final outfitting taking place at B&W in Copenhagen, meaning that the vessel was not completed until 1954.

Unfortunately, like many another established short-sea operator, the '66' Company had not reckoned on such rapid growth as was experienced during the latter 1950s and so, very quickly, both the *Kongedybet* and *Østersøen* were found to have insufficient capacity. Consequently, Knud E. Hansen A/S was appointed to redesign them in lengthened form. The two were sent to B&W in 1958 and 1960 respectively, where they were cut amidships and new sections were inserted.

In the same year as the *Østersøen* was delivered, the first oil tankers drawn up by Hansen's office were also nearing readiness. The urgent need for these related to growth in car ownership throughout the Western World and, more generally, an expanding usage of internal combustion and jet engines, as well as the increasing use of oil for central heating and electricity generation. Many shipping companies, hitherto best known for operating dry cargo vessels in the tramping and liner trades, decided, additionally, to invest in tankers to carry Gulf crude to Europe, the Americas and elsewhere. Thus, in 1952, Knud E. Hansen A/S designed its first tanker. The 18,000 dwt vessel was launched at the Kaldnes Mekaniske Verksted in December 1954 as the *Antarctic* for the Hvalfangerselskapet Antarctic A/S, a Norwegian whaling company owned by Anton von der Lippe, who had first invested in oil tankers in the early-1930s. The *Antarctic* was a typical motor tanker of her era, fitted with a Barclay, Curle-built Doxford engine and arranged with a 'two island' superstructure. At that time, she was by far the largest ship yet drawn up by Knud E. Hansen A/S. Between launching and taking delivery, however, her owner received an attractive offer from Iberian Tankers Co., which was a subsidiary of the Mobil Oil Corporation and so she actually entered service as their *Victoria*, flying the Liberian flag. The other significant KEH-designed tanker to enter service in 1954 was the 10,534 gt *Pacific Clipper*, built by Oskarshams Varv in Sweden for Rederi AB Clipper of Malmö.

As Knud E. Hansen A/S' workload grew, more assistants were taken on and the offices expanded to occupy the entirety of a grand-looking five-storey building at 75 Bredegade in central Copenhagen. This address was well located, being close to the headquarters of several of Denmark's leading shipping companies.

Dag Rogne. (KNUD E. HANSEN Archive)

In 1954, the firm was joined by a young Norwegian-born naval architect, Dag Rogne. Born in 1923 on Bygdøy, a peninsula directly opposite Oslo harbour on which a number of museums are located Rogne had spent his late-teens working , he worked in a small boat repair yard and taking part in covert sabotage operations on behalf of the Norwegian Resistance at other yards repairing ship motors for the occupying Germans. After the war, he moved to Copenhagen, where he attended the Teknikum, before moving to Helsingør Teknikum to specialise in naval architecture. He graduated in 1949 with the highest grade of any student in that year and initially found employment with Burmeister & Wain in Copenhagen. It was there that Rogne's interest in ferry design began when, in 1950, he was involved in drawing up a scheme to lengthen Gothenburg–Frederikshavn Linjen's 1936-built car ferry *Kronprinsessan Ingrid*. This required the ship to be cut in half so that a new 7.8 metre mid-section could be inserted. After two years, he moved to Gothenburg to work at Eriksbergs Varv, where he assisted in designing oil tankers mainly for Norwegian ship owners but, as his Danish wife wanted him to return to Copenhagen, he found work there instead with Titan, designing cranes for cargo vessels. In the summer of 1954, Rogne met Svend A. Bertelsen, with whom he had studied at Helsingør, and he was invited to join Knud E. Hansen A/S, initially in the Steel Drawing Department. By the early 1960s, he was switched to specialise instead in producing general arrangements drawings for ferries, many of which were very innovative and economical in terms of their organisation and propulsion. Later in life, Rogne recalled his colleagues from the early years at Knud E. Hansen A/S:

'Svend Aage was known to everybody as 'Bertel'. He had a great knowledge and curiosity about ships and was a prodigious worker. Back then, the important KEH employees were Preben Agner, who dealt with small ships, Gerhard Erichs, who had a good theoretical knowledge in terms of machinery, speed and power calculations, Herluf Lütken, who specialised in general arrangement drawings, Gunnar Toft Madsen and Erik Madsen, who dealt with steelwork drawings. Gunnar Jensen looked after the financial side and Hanne Christensen was the secretary.'

As we have seen, from the very beginning, Knud E. Hansen developed relationships with Norwegian ship owners. Norway, for long one of the world's leading shipping nations, became particularly influential after the Second World War when Britain, France, Belgium and the Netherlands lost most of their colonies and much of their merchant fleets. With America now the leading superpower and with strong industrial growth in the Far East, Norwegian owners prospered by serving these far-flung markets with relatively modern and efficient tonnage. Norwegians were also early to make successes of emerging business areas, such as oil tankers, bulk shipping, ro-ro ferries and the mass-market cruise trade from Miami. During ensuing decades, Knud E. Hansen A/S designed ships for all of these markets and, being Norwegian himself, Dag Rogne was best able to lure potential clients among the Norwegian shipbuilding and ship-owning communities.

Once employed by Knud E. Hansen A/S, Rogne's first task was to produce steel drawings for the *Bastø I*, a new 1,259 gt Oslofjord ferry Hansen had designed for a short crossing over the fjord between

The Swedish-flagged *Pacific Clipper*, a typical large tanker of the 1950s. (KNUD E. HANSEN Archive)

The staff of Knud E. Hansen A/S at their twentieth anniversary party in 1957; Hansen himself is standing second from the left in the back row. (Tage Wandboeg collection)

Top left: The Moss-Horten Oslofjord ferry *Bastø I*. (Bruce Peter collection)
Top right: The *Bastø IV*, another example of the type. (Bruce Peter collection)
Below left: The passenger and cargo vessel *Hoi Kung*. (Karsten Petersen)
Right: The cargo vessel *Arctic Gull*. (Bruce Peter collection)
Bottom: The cargo vessel *Mabella*. (Bruce Peter collection)

Moss and Horten. The operator, Rederi A/S Alpha, would have been familiar with Hansen's *Kronprins Olav* and *Peter Wessel*, which were visitors to the Oslofjord almost on a daily basis. The *Bastø I* was a double-ended craft fitted with a single Sulzer diesel, connected to a propeller shaft at each end, thus enabling her to shuttle back and forth without needing to turn. Ordered from the Moss Verft & Dokk A/S, her construction was subcontracted to the A/S Pusnæs Mekaniske Verksted in Arendal, with delivery in 1956. Three further vessels were subsequently built to essentially the same design in 1961, 1964 and 1968 respectively.

Hansen's relationship with Moss Verft & Dokk A/S proved fruitful and, during ensuing years, his company was contacted at regular intervals by the yard to provide general arrangement and detailed construction drawings for various general cargo ships, small bulk carriers and tankers. Most of these projects were carried out under the direction of Gerhard Erichs, who made a speciality of designing freight vessels. Such schemes included the 18,776 dwt iron ore carrier *Margit Brøvig* (1956) for Th. Brøvig of Farsund, plus two 4,500 gt general cargo ships, the *Arctic Gull* (1959) for Odd Berg of Tromsø and the *Mabella* (1960) for A/S Mabella, a company owned by Karl Bruusgaard of Drammen. As with the *Bastø I*, the construction of the *Mabella*'s hull was subcontracted to Pusnæs Mekaniske Verksted. The vessel's hull lines were subsequently re-used by Moss Verft & Dokk A/S as the basis for the H.M. Wrangell A/S-owned passenger and cargo liner *Hoi Kung*. Although planned only as a freighter, she was instead completed in 1964 as a combined passenger and cargo vessel for the company's coolie and pilgrim trade in the Far East, accommodating 10 in First Class and more than 1,000 amid the Spartan conditions of the 'tween-deck.

Meanwhile, Hansen himself was designing a new ferry for Grenaa-Hundested Færgefart A/S, which had been a client of his since the latter 1930s. The 1,619 gt *Djursland* was built by Aalborg Værft and,

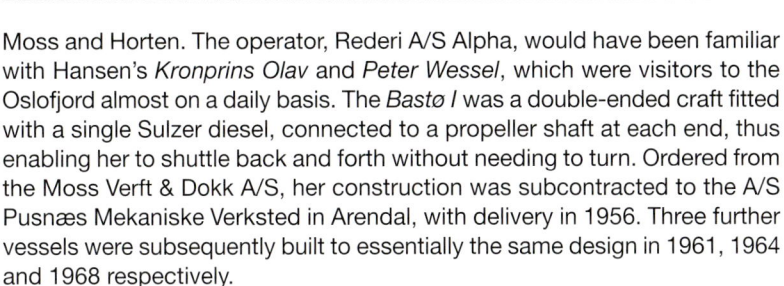

Top left: The Grenaa-Hundested ferry *Djursland*.
(Bruce Peter collection)

Top right and above: The Skagerrak car and train ferry *Skagen* at Hirtshals.
(Bruce Peter collection)

Bottom left: The Norwegian coastal ferry *Hardangerfjord*.
(Bergen Maritime Museum)

Bottom right: The *Hardingen*, dressed overall shortly after delivery.
(Bergen Maritime Museum)

Above: Tage Wandborg (Tage Wandborg collection)

Below: The trial of Poul Erik Rasmussen and Tage Wandborg's self-righting lifeboat design in Esbjerg harbour in 1969. (Tage Wandborg collection)
Bottom right: Three Knud E. Hansen A/S-designed vessels at Helsingborg in the mid-1960s: in the background are the car ferries *Carola* and *Kronprins Carl Gustav* while, in the foreground, the *Sundbuss Jeppe* leaves for Helsingør. (Bruce Peter collection)

upon entering service in 1958, provided substantial additional capacity supplementing the route's existing pre-war-built *Isefjord* and *Marsk Stig*. The *Djursland* had a remarkably high capacity despite her compact size, carrying 1,100 passengers and 95 cars.

Shortly thereafter, Hansen designed the broadly similar 1,870 grt *Skagen*, a combined passenger, car, and train ferry, capable of transporting 505 passengers and either 75 cars or six railway wagons on the Kristiansand Dampskipsselskap's Kristiansand–Hirtshals route. Her hull was constructed by Pusnæs Mekaniske Verksted at Arendal with outfitting taking place thereafter at Kristiansands Mekaniske Verksteder, both in Norway and she entered service in 1958. Hansen then oversaw the planning of a 883 grt Norwegian coastal ferry, the *Hardangerfjord*, which was built by A/S Stord Verft in Norway for the Hardanger Sunhorlandske Dampskipsselskap (HSD). Delivered in 1958, she operated the 'Odda Express' overnight route from Bergen. Some years later in 1966, Knud E. Hansen A/S designed a further smaller ferry for HSD, named the *Hardingen*, for local service across the Hardangerfjord.

In November 1955, Knud E. Hansen A/S gained a further two significant employees – Tage Wandborg and Poul Erik Rasmussen. Wandborg was born in Snekkersten near Helsingør in 1923, where he and Svend A. Bertelsen were childhood friends. Having worked as an apprentice at the Helsingør Skibsværft, Wandborg too attended the Teknikum, graduating in 1944. Due to the war, he was unable to find work in shipbuilding, and so he moved to Randers in Jutland, where he designed railway vehicles for the train builder Scandia. Thereafter, he served in the Royal Danish Guard as the regiment's youngest Second Lieutenant before moving to Stockholm in 1947, where he joined the Drawing Office of the Finnboda Varv at Nacka. There, he assisted in designing the 2,798 grt Baltic passenger steamer *Birger Jarl* for Stockholms Rederi AB Svea. She was one of a trio of similar vessels ordered by various established cross-Baltic operators and intended to enter service in time to carry the increased traffic expected in connection with the Helsinki Olympic Games (1952). In the end, she was not completed on time but nonetheless all three did become known as the 'Olympic Ships.' With her streamlined funnel, the Birger Jarl was the most modern looking of them and is the only one to survive today, albeit re-engined as a motor vessel.

Having joined Knud E. Hansen A/S, Wandborg initially made only small contributions mainly to cargo ship projects. He remembers Hansen as having been:

'… A very refined and sensitive man, softly spoken and genteel in manner. He was very proper in his dealings with others and he addressed all of his assistants and colleagues by their professional titles. I, for example, was always 'Engineer Wandborg'. He paid great attention to the details of his work and he discussed what was being done by each person in the office at the beginning and end of the day, questioning the development of an individual's ideas and offering suggestions of his own. Hansen wanted originality from his people and would reassign work that he thought did not measure up creatively.'

Wandborg recalls that Hansen soon noted his design talents and he was given more challenging work:

'With colleagues, I speculatively designed a new type of cargo crane and we made a wooden model to demonstrate how it would work. When we were experimenting with this, Hansen walked past and said half-jokingly "Playing with your toys, are you, Engineer Wandborg?" Later that day, he had an important client in his office with whom he was apparently discussing a possible order for a cargo ship. His secretary called for me to come at once and to "bring your toy crane with you". Hansen was actually delighted with the crane and so it was not long before I was being allocated complete ships to design.'

As well as being a naval architect of considerable skill, Wandborg was also a great aesthete with wide-ranging interests in architecture, design and transport of all kinds. As his talent for designing elegant silhouettes and harmonious details came to be appreciated, he was asked to shape and refine the topsides, superstructures, funnels of much of Knud E. Hansen A/S's subsequent passenger ship design output, particularly from 1960 onwards. Søren Bech, the company's former archivist recalls that vessels drawn up by Wandborg's colleagues were often subjected to quite radical reconfiguration once he became involved:

'Tage was among the best people we had – delightful to work with but also with very strong ideas about how things should be done. Back then, unlike today, all of the drawings were painstakingly drafted by hand. Sometimes, the naval architect responsible would realise that the result didn't quite look right and so Tage would make sketches with a different profile or with a longer hull. Once this happened, it was necessary to cut the existing drawings up and to tape them together again with strips of new drafting film inserted to make space for Tage's improvements. Often, these aesthetic and planning decisions took place around my table because it was the largest in the office, and so it was possible for me to witness this aspect of the design process at first hand without actually being involved.'

Wandborg speaks about ships and naval architecture with passion and enthusiasm and clearly enjoys recounting how he persuaded ship owners, many of whom are naturally conservative in outlook, to trust him. He believes that:

'To persuade a ship owner to believe in your designs, first of all you must fascinate and enchant him with your work to gain his respect and trust. You have to paint a beautiful mental picture through sketch drawings, the use of evocative language and by rattling off statistics ... For example, you wouldn't simply point out a promenade deck, that's dull. Instead, you would describe a busy scene full of happy people relaxing on sun loungers with potted palm trees, Jacuzzis, swimming pools, a bandstand with Caribbean music ... anything to make the client immerse himself in your vision of how the ship should look and feel.'

Listening to Wandborg waxing lyrical about the many designs for famous ships in which he was involved, it can be imagine how Knud E. Hansen A/S gained a group of loyal clients who came back time and time again to commission designs for ever larger and more elaborate vessels. Indeed, for around a quarter of a century from the latter 1950s until the early 1980s, Wandborg was Knud E. Hansen A/S' most significant and prolific naval architect and his distinctive and highly refined approach to ship aesthetics became synonymous with the company's output.

Wandborg found that the first noteworthy design project allotted to him by Knud E. Hansen in 1958 was to draw up two small passenger ferries, the 98 grt, 100-passenger *Sundbuss Henrik* and *Sundbuss Pernille*, for a Norwegian ship owner, Ragnar Moltzau, to operate between Helsingør and Helsingborg. Moltzau was primarily an operator of oil tankers who, in the 1960s, invested profits in ferry services from Denmark. Built by Alssunds Skibsværft, near Sønderborg in Denmark, their elegant streamlined design was typical of Wandborg's approach. Upon the vessels' successful entry into service, Moltzau ordered a third, larger example, the 75 grt *Sundbuss Jeppe*, which was built by Westermøen Slipp in Mandal, Norway again to a design by Wandborg. Subsequently, Moltzau became one of Knud E. Hansen A/S' best clients. For the next half-century, the 'Sundbusserne', as they were known, traversed The Sound, carrying millions of day-trippers between Sweden and Denmark.

Whereas Wandborg's principal area of interest was ships' upper works, Poul Erik Rasmussen's speciality was devising efficient hull forms, with particular attention being paid by him to their hydrodynamic performance at and below the waterline. Born in Hundested, he had first learned the fundamentals of boat building by working in a small privately owned yard there. Subsequently, he too studied naval architecture at the Helsingør Teknikum. For more than 40 years, nearly all KEH projects had hull lines devised or refined by Rasmussen. Wandborg observes that:

The *Skaw Pilot* was designed by Wandborg and Rasmussen in the early-1960s for pilotage duties in the sometimes rough waters off Skagen at Denmark's northern tip. The vessel remains in service there at present. (KNUD E. HANSEN Archive)

'He was a master in this field and his exceptional skill was recognised worldwide. He had a very refined sense of the best shapes for hulls and the associated values of their stability characteristics, as well as the right location of their centres of buoyancy.'

While much of Rasmussen's work related to hull design for ferries and other types of sea-going merchant ship, he also was involved in numerous special projects. For example, in 1967, together with Wandborg, he developed a revolutionary prototype for a 180-degree self-righting life rescue cutter for use on the Danish West Coast, which was tested in Esbjerg harbour in 1969 and proved extremely successful.

Designing large modern vessels is a team effort with a variety of complementary skills required, but Tage Wandborg emphasises the need for strong leadership to focus attention on achieving a well-resolved and harmonious outcome. Thus, each project was assigned to a senior naval architect, who was responsible for supervising other colleagues with expertise in specific areas; general layout planning, the application of relevant safety regulations, hydrodynamics, weight calculations, technical specifications, exterior styling or interior design. These many diverse strands had to be integrated into the overall scheme in the most effective way to give clients the best possible value. Small ships could be designed entirely by a single employee. Either work was allocated by chance, or because a particular staff member was well-known to a ship owner who specifically requested them.

Freighters and tankers

During the 1950s, Knud E. Hansen A/S produced numerous cargo ship designs for Danish owners, ranging in scale from small coasters to relatively large freighters for international 'deep sea' trades. The majority of these vessels had in common an aft-located engine room and superstructure, enabling a shorter propeller shaft and freeing up more space amidships for cargo. Such layouts became standard

Above: The launching of Knud E. Hansen's own ship, the motor coaster *Clipperen*, at Alssunds Skibsværft. (KNUD E. HANSEN Archive)

Above right: The completed *Clipperen* in service in the latter-1950s. (KNUD E. HANSEN Archive)

Right: An original design drawing for the *Clipperen*. (KNUD E. HANSEN Archive)

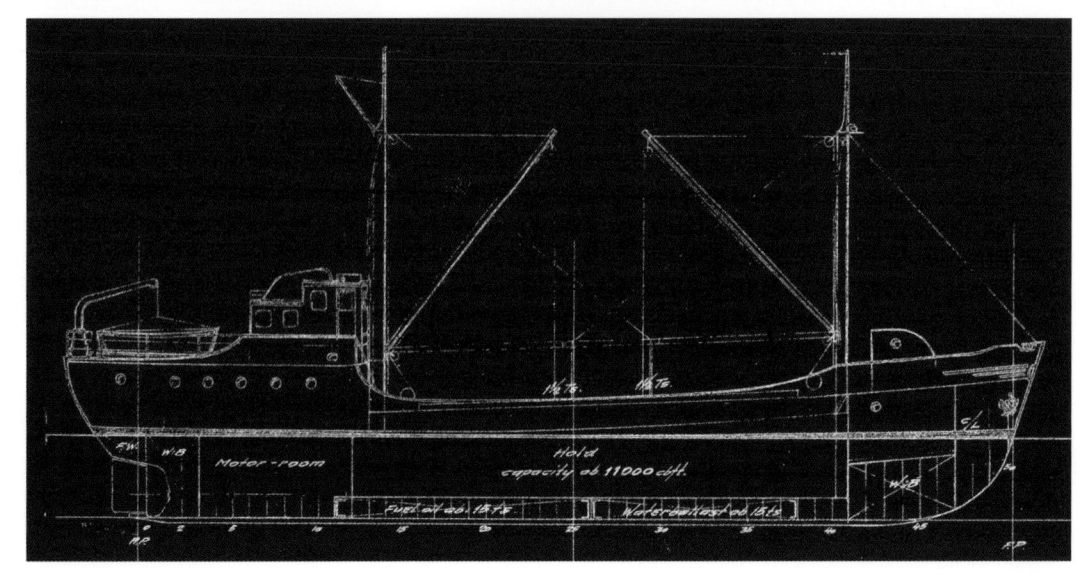

The *Hans Mærsk*, fully loaded with cargo. (A.P. Møller-Mærsk A/S)

Above: The *Robert Mærsk* at sea with some containers placed on the hatch covers. (A.P. Møller-Mærsk A/S)

Left: The A.P. Møller-owned cargo liner *Estelle Mærsk*. (A.P. Møller-Mærsk A/S)

The *Henriette Mærsk* entering port, her cranes raised in preparation for handling cargo.
(A.P. Møller-Mærsk A/S)

Below: The newly-completed Dampskibsselskabet Jutlandia cargo vessel *Inge Toft* as she appeared upon delivery to her owner. (Museet for Søfart)

Bottom: A design drawing for the *Inge Toft*. (KNUD E. HANSEN Archive)

for most liner companies later in the 1960s but, as was typical, Knud E. Hansen A/S was at the leading edge of their development. A majority of these projects were handled by Gerhard Erichs and Herluf Lütken – who drew up for sea-going freighters, tankers and bulk carriers – and Preben Agner, who designed coasters and other small craft. Tage Wandborg recalls:

'Gerhard Erichs … was very pleasant with a good sense of humour and also was a fast worker, brilliant at calculating capacity, displacement and the propulsion power needed for freight ships. In terms of Knud E. Hansen A/S' design output, he was one of the most important people when I joined. His colleague was Herluf Lütken, a Copenhagener who was a very charming and cultured gentleman. He drew up general arrangements and was not a fast worker like Erichs, but very methodical in his approach. Preben Agner designed mainly small coasters. He was in my year at the Helsingør Teknikum but, unfortunately, he decided quite early on that he didn't like me and so I found him quite a hard character to work with. Most of his coaster designs were attractive and successful and many were built in small shipyards all over Scandinavia, West Germany and the Netherlands.'

In 1955, Agner designed a standard coaster type to be built by Alssunds Skibsværft. Examples included the *Stensnæs*, *Elly Jensen* and *Clipperen*, the latter owned by Rederi Clipperfart A/S, a

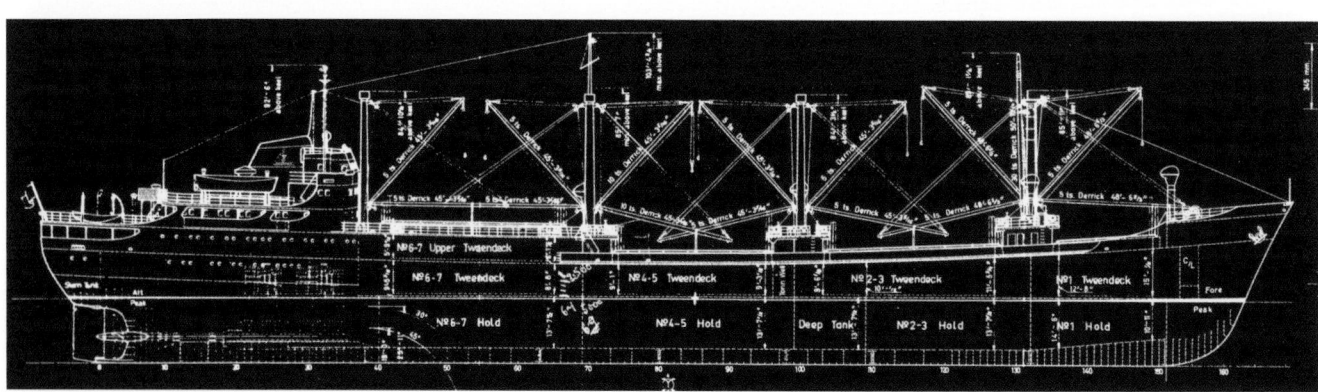

KNUD E. HANSEN • 80 YEARS **41**

The *Kongsholm*, dressed overall upon completion by Stord Værft. (KNUD E. HANSEN Archive)

Right: The Norwegian cargo liner *Fernwood*. (KNUD E. HANSEN Archive)

Below: The *Bambi*, a smaller West German-built cargo vessel, similarly decorated for handing over. (KNUD E. HANSEN Archive)

The cargo vessel *Ailsa*. (Bruce Peter collection)

42 KNUD E. HANSEN • 80 YEARS

Right: The J. Lauritzen ice-strengthened cargo vessel *Varla Dan*. (Bruce Peter collection)

Left: The hull of the *Hans Hedtoft* in the dock at Frederikshavn. (Museet for Søfart)

A rare image of the *Hans Hedtoft* in Greenland waters, shortly before her tragic and untimely loss. (Museet for Søfart)

company set up by Knud E. Hansen himself to engage in shipping trade around the Danish and Swedish coasts. While Hansen's operation of the *Clipperen* generally broke even, so far as can be ascertained, it did not earn him any substantial profits. Its construction and operation does, however, illustrate Hansen's personal enthusiasm for ships in that he too wanted to be able to claim to be a ship owner.

During the second half of the 1950s, Gerhard Erichs designed several series of medium-sized, aft-engined, cargo liners for A.P. Møller, one of Denmark's most important liner companies and at that time rapidly expanding in the USA–Far East and Far East–Bay of Bengal trades. Frederikshavn Værft & Flydedok A/S constructed the 3,218 grt *Ras Mærsk*, *Robert Mærsk* and *Romø Mærsk*, delivered in 1957–59, while the 3,646 grt *Hartvig Mærsk*, *Hans Mærsk* and *Estelle Mærsk* were built concurrently by Burmeister & Wain in Copenhagen. Meanwhile, Bijkers Aannemingsbedrijf in the Netherlands delivered the smaller 1,985 grt *Nelly Mærsk* and *Niels Mærsk*. Knud E. Hansen A/S's list of projects for 1957 also includes a design for a considerably larger 10,000 gt cargo liner for A.P. Møller and it seems likely that this might have been an initial project for the vessels built as *Anette Mærsk*, *Henriette Mærsk* and *Torben Mærsk* in 1962–63. The first of this series of liners for round-the-world service via South Africa was built in Japan, while the other two came from Helsingør.

The 4,632 gt tramping cargo vessel *Inge Toft*, completed in 1957 for Dampskibsselskabet Jutlandia, had a very similar hull to these A.P. Møller cargo liners, but a somewhat smaller superstructure. The *Inge Toft*'s hull was built at Valmet in Finland, a builder which at that time only produced steelwork, leaving others to complete vessels' outfitting. Thus, she was towed in an incomplete state to Langesund in Norway where she was completed. Shortly after delivery, the *Inge Toft* became mired in controversy when, carrying a cargo of phosphates from Israel in May 1959, she was seized by the Egyptian

Below left: The cargo vessel *Cabo Frio*. (Bruce Peter collection)

Below right: The Norwegian-owned tanker *Beauval*. (Bruce Peter collection)

Bottom: The cargo vessel *Bessegen*. (KNUD E. HANSEN Archive)

authorities in the Suez Canal, her cargo was confiscated and she was held in Port Said until February 1960, upon release returning empty to Haifa.

For Norwegian owners, Knud E. Hansen A/S designed the 6,800 dwt cargo liner *Fernwood*, completed in 1957 by Stord Verft in Leirvik for Fearnley & Eger's Mediterranean service, plus the *Kongsholm*, also delivered by Stord Verft in the same year and owned by Brødrene Olsen of Stavanger. The *Bambi* was the first of three similar 3,000 dwt cargo vessels designed for clients of the Hanseatische Werft in Hamburg. She was delivered in 1957 to L. Harboe Jensen and, thereafter, the yard re-used her design when building two vessels as wartime reparations for Israel, the *Amal* and the *Atid*, owned by Atid Mediterranean Lines of Haifa.

The 18,650 dwt tanker *Edith Borthen* was built at Marinens Hovedverft at Horten for Harry Borthen & Co of Oslo and completed in 1958, as was the *Ailsa*, a 4,500 grt cargo liner built at Sarpsborg for Sigurd Bruusgaard of Drammen. These contracts show the continuing importance of Norwegian shipyards and owners to Knud E. Hansen A/S.

In 1956, Knud E. Hansen A/S was called upon to provide a general arrangement and hull lines for the *Hans Hedtoft*, a 2,875 grt passenger and cargo vessel for Greenland service built by Frederikshavn Værft & Flydedok A/S and delivered in 1959 to the Danish State-owned Kongelige Grønlandske Handel. Unfortunately, she is best remembered for tragically sinking when on her maiden voyage with the loss of 95 lives.

The original intention was that the *Hans Hedtoft* would carry passengers only in summer when the seas around Greenland were guaranteed ice-free but, owing to political pressure, her owner was forced to transport them all year round. In line with typical shipbuilding practice for vessels of her type, her hull plates were welded together but riveted to the frames, which also were of riveted construction, a method of building that may possibly have resulted in her hull partially disintegrating on hitting submerged ice. In the mid-1950s, many ships were of such hybrid construction, though riveting still tended to be favoured for critical areas of their structure. The loss of the *Hans Hedtoft* was a national scandal, the consequences of which continue to reverberate. There is no doubt that the vessel was correctly designed for summer service and, had her operator not been forced to take risks by sailing her through winter ice, she would probably have had a lengthy and successful career.

At around the same time, Knud E. Hansen A/S also produced plans for the *Besseggen*, a 5,800 dwt paper and forestry products carrier built by Stord Verft in Leirvik and delivered in 1958 to Christian Østberg of Oslo. Meanwhile, the large 9,262 gt general cargo vessel *Anne Reed* was built by Marinens Hovedverft at Horten for Dampskipsselskapet Ibis of Bergen. Unusually for a KEH-designed freighter her superstructure was located amidships, probably at the behest of the owner. Shortly thereafter, the 2,353 gt ice-strengthened cargo vessels *Perla Dan* and *Varla Dan* were completed by Pusnæs Mekaniske Verksted and delivered in 1959 to J. Lauritzen for the carriage of timber and wood pulp from Finland to the British and French ports. As with J. Lauritzen's other ice-strengthened vessels, Det Kongelige Grønlandske Handel often chartered them for Denmark–Greenland service. Unlike the unfortunate *Hans Hedtoft*, their hulls were of entirely welded construction, this being J. Lauritzen's standard specification for vessels of this type. The *Cementine*, constructed by Langesunds Mekaniske Verksteder, was a compact 1,100 dwt cement carrier for A/S Dalen Portland Cement Fabrik. Remarkably, she continues to trade presently as the British-owned *Cementina*, after a career of over 50 years.

A 36,000 dwt steam turbine-driven tanker, the *Beauval*, for Bjørn Bjiornstad & Co of Moss and Oslo was built at Kristiansands Mekaniske Verksteder. Delivered in 1964, she was a typical 'two island' design of her era. The reason for the delay in construction was the need first to fix a long-term charter contract with an oil company. Eventually, Shell agreed to use the ship for a seven-year period at an acceptable rate. In the time between being designed and built, her owner realised that it would have been wiser to have specified more fuel-efficient diesel propulsion and so, while under construction, she was sold.

While the plans for the *Beauval* were being prepared, KEH also produced drawings for a refrigerated cargo vessel, the *Cabo Frio*, which was completed by Langesunds Mekaniske Verksteder in 1960. Another concurrent project was the liquefied natural gas tanker *Mundogas Brasilia*, built by Frederiksstads Mekaniske Verksteder for the Norwegian Øivind Lorentzen Group, which chartered her to Mundogas. Styled externally by Tage Wandborg, she was a striking-looking ship and, although quite small by today's standards, upon delivery, she was one of the largest gas carriers in the world.

Other projects of the latter-1950s included the fishing trawlers *Brandur Sigmundarson*, constructed by Frederikshavn Værft & Flydedok A/S for Icelandic owners and the *Olavur Halgi* and *Leivur Ossursson*, built in Viana-Castelo in Italy for the Faroese government. The trawler *Ulla Skagbo* was the first of a series constructed by Ørskov in Frederikshavn for the Danish owner Otto Danielsen and his business associates of which later examples were the *Copemar 1*, *Tronoen* and *Buen Provecho*. Knud E. Hansen

A/S also provided Ørskov with a layout design for the expansion of their yard into a newly-acquired site adjacent to the existing facility.

Ferry projects

In post-war Denmark, car ownership shot up from just below 200,000 in 1946 to 370,000 in 1959. Over the same period, there was also a steep increase in the number of lorries and so the Danish Ministry of Transport's Road Directorate published a long-term plan to improve and increase the country's road network. At the same time, Scandinavians had greater wealth and disposable income to spend on holidays and short trips. Very quickly, a number of new entrepreneurs became involved in the ferry business and it was in this process that Knud E. Hansen found a lucrative niche, as his consultancy could offer ferry owners complete designs and construction supervision, leaving them to concentrate on developing and promoting their businesses. Apart from large vessels for domestic and international routes, Knud E. Hansen A/S also designed little wooden-hulled ferries to serve Denmark's many small islands and these were often constructed in shipyards which otherwise built fishing cutters. From the mid-1950s onwards, however, designing larger ferries became the company's speciality and, as there was an increasing demand for these vessels, the firm's workforce also grew further.

Knud E. Hansen A/S' first significant car ferries of the 1960s, the 1,064 gt *Primula* (delivered in 1960) and the 2,375 gt *Kattegat* (completed in 1961), set the tone for subsequent output during the first half of the decade. The former was built for Linjebuss, a subsidiary of Stockholms Rederi AB Svea, which operated between Helsingør and Helsingborg in competition with the state-owned car and train ferries of DSB and Moltzau's passenger-only 'Sundbusserne'. Constructed by the Finnboda Varv at Nacka in Stockholm, KEH gained this and subsequent contracts from Linjebuss as a result of Tage Wandborg's previous employment there, during which time he had been involved in designing several ships for Stockholms Rederi AB Svea and was thus well-regarded by its senior management.

Left: A stern-quarter view of the Grenaa-Hundested ferry *Kattegat*. (Jan Vinther Christiansen collection)

Bottom left: The Swedish passenger vessel *Öresund*. (Bruce Peter collection)

Bottom right: The *Primula* cuts through ice off Helsingør during a cold winter in the early-1960s. (Bruce Peter collection)

Above: The DSB ferry *Prinsesse Elisabeth*. (Bruce Peter collection)

Right: The *Prinsesse Anne Marie*. (Bruce Peter collection)

The *Primula* was short and broad, measuring only 48 metres in length, yet was 15.36 metres wide. Nevertheless, she could manoeuvre quickly and easily in what were relatively confined harbours. In order to speed up loading, her car deck was a single span from side to side, the superstructure above being of a web-frame construction. The *Primula* was the first of numerous short and broad ferries designed by Knud E. Hansen A/S in the 1960s for routes across the Øresund, not only between Helsingør and Helsingborg but also from Tuborghavn to Landskrona and from Dragør to Limhamn.

Simultaneously, Knud E. Hansen A/S designed the hull for the 2,214 grt Swedish passenger motor vessel *Öresund* for Öresundsbolaget's Copenhagen–Malmö route. The Swedish State Railways (abbreviated as SJ) and DSB jointly operated Öresundsbolaget, each contributing a couple of vessels to the service. The *Öresund* was otherwise the work of SJ's own technical staff and so, externally, she appeared as a miniature version of the most recent Swedish train ferries. Ordered from Aalborg Værft, due to a lack of capacity there, the construction of her hull was subcontracted to Sölvesborgs Varv in Sweden with outfitting being carried out in Aalborg. Inboard, she was comfortably appointed and, just like the *Primula*, attracted large numbers of day-trippers who crossed between Copenhagen and Malmö to stock up with cigarettes and alcoholic drinks at tax-free prices.

Shortly thereafter, Knud E. Hansen A/S won a design contract from DSB, which was now investing seriously in a new generation of car ferries for Danish domestic routes to supplement its already large train ferry fleet. The 3,412 grt *Prinsesse Anne-Marie* was completed in 1960 by Aalborg Værft to serve on DSB's relatively lengthy northerly Århus–Kalundborg route, requiring a relatively high service speed of 20 knots. Subsequently, in 1964, a near-sister, the *Prinsesse Elisabeth*, was also built in Aalborg as her running mate.

An additional ferry for Grenaa-Hundested Færgefart A/S, the 2,375 gt *Kattegat*, became the prototype for numerous similar vessels designed thereafter by Knud E. Hansen A/S for various privately-operated Danish domestic routes across the southern Kattegat. Built by Marinens Hovedverft at Horten in Norway, she could carry 1,500 passengers and 120 cars. An aft docking bridge was fitted and there was also a solarium in front of her funnel, enclosed by Perspex panels to give passengers a fine view forward while they sunbathed. Another novelty was a fully-enclosed wheelhouse, extending over the bridge wings.

Tage Wandborg gave the Kattegat a slightly forward-weighted 'teardrop'-shaped silhouette, accentuated by the horizontal elongation of the solarium, funnel and aft sun-decks – a form he describes as his 'hungry look'. He observes that 'modern ferries such as these should look eager to proceed and should, in fact, appear to be proceeding, even when tied up at their moorings.' This became the signature of all subsequent Knud E. Hansen A/S ferry designs until the latter 1960s.

In 1959, Knud E. Hansen A/S was contacted by the owner of Skandinavisk Linjetrafik, Jørgen Jensen, a ferry company linking Tuborghavn and Landskrona to request a design for a new ferry which was subsequently built by Hansa Stahl & Schiffbau, a yard in the unlikely location of Cologne on the River Rhine in West Germany. Launched in a largely complete condition as the *Tina Scarlett* on 7 October 1960, just minutes after she settled in the water, disaster struck. While being manoeuvred by tugs in the fast-moving river, the vessel swung unexpectedly into the shipping lane where she collided with a fully-laden Belgian petrol tank barge. Immediately, there was a massive explosion and both ships caught fire. Nineteen people were injured and two, on the *Diamant*, were killed. The unfortunate *Tina Scarlett* was damaged beyond repair.

Remarkably, she was uninsured and Skandinavisk Linjetrafik was sued for seven million Danish kroner, leaving the company on the verge of bankruptcy. The Tuborghavn–Landskrona service remained lucrative, however, and merely required a new owner with sufficient capital to invest in a replacement ferry. The owner of Linjebuss, Stockholms Rederi AB Svea, stepped in, ordering again from Hansa Stahl & Schiffbau. On this occasion, the steelwork was subcontracted to Schiedam Scheepswerf at Groot-Amers, also on the Rhine but located across the Dutch border. The 1,492 grt *Linda Scarlett* was delivered in August 1961 and thereafter served Skandinavisk Linjetrafik until the early-1970s.

While Hansen was overseeing the *Linda Scarlett*'s design, his colleague, Erik Møller, was given the task of preparing plans for a combined car and train ferry for the Ærøskøbing–Svendborg route of the Dampskibsselskabet Ærø. This firm had recently appointed a new managing director called Jørgen Svarer, who proved to be a good customer for Knud E. Hansen A/S ferry designs, notwithstanding his strictly limited budget which meant that not all of the proposals devised by KEH were actually realised.

Delivered in May 1960 by the Husumer Schiffswerft in West Germany, the *Ærøsund* measured only 373 grt but was nonetheless capable of carrying 400 passengers, 35 cars or around five railway goods wagons. Because of her unusual multi-purpose specification, she had a rather bluff and broad hull to maximise her vehicle capacity while enabling her to fit the rather constricted dimensions of Ærøskøbing harbour. Given that it was necessary to have an unobstructed centreline for the carriage of railway wagons, the exhausts from her two MaK diesels were routed up though side-casings to twin exhaust stacks. Visual balance was achieved through the fitment of a dummy funnel above the bridge and this layout was from then on to form the basis of a majority of Knud E. Hansen A/S' subsequent ferry designs of the 1960s.

Concurrently, Knud E. Hansen's original client, Larvik-Frederikshavn Fergen, requested a design for a new ferry for the increasingly popular route between Denmark and Norway. Notwithstanding having been lengthened, the old *Peter Wessel* was struggling to cope, especially during the peak holiday season. The new 2,903 grt ferry was built by Trondheims Mekaniske Verksted and delivered in June 1961 as the *Cort Adeler*. She offered a greatly enhanced overnight capacity in cabins and reclining seats, plus parking for 140 cars.

Knud E. Hansen A/S next assisted a new entrant into the Scandinavian ferry market, Jahre Line – owned by the Norwegian ship owner, Anders Jahre of Sandefjord, who had made his money in the whaling industry and subsequently operated oil tankers – to develop an innovative design for a large overnight ferry for service between Oslo and Kiel. With the West German economy booming and

Below left: The *Linda Scarlett*, crossing the Øresund in the mid-1960s. (Bruce Peter collection)

Below right: The small Danish domestic car and train ferry *Ærøsund*. (Bruce Peter collection)

Bottom left: The Norwegian ferry *Cort Adeler* is seen off Larvik. (Bruce Peter collection)

Bottom right: The Swedish steam turbine passenger vessel *Svea Jarl*. (Bruce Peter collection)

48 KNUD E. HANSEN • 80 YEARS

Norway was a popular travel destination, in 1959, Jahre ordered the 7,034 grt *Kronprins Harald* from the Howaldtswerke Deutsche Werft (HDW) shipyard in Kiel.

According to Tage Wandborg, Jahre was determined that the ship should have a 'traditional' silhouette, rather than one of Wandborg's increasingly futuristic designs, and naval architects at the shipyard also had significant inputs. Powered by four MAN medium-speed diesels, coupled in pairs to each shaft via gearboxes, the vessel maintained a 20-knot service speed. The four-engine approach effectively solved the fundamental problem faced by naval architects involved in ferry design of finding a suitably compact, yet powerful, propulsion system to fit in the constricted space beneath a ferry's vehicle deck. Slow-speed direct drive marine diesels were relatively tall due to their large cylinders and so ships fitted with such large and powerful machinery, for example DFDS's 22-knot *England*, had a substantial freeboard. This made them less suitable for carrying buses and lorries in significant numbers as such extra weight was best kept low to maintain stability and for ease of loading. Subsequently, Knud E. Hansen A/S specified four-engine solutions for most of the ferries they designed until the latter 1960s.

The *Kronprins Harald* had space for 120 cars, loaded through ports in the side of her hull. Cabin berths were provided for nearly all 577 passengers. Jahre Line was a traditional two-class operation with First Class public rooms occupying the forward superstructure on boat deck while those for Second Class were located towards the stern on main deck. There were smoking saloons forward and aft with two restaurants to starboard amidships and a large galley to port.

Soon after the *Kronprins Harald* entered service in 1961, a slightly larger sister ship, the 7,694 grt *Prinsesse Ragnhild*, was ordered from the same builder for delivery in 1966.

While working on the *Kronprins Harald*, Knud E. Hansen A/S was also involved in designing a new overnight passenger ship for Stockholms Rederi AB Svea's jointly-operated Stockholm–Helsinki service. Remarkably, in view of extensive recent advances in the design of marine diesel engines and the obvious fuel economies enabled by motor ships, Stockholms Rederi AB Svea's directors insisted that the 4,334 grt *Svea Jarl* should steam-powered by a single 6-cylinder Skinner Marine steam engine as diesel motors were felt by them to be potentially noisy and intrusive on an overnight vessel. This somewhat complex and temperamental machinery gave a service speed of only 16 knots, very little considering the route's length and the emerging threat from airline competition. As

Above: The *Kronprins Harald* is seen during the final stages of outfitting at the HDW shipyard in Kiel. (Bruce Peter collection)

Opposite: The newly-delivered *Kronprins Harald* is seen at Oslo. (Bruce Peter collection)

Left: Upon entering service in 1961, the Silja Line ferry *Skandia* revolutionised traffic between Sweden and Finland. (Marko Stampehl collection)

50 KNUD E. HANSEN • 80 YEARS

Top left: The Iraqi harbour tug *Saad*. (KNUD E. HANSEN Archive)

Top right: A patrol boat for Iraq. (KNUD E. HANSEN Archive)

Above left: The buoy maintenance vessel *Al Waleed*. (KNUD E. HANSEN Archive)

Above right: The large pilot boat *Al Rasheed*. (KNUD E. HANSEN Archive)

Right: The Iraqi cargo vessel *Kassim* during sea trials and prior to her re-naming. (KNUD E. HANSEN Archive)

Above left: Two fast harbour launches for Iraq. (KNUD E. HANSEN Archive)

Above right: The harbour launch *Tikreet*, the design of which resembled the 'Sundbusserne' in compressed form. (KNUD E. HANSEN Archive)

the vessel would sail from a historic quay at Skeppsbron in Stockholm's picturesque Gamla Stan area, any cars carried would need to be side-loaded through hatches in the shell plating. As the project developed, the design that emerged showed some similarities to her owner's existing *Birger Jarl* and to the *Kronprins Harald*. The *Svea Jarl* was completed by the Finnboda shipyard at Nacka in 1961. Elegantly appointed through she undoubtedly was, within little over a decade, her essentially conservative design meant that she was no longer economical as a ferry and so she was converted for cruising instead.

As elsewhere in Northern Europe, during the latter 1950s, there was a surge in passenger and car traffic across the Central Baltic corridor and so in 1957 Stockholms Rederi AB Svea and its partners in the Sweden–Finland trade – Finska Ångfartygs Aktiebolaget and Ångfartygs AB Bore – decided to establish a fourth jointly-owned company, Siljarederiet, to develop a cross-Baltic car ferry service. between Norrtälje, a town to the north-east of Stockholm, Mariehamn in the Åland Islands and Turku.

From early on, Knud E. Hansen A/S advised on the initial design development of Siljarederiet's new ferry. At first, the owners requested a side-loading vessel, similar in layout and appearance to the *Svea Jarl*. Soon, a much more practical bow- and stern-loading drive-through design with space for 175 cars came to be favoured. Knud E. Hansen's basic design was further developed by the vessel's builder, the Wärtsilä Helsinki Shipyard. Wärtsilä's particular expertise was in the design of icebreaker hulls but, as the company had never previously designed a ferry, Knud E. Hansen A/S was re-engaged to advise on matters of detailed design before and during the construction phase.

The 3,593 grt *Skandia* was powered by twin 9-cylinder Wärtsilä-Sulzer diesels, located towards the stern, enabling an 18-knot service speed, and the exhaust uptakes were routed though a narrow centre casing. An icebreaker bow made a 'knife edge' to smash through sheet ice in winter.

Inboard, the *Skandia* was a one-class vessel, her entire passenger accommodation being air-conditioned and outfitted in light, contemporary colours and with comfortable furniture in which to relax. An outstanding feature perpetuated by Tage Wandborg on numerous subsequent Knud E. Hansen A/S-designed ferries was an oval-shaped observation lounge in a 'dummy funnel' amidships, giving passengers panoramic views of the passing archipelago scenery. Elsewhere on board, eating, drinking, shopping and a visit to the sauna were welcome attractions for adults, while children could enjoy the playroom. Yet, reflecting Siljarederiet's predominant budget-conscious clientele, the majority of overnight accommodation was in the form of reclining seats rather than berths in cabins, there being

A design drawing of the *Farsea*, a typical Knud E. Hansen A/S bulk carrier of the early-1960s. (KNUD E. HANSEN Archive)

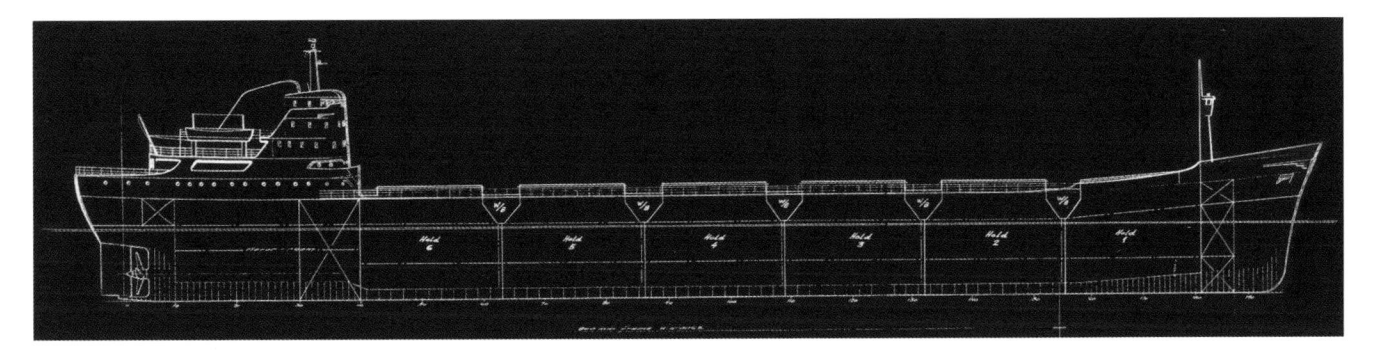

The geared bulk carriers *Polarland* (1), *Cape Clear* (2), *Baron Forbes* (3), *Mineral Ougree* (4), *Lysland* (5) and *Skausund* (6) were all variations on the standard KEH design for the Haugesund shipyard. (Bruce Peter collection)

The bulk carrier *Gerore*, built in Kristiansand for the locally-owned Johan Gerrards Rederi. (KNUD E. HANSEN Archive)

only 136 berths out of a total passenger capacity of 1,200. This was also partly because the majority of crossings were expected to take place in daylight hours.

Even before the *Skandia* entered service, Siljarederiet ordered a sister, the *Nordia*, which was completed in 1962.

While the *Svea Jarl* and *Skandia* were being built in Sweden and Finland respectively, a new Stockholms Rederi AB Svea cargo vessel, the 2,400 grt *Garm*, was under construction to a Knud E. Hansen A/S design at Helsingborgs Varv. Meanwhile, at the Valmet shipyard in Helsinki, the broadly similar 2,300 grt *Pulptrader* was being built for Pulpships AB, owned by Harry Nielsen of Helsinki. As her name suggested, she was designed to carry wood pulp for the paper industry. Both the *Garm* and the *Pulptrader* followed Knud E. Hansen A/S' usual machinery- and superstructure-aft layout pattern for vessels of their type.

A much smaller concurrent project was the *Sønderho*, a small passenger and mail launch for Post & Telegrafvæsnet (the Danish postal service) to connect the port of Esbjerg on Denmark's West Coast with the offshore island of Fanø. Built by Esbjerg Jernstøberi & Maskinfabrik A/S, the completed vessel was transported carefully from their factory through the streets of the town and down to the port. Today, after over half a century of use, she continues on the Esbjerg–Fanø route.

Iraqi projects

In the 1960s–70s period, Knud E. Hansen A/S carried out a great many projects in Iraq for the state-owned Iraqi Port Administration and Iraqi Maritime Transport Company. Knud E. Hansen visited the country on a business trip to the Middle East in the autumn of 1958, shortly after the Iraqi Revolution.

In July that year, a coup d'etat had overthrown the Hashemite monarchy which had ruled since the early 1930s and which was regarded by many as a means by which the West could retain imperial control. A new Iraqi Republic was established and this was ruled for the next 40 years by the Socialist Ba'ath party. For the first two decades, this government invested substantially in Iraq's national infrastructure. The oil industry was greatly expanded and profits were invested in shipping, both deep sea and on the Tigris and Euphrates rivers.

Hansen's visit to Baghdad happened at a most opportune moment. As Knud E. Hansen A/S was a Danish company and therefore without colonialist associations, it became the Iraqi government's favoured designer, not only for all of the vessels it required, but also for substantial amounts of port infrastructure. Indeed, during the ensuing 20 years, the Iraqi government commissioned Knud E. Hansen A/S to design no fewer than 157 ships of all sizes, ranging from workboats, tugs, barges, dredgers and passenger launches to cargo liners, tankers, floating cranes and floating docks. Additionally, layout designs were provided for harbour installations in Baghdad and Basra. The first projects to materialise from Hansen's trip were small passenger launches, harbour master launches, mooring boats, tugs and four pilot boats. The first tug was the *Al Omarah*, designed in 1959 and built by Kremer & Sohn in Elmshorn in West Germany. A large pilot boat, the *Al-Rasheed*, was designed by Tage Wandborg for the new Port of Basra and built by Meyer Werft at Papenburg on the River Ems in West Germany. The intention was that she would be stationed offshore for weeks at a time with several pilots on board but the Iraqi government's ministers so admired Wandborg's design that they decided instead to use the vessel as their State Yacht. Wandborg also drew up a buoy maintenance vessel, the *Al-Waleed*, which was completed in 1964 by Rolandwerft in Bremen to service the buoys marking the navigation channel leading to the Port of Basra and she too was notable for her stylish appearance.

Meanwhile, Gerhard Erichs designed two general cargo liners, the 5,701 grt 1*4 July* and the *Kassim*, names chosen to commemorate the Iraqi Revolution. Once again, these vessels followed KEH's favoured 'engines-aft' layout. They were built by the Hitachi shipyard at Sakurajima in Japan – the first time Knud E. Hansen A/S had been involved in projects to be realised so far away from Denmark. They did, however, begin a trend whereby KEH naval architects found themselves working for extended periods in shipbuilding towns and cities all over the world as the industry became increasingly globalised.

By the time the *Kassim* was ready to commence sea trials in 1963, however, the Iraqi Prime Minister Abd al-Kaim Qasim, a former army general in whose honour she was named, had been overthrown by the Ba'ath party hierarchy and so, prior to delivery, she was renamed *14 Ramadan*.

Haugesund bulk carriers

In 1960, Knud E. Hansen A/S began a lengthy and successful relationship with Haugesunds Mekaniske Verksted in Norway, for which complete designs for bulk carriers and tankers were produced. Such vessels became the yard's staple output throughout the 1960s and well into the seventies. At first, the Haugesund projects were coordinated by Gerhard Erichs but, from the mid-1960s onwards, his colleague Erik T. Møller took over, initiating new research to optimise payload, steel weights and production methods for these vessels. Møller, who joined Knud E. Hansen A/S in 1959, was, like most of his colleagues, a Helsingør Teknikum graduate. He became a specialist in tanker and bulk carrier design while Erichs grew more interested in issues relating to the calculation of vessels' speed and power. Svend A. Bertelsen also was very interested in this work as, in addition to his all-consuming work as KEH's managing director, he sat on the board of the Burmeister & Wain shipyard in Copenhagen, which made a speciality of building bulk carriers in the 1970s–90s period.

The reasoning underpinning Haugesunds Mekaniske Verksted's decision to franchise out all design work to Knud E. Hansen A/S was economic. In 1969, *The Motor Ship* observed that most Scandinavian shipyards employed a ratio of office staff to manual workers of 1 to 4 whereas, at Haugesund, it was 1 to 10. By not providing full-time jobs for relatively well-paid naval architects, drawing office technicians and administrators, the yard saved a lot of money, enabling it to focus instead on mass-producing standardised ship types designed by others as cheaply as possible.

The first collaboration between Knud E. Hansen A/S and Haugesunds Mekaniske Verksted was the design and construction of an 18,830 dwt gearless motor bulk carrier named the *Farsea*; she was built for the Norwegian owner Sverre Farstad of Ålesund and delivered in 1962. Typical of her generation and type, she had straight hull lines with six hatch openings, the topsides curving inward at main deck to provide extra stiffening. Her superstructure was fully aft and elegantly streamlined in a manner somewhat reminiscent of KEH's concurrent treatment of the Oslo–Kiel Jahre Line ferry *Kronprins Harald* – a surprisingly costly approach for a very functional ship destined to have a relatively short active life.

A further seven bulk carriers shared the *Farsea*'s hull design; these were the *Tonto* of 1963, a geared bulker (i.e. fitted with cranes) owned by Rederiet Tønseth of Bergen, the *Bris* (1964), belonging to Thorviks Rederi A/S of Oslo, the *Valhall* (1966) of Valdemar Skogland A/S, Haugesund, the *Polarland* (1966) of Richard Amlie, also of Haugesund, plus three examples for Scottish Ship Management, the *Cape Clear*, *Baron Forbes* and *Baron Dunmore* of 1967–68. This owner was formed through the combination of two long-established Glasgow-based tramp shipping companies, Lyle and Hogarth, both of which entered the bulk trades in the post-World War 2 era. Scottish Ship Management's relationship with Norwegian shipyards began when, in the early 1960s, representatives of Lyle and Hogarth appeared unannounced at Marinens Hovedverft in Horten, where there was also a shipyard capable of building bulk carriers. Ensuing discussions led to contracts being signed not only with Marinens Hovedverft, but also with Kaldnes Mekaniske Verksted at Tønsberg as well as the yard at Haugesund. The Scots wished to enter the so-called 'Handy size' bulk carrier market, a sector in which Norwegian yards and ship owners already were excelling.

Essentially similar KEH-designed bulk carriers of slightly varying dimensions were the *Lysland* (1964) of Halfdan Grieg, Bergen, the *Mineral Ougree* (1965) of Armement Deppe SA, Antwerp, the *Skausund* (1966) of I.M. Skaugen & Co, Oslo, the *Rolwi* and *Nanfri* (1968) plus the *Andwi* (1969) for a subsidiary of Rolf Wiglans Rederi A/S, Bergen, all of which were built in Haugesund. Examples of the type built elsewhere were the *Norbella* (1966) of I/S Norbella, Tromsø, constructed by Bergens Mekaniske Verksteder and the *Gerore*, completed in 1969 for Johan Gerrards Rederi, Kristiansand by Kristiansands Mekaniske Verksteder.

Alas, Knud E. Hansen did not survive to enjoy the growing reputation of his naval architecture consultancy because, tragically, he drowned in July 1960 while sailing his yacht, the *Sollys*, through rough weather in the Kattegat. This vessel had been designed by Hansen to replicate a nineteenth century prototype. Off the island of Anholt, her boom moved suddenly, knocking Hansen overboard. As the *Sollys* had been designed to be as authentic as possible, there was no motor, and so it proved impossible to turn quickly to rescue him and his family could only watch in horror as he disappeared in the sea. Three weeks later, Hansen's body was washed ashore at Kullen on the Swedish Coast. In his will, he left his business and the building it occupied at 75 Bredegade in Copenhagen to 10 of his employees. They were Svend A. Bertelsen, Dag Rogne, Gunner Jensen, Gunnar Toft Madsen, Preben Agner, Gerhard Erichs, Erik Madsen, Finn Aalsgaard, Herluf Lütken and Hanne Christensen, who had been his secretary. As Hansen apparently had not adjusted his will since Tage Wandborg's appointment, he was not included in this new board of directors. This anomaly meant that, although Wandborg was Knud E. Hansen A/S' most prominent employee, his status within the company's hierarchy was less central than it ought to have been.

Top: The bulk carrier *Rolwi* at the fitting out quay in Haugesund. (Bruce Peter collection)

Above: The sister ship, *Andwi*, as she appeared upon delivery. (Bruce Peter collection)

Below: How the Danish newspaper *Berlingske Tidende* reported on the untimely death of Knud E. Hansen. (KNUD E. HANSEN Archive)

The Bertelsen era

KNUD E. HANSEN
SHIP DESIGN SINCE 1937

The *Viking I* in Southampton Docks during the mid-1960s. (Bruce Peter collection)

Above left: The Esbjerg-Fanø ferry *Esbjerg*. (John Peter)

Above right: The Dutch-built Iraqi dredger *Hillah*. (KNUD E. HANSEN Archive)

Svend A. Bertelsen, the new Managing Director of Knud E. Hansen A/S, had a much less formal style than had been typical of Hansen himself. Everyone was now on first name terms, or called by their nicknames, but just as before, Bertelsen inspired his colleagues to produce good work, leading by example. Tage Wandborg recalls that:

'Svend Aage was my close friend and advocate. He was a charming gentleman, a good leader and a mathematical genius with his slide rule. He was also a workaholic and he expected a similarly high output from the rest of us. Not only was he an excellent naval architect with a particular gift for complex weight and stability calculations, but he was also very good at drumming up new business and, typically, he would work over weekends at home in order to prepare detailed specifications to form the basis of design work to be carried out by his colleagues the following week. In consequence, Knud E. Hansen A/S never advertised its services. Clients came knocking on the door because of its existing reputation.'

Under Bertelsen's leadership, Knud E. Hansen A/S enjoyed considerable success. In 1960, further Iraqi contracts were secured for the design of additional harbour craft plus a very substantial project to design the world's largest floating crane, the *Al Miqdad*. Having carried out initial conceptual studies, Svend A. Bertelsen eventually allocated the task of designing the crane as a challenge for a recently appointed staff member, Holger Terpet, who joined the firm in 1962. A small, intense, lively man Terpet was born near Hirtshals in North-Western Jutland in 1932. There, he became a joiner at the local Hansen and Bilde shipyard, which specialised in building fishing cutters. After military service and short spells working in shipyards at Karlstad in Sweden and in Aalborg in Denmark, he studied naval architecture at the Helsingør Teknikum and, from there, was appointed by Bertelsen to Knud E. Hansen A/S, where he remained well beyond the usual age for retirement (he died in 2008).

Prior to designing the floating crane for Iraq, Terpet's previous work at Knud E. Hansen A/S had been quite different as he had drawn up plans for two small double-ended ferries, the 399 gt *Esbjerg* and *Nordby*, built respectively by Aalborg Værft and Århus Flydedok og Maskinkompagni for Post & Telegrafvæsnet's short route between Esbjerg and Fanø.

For Terpet, the *Al Miqdad* project proved tough. Partly this was due to the specified 1,000-tonne lifting capacity and partly it was because the Iraqi Port Authority ordered it from an Austrian shipyard, the Österreische Shiffswerften AG Linz-Korneuburg, located on the bank of the River Danube just north of Vienna. This yard normally constructed river craft and, due to the shallows at the Danube's mouth, it was only possible to get large 'deep sea' vessels out in the spring when glacial snow melt from the Alps caused the river to swell significantly. Furthermore, instead of specifying a crane with wires, the Iraqis insisted that it should have a spindle, a solution usually chosen for cranes of far smaller lifting capacity. The spindle, with an 11-metre diameter, took a long time to design and was manufactured by Krupp in West Germany.

By the time the crane was completed in 1968, the Suez Canal was closed and so it had to be towed to Iraq via South Africa and the Cape of Good Hope. While crossing the Bay of Biscay, the tow hook broke through the crane barge's shell plating and so it was necessary to carry out repairs in Spain. Once the *Al Miqdad* arrived in Iraq, seven years after it had first been ordered, it was found that, as Holger Terpet had feared, the spindle system could not lift the weights required and so it was converted to a wire system instead. Knud E. Hansen A/S however developed a close relationship with the Korneuburg shipyard and this subsequently led to further KEH-designed vessels being built there, most notably a series of ro-ro freight ferries for Stena Line (see below).

The *Al Miqdad* commission was closely followed by a project to produce a layout for a shipyard in

Basra, which required a floating dock to be designed and built. More conventionally, a 65,000 dwt oil tanker was designed for the Iraqi Maritime Transport Company and several series of dredgers were manufactured in the Netherlands to maintain Iraq's new port and river infrastructure. Of these, the large suction dredger *Hillah*, designed in 1964 and delivered from the IHC Verschure shipyard in Kinderdijk in 1969, was particularly notable.

The production of drawings for drive-through passenger and car ferries dominated Knud E. Hansen A/S design output for the remainder of the 1960s. In this work, Tage Wandborg, Dag Rogne and Poul Erik Rasmussen had dominant roles. Wandborg and Rogne devised general arrangements, while Rasmussen drew up the underwater hull designs. In addition, Wandborg styled nearly all the vessels' silhouettes and livery details, giving most a uniformly sleek identity that was immediately recognised as having emanated from the Knud E. Hansen A/S drawing office. Unless an owner strongly objected, he even had distinctive 'speed flashes' welded on to their bows; he considered these his 'signature' but they were subsequently 'absorbed' into various shipping companies' corporate identities.

While Wandborg was first and foremost an aesthete who applied the same slanted font to his drawings as he favoured for lettering on the hulls of the ships he designed, Rogne's enthusiasms primarily related to technical aspects of naval architecture, although Wandborg was interested in these facets too. Unlike Wandborg, however, Rogne believed that, in order to attract and retain customers, designs should be produced as quickly as possible and with the minimum of work to save money as the shipyards' own drawing offices could attend to the minutiae as necessary. Perhaps unsurprisingly, there was strong competition between the two men, each of whom developed their own groups of important clients for ferry designs. Being originally from Norway himself, Dag Rogne developed particularly close working relationships with Norwegian car ferry operators such as Otto Thoresen, Det Kristiansands Dampskipsselskap and Larvik-Frederikshavn Fergen. Additionally, he was a very good friend of Sten A. Olsson, the founder of Stena Line, for whom Knud E. Hansen A/S designed numerous ferries from the mid-1960s until the present day. According to Rogne:

> 'Wandborg initiated a new style for passenger ferries and I learned to emulate it in my own work. Because we worked in a relatively small office, we all knew what each other was doing and we would instinctively spot good ideas from our colleagues and incorporate these in our own work. The 1960s and 70s were busy years with a great deal of activity as one ferry after another came off the drawing boards, as well as many other kinds of ships. In terms of moving passenger ship design forward, Knud E. Hansen A/S was a hotbed of creativity and often we surprised each other with what we produced.'

Wandborg, in contrast, contends that the few ferries styled by Rogne were pale imitations of his own work and that they lacked his own signature attention to proportion and design detail – even although admittedly they generally functioned remarkably well. A further employee, Morten Skrydstrup, who first joined Knud E. Hansen A/S in 1968, recalls:

> 'I shared an office with Wandborg, Rogne and Rasmussen. Wandborg and Rogne were highly competitive but were very different characters. Rogne was quite small, quiet and studious, whereas Wandborg was very outgoing. The two respected each other but, below the surface, one could tell that Wandborg considered Rogne's designs to be very inferior to his own, while Rogne probably thought that Wandborg put in too much effort to beautify everything beyond what he was actually paid to produce.'

The first ferries of what was soon to become a large series of similar designs by Knud E. Hansen A/S were the 2,301 grt *Julle* and *Kalle* of Juelsminde–Kalundborg Linien. These were by the Adler Werft in Bremen, West Germany, entering service in 1962 and 1963 respectively. While they had much in common with Grenaa-Hundested Færgefart's *Kattegat*, their vehicle deck casings were on either beam rather than along the centreline. Fold-away platform decks at the upper level enabled either commercial vehicles or two levels of cars to be carried, depending upon the time of year (during the holiday season, there was expected to be less freight traffic and many more cars). Each could transport 1,200 passengers and 120 cars. Their main deck contained a cafeteria forward with a hallway amidships and a restaurant aft. The galley, supplying food to both, was on the boat deck above. Four 9-cylinder MAN medium-speed diesels gave a 16.5-knot service speed and twin rudders were fitted to increase manoeuvrability as, when turned, these forced the wash of each propeller to the side more effectively than a centre rudder. There was also a bow rudder and a lateral-thrust propeller, enabling the vessels to turn quickly within their own lengths. As the exhaust uptakes were routed through side-casings, as with the *Ærøsund*, a streamlined dummy funnel was fitted slightly forward of amidships between the foremast and exhaust stacks, housing ventilation equipment and generators.

Following hard on the heels of the *Julle* and *Kalle* projects, Knud E. Hansen A/S next was approached by the West German excursion ship operator Schiffahrts-Gesellschaft 'Jade' GmbH of Wilhelmshafen to design a passenger-only motor vessel to link the town with the North Sea island of

Top left: Juelsminde harbour in the mid-1960s with the ferry *Julle* at the berth. (Bruce Peter collection)

Top right: The Bornholm ferry *Jens Kofoed*. (Bruce Peter collection)

Centre: The Helgoland excursion vessel *Wilhelmshafen*. (Ambrose Greenway)

Bottom left: The Gedster-Travemünde ferry *Gedser*. (Bruce Peter collection)

Bottom right: The *Lasse*, built by Aalborg Værft, which acquired a license to use a modified version of Knud E. Hansen A/S' standard ferry design.
(Bruce Peter collection)

Helgoland. This can be a stormy passage and so the new *Wilhelmshaven* was robustly designed. Built by the Rolandwerft in Bremen, she was only around 10 metres shorter than these ferries and, although her passenger capacity was about the same, her gross tonnage was nearly half at only 1,418 grt. The lack of car deck space made a big difference to the overall volume and served to illustrate that, were it not for their vehicle capacity, the first generation of KEH-designed car ferries would actually have been very small ships indeed.

Thanks to Tage Wandborg's styling, the *Wilhelmshaven* had the sleek appearance of a modern motor yacht and was immediately acclaimed by tourists and regular travellers alike. Her two MAN diesels were located aft of amidships and the exhaust was carried up through the lower part of her rear mast. As with the Siljarederiet ferry *Skandia*, the *Wilhelmshaven* had an observation lounge, known as the 'skybar' located in a dummy funnel on the topmost deck. It was the perfect spot from which to watch the ship's progress towards the vertiginous red sandstone mass of Helgoland and the feature was replicated on many subsequent KEH ferry designs.

Subsequently, Tage Wandborg made styling drawings for another operator involved in the tourist trade to Helgoland, the Hafen Dampschiffart AG (Hadag) of Hamburg. He was asked to devise silhouettes for two of its ships, the *Wappen Von Hamburg* of 1962 and her larger 1965 namesake.

The *Wilhelmshafen* project was followed by a commission to design a 2,964 grt car ferry of broadly similar design to the *Julle* and *Kalle* for overnight service between Copenhagen and Rønne on Bornholm, a Danish island in the Southern Baltic. During daytime, the vessel would additionally make two return sailings to Ystad in Sweden. The venture's backers were A/S Bornholm-Færgen, a newly-established operator owned by various private interests on Bornholm which sought to break the monopoly of the long-established Dampskibsselskab på Bornholm af 1866 on routes to the island.

Named the *Jens Kofoed*, the vessel's interiors were arranged much like that those of the Cort Adeler with cabins in the forward superstructure and on either side of the vehicle deck. That there was space for 1,000 passengers, with no fewer than 268 berthed for overnight sailings and 100 cars in a vessel measuring only 88.10 x 16.21 metres was a triumph of rational and ingenious planning. Because there was no available linkspan in Copenhagen, the ship was fitted with two stern ramps, each at approximately a 45-degree angle to the quay, enabling, if not exactly side-loading, then stern-quarter access there.

Once again, the construction contract was placed with a West German shipyard, the Bremer-Vulkan GmbH of Bremen, but, as it already had a full order book and Bornholms-Færgen demanded a quick delivery time, the best option for Bremer-Vulkan was to subcontract the steelwork to another yard, Bartram and Sons Ltd of Sunderland on the River Tyne. Tage Wandborg recalls that:

'I was not entirely happy about this sub-contracting because it made our supervision of the project that bit more difficult and Bartrams had never built a ship of this type before. Immediately, we noticed several interesting differences between shipbuilding methods in West Germany and in Britain. The British appeared to use a much more springy type of steel that was very difficult to work into the elegant double-curvatures that we took for granted when designing ferries to be built in Germany. When you looked closely at the hull and superstructure of the ship, you could see that it had been a struggle to build as it had a slightly rippled surface. Although the detailed build quality was not quite what we were used to from the Germans and the British shipyard was probably using antiquated equipment, one could not fault its solidity.'

The incomplete shell was towed across the North Sea to Bremen for fitting out and the vessel was delivered in August 1963. Notwithstanding Wandborg's anxieties, the entire process from ordering to completion had taken just under a year – a model of efficiency by all concerned.

While the *Jens Kofoed* was under construction, Ragnar Moltzau, the Norwegian owner of the Helsingør–Helsingborg 'Sundbusserne', decided commence ferry route between Gedser in Denmark and Travemünde in West Germany. Moltzau was attracted by the possibility of making good profits from duty free sales to day-trippers taking advantage of price differentials between the two countries. The Moltzau ferries, the 2,494 grt *Gedser* and the *Travemünde*, ordered from the Orenstein & Koppel und Lübecker Machinenbau of Lübeck, were similar to the *Julle* and *Kalle* and the first entered service in May 1963.

Aalborg Værft subsequently was licensed by Knud E. Hansen A/S to construct a further series of five ferries from 1964 onwards to designs modified by their own drawing office from those of the *Gedser* and *Travemünde*. The first of these, the 2,360 gt *Lasse*, joined the Juelsminde–Kalundborg service, while the remaining four, named the *Mette Mols*, *Maren Mols*, *Mikkel Mols* and *Morten Mols*, were built in two batches for DFDS' Mols Linien subsidiary, which operated between Ebeltoft and Sjællands Odde. Their initial pair entered service in 1966, the other two following in 1969 to cope with rapidly expanding custom on the route.

Two new ferries for Grenaa-Hundested Linien, the 3,061 grt *Grenaa* and the *Hundested*, built by the

62 KNUD E. HANSEN • 80 YEARS

Left: The *Grenaa*, seen shortly after entering service in 1964. (Jan Vinther Christiansen collection)

Below: The launching of the *Gotland* at De Mervede Van Vliet & Co on 5 June 1964. (Bruce Peter collection)

Right: The completed *Gotland* as she appeared upon entering service. (Bruce Peter collection)

Bottom left: The *Gotland*'s fleet-mate, the *Visby*, had a larger number of passenger berths – consequently, her casings were broader and her exhaust stacks were slightly inboard of the shell plating.
(Bruce Peter collection)

Bottom right: A portside view of the *Gotlandia*. (Bruce Peter collection)

KNUD E. HANSEN • 80 YEARS **63**

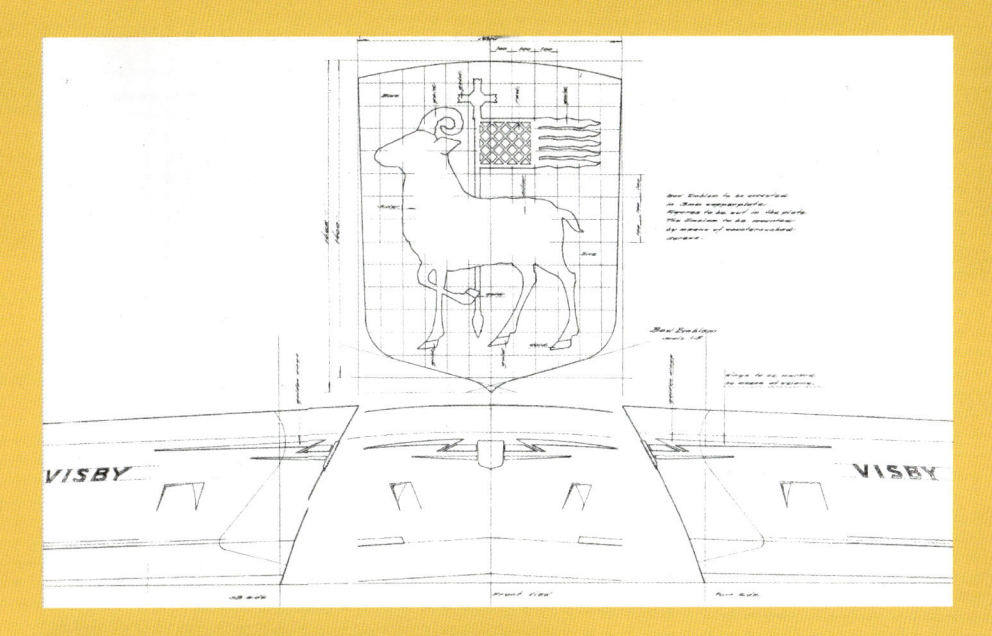

Left: Drawings by Tage Wandborg of the bow decoration on the *Visby*. (KNUD E. HANSEN Archive)

Below left: The *Dana Scarlett*, which operated between Tuborghavn and Landskrona. (Bruce Peter collection)

Below right: A stern-quarter view of the Helsingør-Helsingborg ferry *Carola*. (Bruce Peter collection)

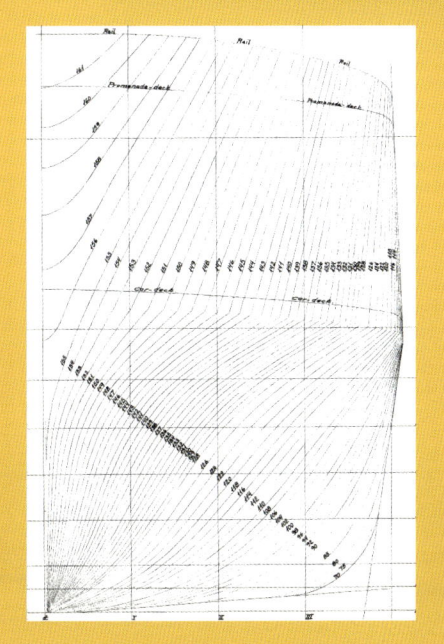

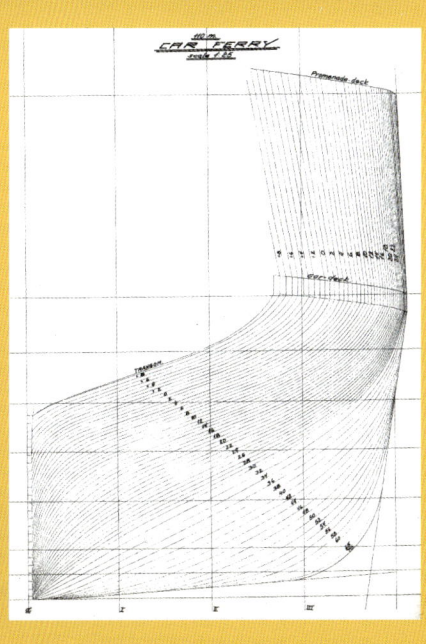

Bow and stern lines of the Thoresen-owned *Viking II* and *Viking II*, drawn by Poul Erik Rasmussen and showing the typical KEH solution with a knuckle-joint at vehicle deck height. (KNUD E. HANSEN Archive)

Schiffbau-Gesellschaft Unterweser AG in Bremerhaven and delivered in 1964, represented the next stage in the development of Knud E. Hansen A/S' 'standard' short-sea ferry type. At 17.7 metres wide, they were slightly broader than existing examples to give room for two lines of commercial vehicles between the hanging car decks.

Ferries for Gotland

In the early 1960s, curiosity about the proficiency of Knud E. Hansen A/S's ferry designs spread rapidly throughout the Scandinavian shipping community. In the ensuing years, Rederi AB Gotland (otherwise known as Gotlandsbolaget), based in Visby on the Island of Gotland in the Baltic Sea, became one of the firm's best customers. The company had been founded in 1865 and its handsome ships with their black-topped red funnels embellished with a white letter 'G' had served the island ever since. In 1962, however, an unwelcome competitor emerged in the form of Rederi AB Nordö, a ship owner only since 1949, which introduced a summer-only ferry route between Oxelösund, Klintehamn and

The launching of the *Viking III* at Lübeck on 10 March 1965. (Bruce Peter collection)

Above: The *Viking I* is seen in the Solent in the mid-1960s. (Bruce Peter collection)

Below left: The cafeteria of the *Viking I* showing passengers whiling away the hours of a night crossing of the Channel. (Bruce Peter collection)

Below right: A stern-quarter view of the *Viking II* off her Southampton berth. (Bruce Peter collection)

KNUD E. HANSEN • 80 YEARS **65**

Left: The *Svea Drott* at her berth in Helsingborg with the *Ursula* in the foreground.
(Bruce Peter collection)

Centre images: The launching of the *Queen of Prince Rupert* at the Victoria Machinery shipyard in Canada on 15 October 1965.
(Bruce Peter collection)

Left: The Spain-Morocco vessel *Ibn Batouta* early in her career at the commencement of a crossing of the Strait of Gibraltar. (Ambrose Greenway)

Above: The *Queen of Prince Rupert* is pictured *en route* through the Inside Passage on Canada's Pacific seaboard. (Bruce Peter collection)

Oskarshamn. Consequently, Rederi AB Gotland felt obliged to respond and one of its managers, Eric D. Nilsson, who had previously worked for Stockholms Rederi AB Svea and consequently had connections with Knud E. Hansen A/S, invited the firm to produce designs for new ferries. Already in 1960, KEH had been commissioned redesign the aft car deck on the company's 1936-vintage *Christofer Polhem* (ex *Kronprinsessan Ingrid*) to accommodate more cars and to fit a stern door – a project carried out by Tage Wandborg.

For the new Gotland ferries, Knud E. Hansen A/S produced two different designs. The 2,990 grt *Gotland* was primarily a daytime ferry, based on the design of the *Gedser* and *Travemünde*, whereas the 2,825 grt *Visby* had a higher number of cabin berths for night sailings, more like the *Jens Kofoed*. While Wandborg designed the former, Dag Rogne had overall responsibility for the latter, although Wandborg's distinctive styling was applied to both vessels. He recalls that:

> 'Eric D. Nilsson got very good quotations for the construction of the ships from two yards in the Netherlands. The trouble was that neither had ever attempted to build this kind of ferry before. De Mervede Van Vliet & Co at Hardinxveld on the River Rhine built the *Gotland* but, for the ship to reach the sea, it was necessary to remove temporarily a vast steel box-girder railway bridge across the river and so the contract price included the hire of a crane barge for a day.'

The *Visby*, meanwhile, was ordered from the Zaanlandse Scheepsbouw at Bolnes and outfitted at its sister yard in Zaandam. Nonetheless, the two ferries were completed in a timely manner in 1964 and the railway bridge was indeed removed to let the *Gotland* out to sea.

Subsequently, De Mervede Van Vliet & Co won an order for a similar ferry from Jadrolinija, the Yugoslavian state-owned shipping company, for Adriatic service on the Dalmatian Coast and overnight to Italy. Although Knud E. Hansen A/S was not involved in planning the *Liburnija*, De Mervede Van Vliet very obviously used the *Gotland*'s design as their starting point.

Shortly after Rederi AB Gotland had taken delivery of the *Gotland* and *Visby*, Rederi AB Nordö hit back with its own duo of Knud E. Hansen A/S-designed ferries, the 1,959 grt *Ölanningen* and *Gotlandia* which were delivered in 1965 by Langesunds Mekaniske Verksteder in Norway for routes from Södertälje to Kappelshamn and Oskarshamn to Klintehamn respectively. Notwithstanding their compact size, each could carry 120 cars each due to being fitted throughout with hanging decks.

Knud E. Hansen A/S next designed more ferries for the Stockholms Rederi AB Svea-owned Linjebuss and Skandinavisk Linjetrafik subsidiaries operating across The Sound. One was to supplement the *Primula* between Helsingør and Helsingborg and the other was to augment the *Linda Scarlett* between Tuborghavn and Landskrona. Delivered in 1964 by Öresundsvarvet in Landskrona, the 1,721 grt *Carola* and *Dana Scarlett* were hybrids of the *Primula*'s relatively short and broad dimensions combined with the aesthetic elements of the larger *Kalle/Julle* ferry type.

A further, larger, ferry for the same owner was the 2,505 grt *Scania*, intended for Baltic service between the Swedish port of Gräddö and Mariehamn in the Åland Islands. Between ordering her from Uddevallavarvet and her delivery in 1964, Stockholms Rederi AB Svea decided instead to place her with their Skandinavisk Linjetrafik subsidiary on a new route from Korsør in Denmark to Kiel in West Germany.

The Thoresen Vikings

In the summer of 1962, Knud E. Hansen A/S designed their first ferries for use outside of Scandinavia. Their client was Otto Thoresen, a Norwegian ship owner who had the idea of operating frequent cross-

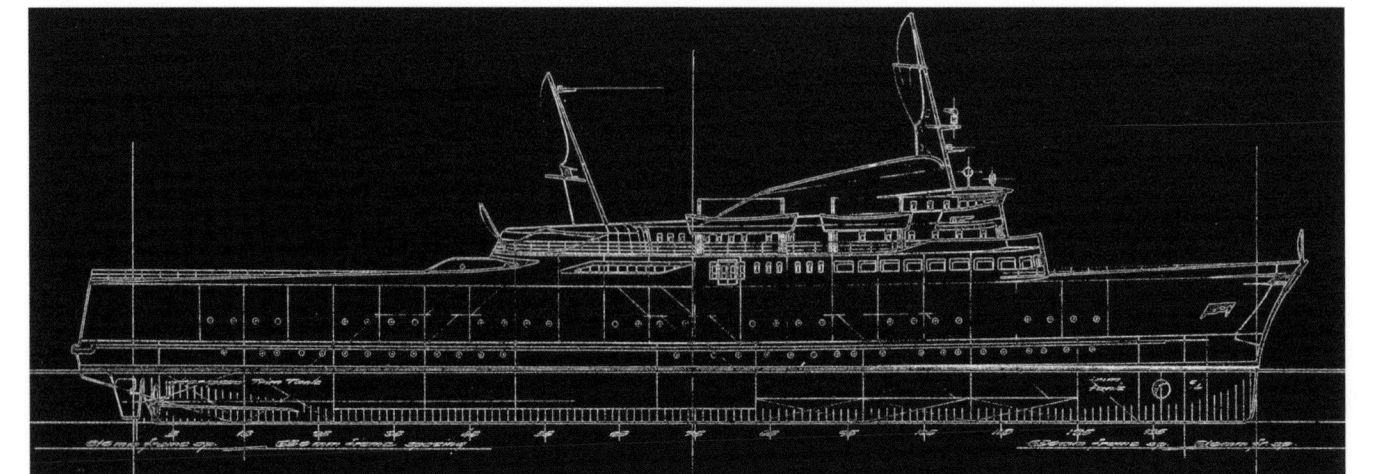

An early design drawing for the *Prins Bertil*, emphasising that the concept was significantly geared towards freight traffic.
(KNUD E. HANSEN Archive)

Channel services between Southampton, Le Havre and Cherbourg when he experienced a severely delayed crossing on a down-at-heel British Railways steamer.

The 3,670 grt *Viking I* and *Viking II* were delivered by the Kaldnes Mekaniske Verksted at Tønsberg in Norway in 1964, and thereafter the 3,824 grt *Viking III* was built by the Orenstein & Koppel und Lübecker Machinenbau of Lübeck, appearing in June 1965. All three were somewhat larger than previous KEH ferries and had overnight berths for 300 out of a total capacity of 940 and space for 180 cars, loaded through both bow and stern doors. They were, in fact, the first drive-through ferries to serve international routes from a British port, albeit flying the Norwegian flag and therefore exempt from British safety regulations. Nonetheless, their introduction gave rise to a vigorous debate within the British naval architecture profession regarding the safety of drive-through ferries with bow doors.

So far as the British travelling public was concerned, however, the advent of the Thorsesen 'Vikings' was very welcome. Indeed, when the *Viking I* made her maiden arrival in Southampton in April 1964, she caused a mild sensation. Apart from the striking modernity of her design, she was painted in a remarkable livery. Her hull was bright orange with the company name 'Thoresen Car Ferries' painted along either side – the first time that this had been done on a passenger ship sailing from Britain – while the topmost decks of her superstructure and her exhaust stacks were a fresh turquoise green.

A further similar vessel to the Thoresen 'Vikings' was the 4,018 grt *Svea Drott*, built by Öresundsvarvet in Landskrona in 1966 for Stockholms Rederi AB Svea's newly-established Trave Line overnight service linking Malmö and Travemünde. At the same time, BC Ferries in Canada commissioned a slightly shorter version in the form of the 3,500 grt *Queen of Prince Rupert*, constructed by the Victoria Machinery Company and also delivered in 1966 for operation on the scenic 'Inside Passage' route from Prince Rupert to Port Hardy. Otto Thoresen, who lived in Spain, was subsequently involved in the establishment of a new ferry company – Lignes Maritimes du Detroit, known as 'Limadet' – to connect Malaga and Algeciras with Tangier in Morocco and he commissioned Knud E. Hansen A/S to design the 2,890 grt *Ibn Batouta*, which was built by Ateliers et Chantiers de la Seine-Maritime at Le Trait in France and also delivered in 1966.

Sweden's ferry entrepreneurs

Lion Ferry, a subsidiary of the Bonnier newpaper and publishing empire based in Halmstad, meanwhile had also contacted Knud E. Hansen A/S to request plans for what turned out to be only the first of a series of new ferries. In Sweden, the government provided tax breaks for investors in shipping and so Bonnier must have thought that it would be lucrative to become involved in the ferry business. Moreover, alcoholic drinks and tobacco products were subject to progressive taxation and this had created an opportunity for entrepreneurs to provide short day cruises to buy these and other 'luxury' goods at tax-free prices.

Lion Ferry had been established in 1958 and initially had sought to establish a ferry route from Halmstad to Grenaa, but the Town Council there had already entered into an agreement with a Norwegian company, A/S Europafergen, and so demanded that Lion Ferry should pay compensation to break the Norwegians' exclusive right to operate to Sweden from the port.

The alternative for Lion Ferry was to develop a Halmstad–Århus service. This was not an obvious ferry link as it was somewhat longer than other established Sweden–Denmark crossings and, therefore, difficult to timetable attractively. Fortunately for Lion Ferry, the lure for Swedes of tax-free shopping on board the ferry, and of Århus as a destination, made the operation a success, at least for a time. In addition, the company's dynamic managing director, Henrik Meijer, who was a lawyer by training, was particularly effective in drumming up freight business.

Another of Meijer's business avenues, subsequently emulated by another up-and-coming Swedish ferry entrepreneur, Sten Allan Olsson (see below), was to earn money by selling and chartering ships and so few of Lion Ferry's vessels lasted long in the fleet. Knud E. Hansen A/S's first design for Lion Ferry, the 3,625 grt *Prins Bertil* of 1964, was, in fact, to become a standard type for Lion Ferry and for other clients of her builder, Werft Nobiskrug at Rendsburg in West Germany. Her vehicle deck had a clear span for almost the entire hull length, save for a short, narrow casing aft of amidships. This arrangement provided five unobstructed lanes on which lorries could be parked. Indeed, her vehicle capacity of 162 cars or 24 trucks represented a significant increase over previous KEH designs. As there was very little supporting framework in the hull, it was necessary to build robust diagonal cross-bracing into the deckhead to keep the structure from flexing unduly. The superstructure only covered two-thirds of her hull with an open deck to the rear, upon which cars could be loaded via a side-ramp. The principal saloons were on the main and boat decks, with a large restaurant located forward, overlooking the bow.

Externally, the *Prins Bertil*'s superstructure was built up in layers and the effect was accentuated by a large 'skybar' above the bridge, the exhaust being routed through a broad rear mast with a tapering

The *Poseidon* is seen in Gothenburg harbour in the mid-1960s. (Rickard Sahlsten collection).

KNUD E. HANSEN • 80 YEARS **69**

Right: The *Prins Bertil* makes an impressive sight at speed shortly after completion.
(Werft Nobiskrug, Rendsburg)

Below left and right: The launching of the *Kronprins Carl Gustav* at the Werft Nobiskrug shipyard, Rendsburg, on 26 January 1966.
(Werft Nobiskrug, Rendsburg)

Bottom left: The *Gustav Vasa* in the livery of her charterer, the Swedish State Railway, Statens Järnvägar.
(Bruce Peter collection)

Bottom right: The *Kronprins Carl Gustav* as she appeared upon entering service. (Werft Nobiskrug, Rendsburg)

KNUD E. HANSEN • 80 YEARS **71**

Top left: The *Munster* passes through the Kiel Canal on her delivery voyage in May 1968. (Werft Nobiskrug, Rendsburg)
Top right: The Stena-owned passenger excursion vessel *Poseidon*, the design of which was similar to the *Wilhelmshafen*. (Rickard Sahlsten collection)
Upper centre right: The hull of the *Stena Baltica* touches the water for the first time at Langesund on 27 March 1965. (Rickard Sahlsten collection)
Upper centre left: The launching of the *Stena Danica* at Le Trait on 3 May 1965. (Rickard Sahlsten collection)
Lower centre left: The newly delivered *Stena Baltica*, dressed overall for her maiden crossing of the Kattegat. (Rickard Sahlsten collection)
Lower centre right: A saloon on the *Stena Danica*. (Bruce Peter collection)
Bottom left: An aerial view of the *Stena Danica* crossing the Kattegat in the mid-1960s. (Bruce Peter collection)
Bottom right: The Stockholms Rederi AB Svea-owned *Scania*, which was used as a reference design for the *Stena Danica* and *Stena Nordica*. (Anders Bergenek collection)

black-painted top and a smoke-deflecting fin, somewhat resembling a witch's hat. The sleek external design suggested that she would be fast and, indeed, a relatively high speed of 20.5 knots was achieved by means of four MAN diesels, coupled in pairs to each propeller shaft.

The *Prins Bertil* was followed by two half-sisters, the 1965-built 2,801 grt *Gustav Vasa* and the 4,020 grt *Kronprins Carl Gustav*, delivered in 1966. From the outset, the *Gustav Vasa* was designed to fulfil a charter arrangement between Lion Ferry and the Swedish State Railway, SJ, for its Trelleborg–Travemünde route. Therefore, she had a more extensive superstructure, accommodating 1,016 passengers, and, crucially, an increased vehicle deck height of 4.9 metres (compared to the *Prins Bertil*'s 4.2). The reason was that the *Gustav Wasa* was designed to be retro-fitted with railway tracks and required sufficient headroom to accommodate the European 'Bern Convention' train loading gauge. As with the *Prins Bertil*, the *Gustav Vasa* was fitted with MAN engines but, on the Travemünde service, she did not need such a high top speed as her elder sister. To cut down on power, there was an unusual installation consisting of two larger plus two smaller main engines. The propellers were fixed and so when manoeuvring in ports, the big engines ran ahead and the little ones ran astern. This arrangement reputedly made her tricky to control, as the power ahead was much stronger than astern.

A third ship, the *Kronprins Carl Gustav*, was built for Lion Ferry's own usage between Halmstad, Copenhagen and Travemünde and she combined the most successful elements of both her elder sisters. Delivered in 1966, she was larger again at 4,020 grt, due to her even more superstructure than the *Gustav Vasa* and she also had bigger 9-cylinder engines, which added 2 knots to her speed. Two further similar vessels for the British & Irish Line's Irish Sea ferry routes, the 4,007 grt *Munster* and *Innisfallen*, were delivered in 1968 and 1969 respectively.

In 1962 Sten Allan Olsson, a Gothenburg scrap metal dealer and business entrepreneur, had taken over the operation of tax-free shopping day cruises to Skagen at the northern tip of Jutland in Denmark. This was the beginning of Stena Line which today is one of the world's leading ferry companies.

Soon Olsen began to order new vessels and, as with Lion Ferry, he commissioned Knud E. Hansen A/S to design them. Stena Line's technical director, Captain Helge Olofsson, quickly established a warm personal relationship with the naval architects Tage Wandborg and Dag Rogne. Wandborg speaks warmly of Olofsson, describing him as:

> 'A very skilled and visionary technician, full of experience and innovative ideas. He was certainly one of the pioneers when modern passenger and car ferries were introduced in the 'sixties. I was most inspired to work with him and he gave me a lot of encouragement and enthusiasm about my work, which was to design the upper works of all of Stena Line's ships from the very beginning.'

The first of Stena's new vessels was a small 564 grt passenger ship named the *Afrodite* which was built by D.W. Kremer & Sohn of Elmshorn in West Germany. Immediately after, Stena ordered a larger excursion vessel, the 1,358 grt *Poseidon*, which was built at Ulsteinvik in Norway to a design derived from that of the *Wilhelmshaven*; both were delivered in 1964. They were followed in quick succession by three car ferries, the 2,607 grt sister vessels *Stena Danica* and *Stena Nordica*, built by Ateliers et Chantiers de la Seine-Maritime at Le Trait in France and completed in 1965, plus the smaller 1,156 grt *Stena Baltica*, constructed by Langesunds Mekaniske Verksteder in Norway and delivered in 1966. Tage Wandborg remembers the circumstances surrounding these designs and their procurement:

> 'Sten A. Olsson had a remarkable ability to get exceptional value for money and so he looked at the drawings and kept asking 'couldn't we save more space by making that passage three centimetres narrower, or those stairs a little steeper?' He wanted as much space as possible to be given over to passengers, rather than used for storage and servicing, and had an amazing eye for cost-saving details. Also, he was a shrewd negotiator who only signed contracts with shipyards that were pared to the bone.'

What Sten A. Olsson saved on crew space and building costs, he spent on fairly lavish passenger accommodation and onboard entertainment, the theory being that these aspects would help to attract additional custom and revenue. Thus, he hired an up-and-coming architect called Robert Tillberg to design his ferries' interiors. At that time, Tillberg was also engaged by the Swedish American Line to design the First Class ballroom on the prestigious trans-Atlantic liner *Kungsholm*. Thereafter, he became an important designer of ferry interiors for a variety of Swedish operators and, subsequently, for numerous American-based cruise ships.

The Stena Baltica was planned largely by her builder, Langesunds Mekaniske Verksteder, a yard which had previously built only one ferry, the Norwegian-owned *Kraakerø* of 1964, operating across the mouth of the Oslofjord between Sandefjord and Strömstad. Tage Wandborg was, however, engaged by Stena to carry out superficial aesthetic modifications to the *Stena Baltica*'s funnels and masts to lend her a more purposeful and harmonious silhouette. Inboard, twin medium-speed MAN diesels enabled a service speed of only 14 knots. The *Stena Baltica* should have been Stena's first ferry to

KNUD E. HANSEN • 80 YEARS **73**

Top left: The elegant-looking Gothenburg-Kiel ferry *Stena Germanica* is seen in the archipelago off Gothenburg shortly after entering service in 1967. (Bruce Peter collection)

Top right: One of Tage Wandborg's many detailed drawings of aspects of the *Stena Germanica*'s upper decks, in this instance showing how the funnel was to be built and painted. Note that the Stena 'S' has been skewed to harmonise with the design. (KNUD E. HANSEN Archive)

Above right: Tage Wandborg persuaded ship owners to invest in attractively detailed ships with drawings showing how passengers would perceive them from ashore. An attractive ferry was a good marketing opportunity, he argued, and therefore a more costly funnel casing would be money well spent. (KNUD E. HANSEN Archive)

Centre left, centre right and bottom left: Three of the *Stena Germanica*'s interiors: the shop and reception desk, the lounge with bandstand and dancefloor and the dining saloon. (Bruce Peter collection)

Bottom right: The *Stena Germanica* in Gothenburg harbour. (Bruce Peter collection)

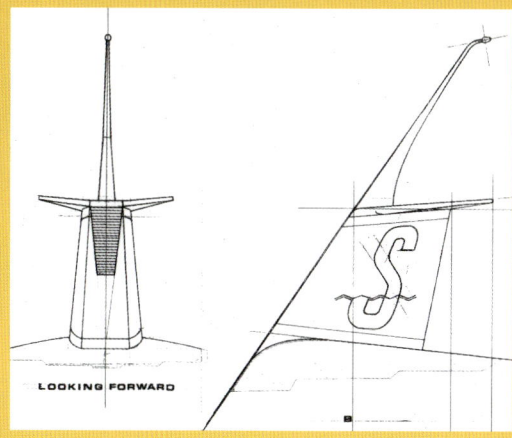

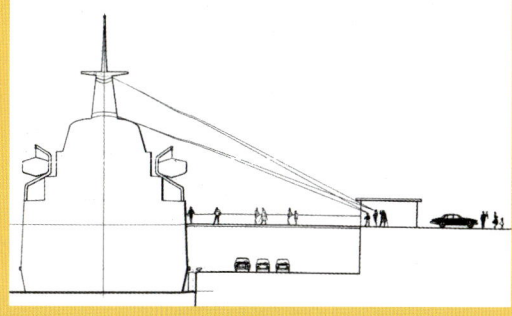

Top left: The *Skagerrak* nears completion at Aalborg Værft in July 1965. (Bruce Peter collection)

Top right: A stern-quarter view of the *Skagerrak*, showing her two-part stern doors. (Bruce Peter collection)

Above left: The stricken *Skagerrak* wallows in heavy swells on 7 September 1966. (Ambrose Greenway collection)

Above right: The *Skagerrak*'s replacement on the Hirtshals-Kristiansand route, the *Christian IV*. (Bruce Peter collection)

Left and above: The forward lounge/cafeteria and the buffet restaurant on the *Christian IV*. (Bruce Peter collection)

enter service and had been intended to operate between Nakskov in Southern Denmark and Kiel in Germany. Unfortunately, her construction was delayed at the shipyard and, in the interim, her owner decided to redeploy her between Gothenburg and Skagen.

In contrast, the planning of the *Stena Danica* and *Stena Nordica* was entirely by Knud E. Hansen A/S, using a layout and dimensions derived from those of the Stockholms Rederi AB Svea-owned *Scania*. The *Stena Danica* was completed in 1965 and, upon delivery she inaugurated Stena Line's new car ferry service from Gothenburg to Frederikshavn, in direct competition with the incumbent Sessanlinjen fleet. The *Stena Nordica*, however, was sent to the Dover Strait to inaugurate a new route from Tilbury to Calais, marketed as 'The Londoner' and aiming to attract British passengers to take tax-free shopping trips to France, a concept probably still slightly ahead of its time for most Britons.

The *Stena Baltica*'s unsophisticated design was atypical of Stena's subsequent approach. By working closely with Knud E. Hansen A/S' naval architects, its later ferries were state-of-the-art both in terms of efficiency and aesthetics, making them very attractive for others to acquire second-hand. Even before the *Stena Danica*, *Stena Nordica* and *Stena Baltica* were completed, in 1964, Sten A. Olsson requested a further substantially larger and more refined ferry design from Knud E. Hansen A/S. Olsson reasoned that West Germany's growing prosperity presented a good opportunity to develop an upmarket overnight ferry service between Gothenburg and Kiel. The initial design was essentially an elongated version of typical KEH ferries of the period, measuring 5,195 grt and with the accommodation arranged much as on the earlier *Cort Adeler*, *Jens Kofoed* and *Visby*. The most noteworthy technical characteristic of the design was the specification of what were at that time exceptionally powerful twin MAN 16-cylinder medium-speed diesels, which could generate 12,891 kW and thereby give a fast 23.5-knot service speed. These engines were relatively long and low with larger-than-usual numbers of smallish cylinders, ideal for fitting beneath a ferry vehicle deck.

Over the ensuing year, the design evolved, with substantial modifications being carried out by Tage Wandborg, the result being a design of very striking appearance. According to Wandborg,

> 'When it came to designing these ships, Sten A. Olsson … wanted quality and comfort. I devised a very streamlined and expressive ship, the lines of which demonstrated that it was fast, as indeed it was. Because the funnel was placed aft, much of the ship's topmost deck was open to passengers, where there was a solarium with floor-to-ceiling windows and a glass-fibre panelled roof to protect them from the elements. I drew a series of parallel horizontal lines and sleek curves to denote the hull, superstructure and deckhouses. The vertical staunchions, supporting the sundecks, were to be plated in and the steelwork cut at a 45 degree angle to give a strong feeling of forward movement …'

Although Stena at first required only one ferry to maintain the Gothenburg–Kiel route, such an attractive price was negotiated with the Langesunds Mekaniske Verksteder that an order was placed for two vessels, the *Stena Germanica* and *Stena Britannica*. Their hulls were assembled at Langesund with outfitting following at the Framnes Mekaniske Verksted in Sandefjord. During the construction phase, however, Langesunds Mekaniske Verksteder got into financial difficulties, a victim of rapidly increasing labour costs and contracts with insufficient margin to take account of wage inflation. Consequently, delivery of the *Stena Germanica* was delayed slightly until 1967. Nonetheless, the Swedish shipping industry magazine *Svensk Sjöfarts Tidning* declared her to be the best looking new Swedish-flagged ship delivered that year.

The Swedish architects Rolf Carlsson and Robert Tillberg designed the interiors, which were very elegant with fine wood veneers and rich colours. The cafeteria was above the dining saloon, located aft, and the same galley on main deck served both with arcades containing comfortable seating on either side to connect the various facilities together. A combined nightclub and smoking saloon was forward on boat deck. The most prominently located facility, however, was the tax-free shop on main deck and beside the entrance hallway.

While these projects were gestating, another client of Knud E. Hansen A/S, the Kristiansand Dampskipsselskap, sought a design for a new 2,703 grt multi-purpose car and rail ferry to supplement their existing vessel, the *Skagen*, on the 'Skagerak Express' service from Kristiansand in Norway to Hirtshals in Denmark. Named the *Skagerak*, she was to have enough vehicle deck space to carry three tracks of railway wagons of Bern Convention dimensions. Largely the work of Dag Rogne, an order was placed with the Aalborg Værft with delivery expected in July 1965.

The major design difference between the *Skagerak* and her predecessors from Knud E. Hansen A/S for usage on international routes was the design of her stern door. Rather than a folding ramp, it was in two halves and slid on rollers into the stern quarters, similar to the doors fitted to the Danish domestic Grenaa–Hundested and Juelsminde–Kalundborg car ferries, which sailed in relatively sheltered conditions. When closed, 28 locking pins, each of which had to be put in place and removed by the

76 KNUD E. HANSEN • 80 YEARS

Top left: The French SNCF-owned Channel ferry *Valencay*, one of two sisters built for service between Newhaven and Dieppe for which Knud E. Hansen A/S were consulted for advice. (Bruce Peter collection)

Top right: The *Saga*, the first of the three large passenger, car and container ferries for operation between Tilbury and Gothenburg. (Alistair Deayton collection)

Above: Hull docks in the latter-1960s with Stockholms Rederi AB Svea's *Svea* loading for Gothenburg and a steam tug of much earlier vintage in attendance. (Alistair Deayton collection)

Left: The Southampton-Bilbao ferry *Patricia* leaves Southampton in the latter-1960s. (Bruce Peter collection)

deck crew, secured it. This arrangement worked well initially but gradually, the crew became sloppy and omitted to lock all of the pins when the vessel put to sea.

During a stormy crossing of on 7 September 1966, the Skagerak's stern door broke open and the vehicle deck began to flood rapidly. The resulting sloshing of water caused a severe list to starboard and so her captain ordered the 97 passengers and 47 crew members to take to the lifeboats, while the Danish and Norwegian coastguards were summoned to mount a major rescue operation. Fortunately the evacuation was largely a success and only one elderly passenger died of a heart attack. For nine hours thereafter, the vessel battled with the elements. A tug arrived and attempted to her to port, but the list gradually increased and she keeled over and sank.

In 1967, the Kristiansand Dampskipsselskap went back to Aalborg Værft to have a replacement ferry constructed to essentially the same design, but with a more conventional design of stern door so that there could be no repetition of the carelessness which led to the Skagerak's demise. The Christian IV was completed in February 1968 and had a lengthy and successful career on the Kristiansand–Hirtshals route.

In addition to providing complete designs for ferries, during the first half of the 1960s, Knud E. Hansen A/S also gave a diverse range of assistance to ship owners and yards executing designs originating elsewhere. Such projects in which KEH naval architects were peripherally involved included work in 1961 on drawings for the Aalborg-designed and built Sessanlinjen ferry Prinsessan Margaretha, plus involvement in 1963 in the development of the Swedish State Railway SJ train ferry Skåne. Knud E. Hansen A/S already had a long-standing relationship with Aalborg Værft, dating back to the 1930s, and they had also previously designed vessels for SJ, such as the Öresund and the Gustav Vasa. Dag Rogne recalled that in the naval architecture, shipbuilding and ship-owning communities in 1960s Scandinavia, everybody knew everyone else, meaning that requests for assistance came quite regularly as though between friends (although, of course, all help provided was invoiced at an hourly rate). Meanwhile, Knud E. Hansen A/S' growing international reputation led builders of ferries overseas also to seek their input – for example, the French national railways, SNCF, to whom hull lines plans and calculations were supplied early in 1964 for the Newhaven–Dieppe car ferries Villandry and Valençay; the former built by Dubigeon-Normandie at Nantes and the latter by Chantiers de l'Atlantique in St Nazaire.

Ferries for England–Sweden service

In 1964, Knud E. Hansen A/S began work for Swedish Lloyd on a design for a new class of large overnight car and container ferry for North Sea service on the lengthy routes from Gothenburg to Hull and Tilbury. Swedish Lloyd, meanwhile, entered negotiations with its old rival in the England–Sweden trade, Ellerman Wilson Line (EWL) to create a joint ferry service. Shortly after, and Stockholms Rederi AB Svea joined the consortium which was henceforth known as England–Sweden Line. Their union was the vision of one of Swedish Lloyd's major shareholders, Torgeir Christoffersen, who believed strongly that containerisation represented the future of short-sea shipping and so was determined that Swedish Lloyd should invest heavily in container-carrying ships. As Swedish Lloyd's existing steamers emphasised passenger comfort and elegance, a majority of the company's directorate wanted a

The Tor Anglia is seen off Immingham in the mid-1960s. (Bruce Peter collection)

Top: The *Sunward* at Nassau in the latter-1960s. (Bruce Peter collection)

Left: The forward lounge on the *Sunward*. (Bruce Peter collection)

Above: The *Sunward*'s shop, located amidships. (Bruce Peter collection)

Bottom: A stern-quarter view of the *Sunward* at Nassau. (Bruce Peter collection)

The *København* of Norge-København Linjen.
(Bruce Peter collection)

miniature passenger liner capable also of carrying containers, whereas EWL and Svea were less keen to abandon the carriage of general cargo in favour of only cars and containers.

The intention was that each partner would order a ship, designed and built to comparable dimensions and with a similar capacity. Both Swedish companies agreed to share the design commissioned by Swedish Lloyd from Knud E. Hansen A/S, while Ellerman Wilson Line developed their own solution.

The new ships were to be stern-loaders with centre casings and only sufficient free height for trucks in the aft-most sections of their vehicle decks. The idea was that, rather than carrying lorries, which Swedish Lloyd's technical staff argued would unnecessarily heighten their centres of gravity, containers would be loaded on palettes and lashed directly to the vehicle deck. Variations on this technique had already been used successfully by the Atlantic Container Line, as well as on ferries in Australia and New Zealand. As events were to prove, however, any benefits were vastly outweighed by the severe disadvantage of increased turnaround times, cancelling out much of the advantage of building ro-ro vessels in the first place. Furthermore, EWL insisted that the new ships should also be fitted with electric cranes and hatches to carry general cargo. Private cars were loaded onto a separate upper car deck, via an independent shore-based ramp and side hatches.

Tage Wandborg recalls that, so far as aesthetic matters were concerned, Swedish Lloyd, in particular, proved to be rather traditionalist in its approach, repeatedly demanding that innovative aspects of Knud E. Hansen A/S' proposals be altered to the extent that the final solution was most atypical of KEH's normal output. As with Jahre Line some years before, the new England–Sweden ferries were instead to resemble conventional passenger liners and so Wandborg's desire to apply his signature styling was frustrated.

Swedish Lloyd's *Saga* and Stockholms Rederi AB Svea's *Svea* were built by Lindholmens Varv in Gothenburg and both were delivered in 1966. They were powered by four 6-cylinder Pielstick diesels, coupled in pairs via gearboxes to the propeller shafts and providing an 18-knot service speed.

Because the London–Gothenburg service involved two nights on board, a key problem for the designers was how to include cabin berths for all 408 passengers in vessels measuring slightly below 9,000 grt. Significant numbers of these were inserted below the vehicle deck and on two levels above. By specifying one-class ships, duplication of public rooms was avoided and this was probably the most progressive aspect of the design at a time when other established North Sea operators still imposed rigorous class divisions. Yet, it was believed by Swedish Lloyd, in particular, that the various age groups and social classes who travelled by ferry would naturally segregate themselves and so the accommodation on the saloon deck was split along the centreline with the most exclusive and luxurious-looking facilities (such as the dining saloon and the cocktail bar) to starboard and the more popular attractions (for example, the cafeteria and the nightclub) to port. That way, boisterous youths and those travelling on a budget would migrate to port, whereas more refined passengers would occupy the starboard side.

The *Saga* and the *Svea* were elegantly appointed, the former's interiors being designed by Rolf Carlsson, and Astrid Sampe, who worked for the Contract Furnishings Department of the Nordiska Kompaniet department store. The Wasa Dining Room, which featured a wrought-iron bas relief of the famous warship by Bertil Vallien, was notably stylish. Further aft, and in complete contrast, the Britannia Room evoked the ornate neo-Tudor atmosphere of the 1929-built Swedish Lloyd packet steamer *Britannia*'s Smoking Room, and even featured some of her richly-patinated leather armchairs. This

The *Sydfyn* and a general arrangement plan of the vessel.
(Bruce Peter collection and KNUD E. HANSEN Archive)

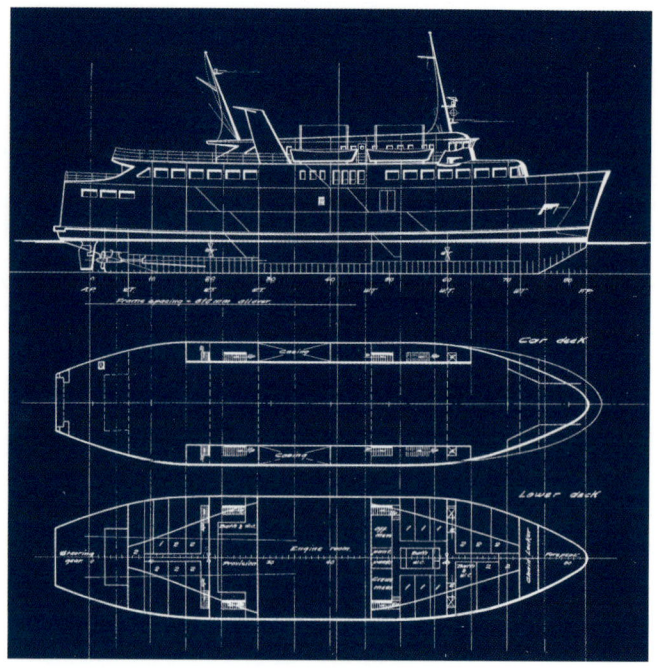

throwback to the 'twenties was perhaps the most unexpected space to be found on any ferry of the era, but its 'folksy' style and fine craftsmanship evidently proved popular with passengers. The *Svea*'s interiors, by Eva Ralf, were considerably more up-to-date in character, with darker veneers contrasting with brightly-upholstered contemporary furniture.

Just as the England–Sweden Line were planning their three-ship service with regular sailings from Hull to Gothenburg by the *Spero* and *Svea* and a weekly return from Tilbury by the Saga, in Stockholm four shipping companies hitherto almost unknown in the passenger transport business were also planning to enter this same market, but using much more efficiently-designed tonnage. Together, Trans-Oil and Bratt-Götha in Gothenburg, Rederi AB Rex in Stockholm and the Dutch firm KNSM formed a ferry-operating subsidiary called Tor Line AB with the intention of developing a triangular service from Gothenburg to Immingham and Amsterdam ('Tor' stood for the initials of the main shareholders, Trans-Oil plus Rex, as well as being the Swedish spelling of the Norse god Thor). The main drivers behind the project were Rederi AB Rex's owner Ragnar Källström and Bratt-Götha's managing director Erik Kekkonius, who had previously assisted the Swedish Bonnier publishing group in setting up their Lion Ferry subsidiary. The Swedish naval architect Åke Törnquist was appointed Project Leader and he was additionally responsible both for Tor Line's graphic identity and the new ferries' stylish interior design.

Given that Kekkonius was familiar with what Knud E. Hansen A/S could achieve by way of efficient ferry design from the Lion Ferry projects, it is not surprising that the firm was retained to provide the basic design for Tor Line's new ferries. According to Dag Rogne, the initial sketches were drawn in a park in Stockholm between meetings with Tor Line's directors at Rederi AB Rex's headquarters. Not surprisingly, Rogne produced a solution which was essentially an enlarged version of the typical KEH short-sea ferry type, then being built in substantial numbers for routes throughout Scandinavia and beyond. In almost every respect, the design was optimised for profitability. Tor Line's ferries were to be significantly faster than those of the England–Sweden Line consortium, their four Pielstick diesels giving a 24-knot speed, thus enabling more crossings to be made per week. Secondly, their drive-through vehicle decks had sufficient free height for significant numbers of lorries to be carried – freight being an important earner of profits all year round. In summer, platform decks could be lowered to increase their car capacity.

Although slightly smaller in terms of tonnage than their England–Sweden Line rivals, the Tor Line ships had a much larger passenger capacity of 980, only half of whom were berthed in cabins, the remainder occupying couchettes and aircraft-style reclining seats. Due to their higher speed, it would only be necessary to spend one night on board and so such cabins as were provided were compact and 'ferry-like', rather than emulating the commodious style of 'deep sea' ocean liners as on England–Sweden Line's vessels. The Tor Line ferries' greater freight and passenger payload enabled them to undercut England–Sweden Line's fares by a substantial margin.

Even though Tor Line received a highly satisfactory design from Dag Rogne, the firm's directors were perturbed to learn that, simultaneously, Rogne's colleagues were working with Swedish Lloyd and Stockholms Rederi AB Svea and so, before an order was actually placed, Knud E. Hansen A/S were fired and the design work was completed by Tor Line's own technical staff, working with the Lübecker Flenderwerke which successfully tendered to build the ferries.

The 7,042 grt *Tor Anglia* was delivered in March 1966 almost two months ahead of Swedish Lloyd's *Saga*, and her sister, the *Tor Hollandia*, was completed the following year – the latter with an enlarged superstructure and consequently increased passenger capacity.

Meanwhile, Swedish Lloyd had ordered from Lindholmens Varv a slightly modified sister to the *Saga* and *Svea* for use on a new route from Southampton across the Bay of Biscay to Bilbao in Spain. The *Patricia* was delivered in 1967 and soon became popular with British holidaymakers. Unfortunately, England–Sweden Line's Hull–Gothenburg route struggled to compete with Tor Line's faster sailings from nearby Immingham. Tor Line's victory in the England–Sweden trade was due to their more cost-effective ships.

The newly-delivered *Sundbuss Pernille II* off Helsingør in 1965. (Bruce Peter collection)

Another significant Knud E. Hansen A/S-designed overnight ferry to enter service in 1966 was the 3,611 grt *København*. Ordered from the Orenstein & Koppel shipyard in Lübeck by Sverre Ditlev-Simonsen for his newly formed Norske Københavnlinje (Norwegian Copenhagen Line), linking Brevik, Gothenburg and Copenhagen, she was styled by Tage Wandborg with sleek and powerful lines. Unlike most previous Knud E. Hansen A/S-designed ferries of the early to mid-1960s, her vehicle deck had a centre casing and so the exhaust uptakes were routed through the rear of the same structure as contained the 'skybar'.

When the *København* was being planned, another ambitious Norwegian ferry entrepreneur, Knut Kloster, was planning Sunward Car Ferries which would operate from Southampton to Vigo, Lisbon and Gibraltar. Kloster, a youthful and dynamic director of the Lauritz Kloster Rederi of Oslo, founded in 1906 and long involved in the bulk cargo and tanker trades, was actually a relative of Sverre Ditlev-Simonsen. He suggested to Kloster that, to obtain a suitable design for a new ferry, he should contact Knud E. Hansen A/S and thus began a long and fruitful relationship with Tage Wandborg.

The 8,666 gt *Sunward* was ordered from Bergens Mekaniske Verksteder and she too entered service in 1966. Designed to traverse the sometimes stormy Bay of Biscay, she was fitted with both fin stabilisers and by a stabilising tank, located high in the superstructure. This consisted of a large water tank with interlaced steel panels to break the natural sloshing of water from side to side, causing the slowed period of its movement to counteract the rolling of the ship.

The *Sunward* and *København* were both stern-loaders but, whereas the former had a vehicle deck with enough free height to carry some freight, the latter could mostly carry cars with only a few trucks parked towards the stern. Cabins otherwise filled the entire deck above and also most of main deck. Her public rooms were at boat deck level and amidships on bridge deck, above which there was a 'skybar'. The main lounge, forward, gave a fine view over the bow and the dining room was located aft. In between these principal rooms there was an arcade on the starboard side, off which a small

Tage Wondborg's striking unbuilt design for the Hook of Holland–Harwich ferry *Koningin Juliana*. (KNUD E. HANSEN Archive)

grillroom was accessed, while the galley space was adjacent on the port side. The interior design was by a Danish architect, Mogens Hammer.

Unfortunately, British Government restrictions on currency for foreign travel and the growing diplomatic tension with Spain over Gibraltar's status quickly caused Sunward Car Ferries to cease operations and so the *Sunward* was laid up in Southampton, awaiting a charterer or buyer. In Miami, meanwhile, an Israeli-American entrepreneur, Ted Arison, was enjoying considerable success in offering short cruises to Floridan holidaymakers using a chartered Israeli-owned ferry called the *Nili*. Arison's venture came to an unexpected abrupt halt, however, when the *Nili*'s owner in Haifa, Somerfin Lines, went bankrupt and the vessel was arrested in Miami. When Arison discovered that the *Sunward* was available, he contacted Kloster and persuaded him to place the vessel in service from Miami to Nassau in the Bahamas, Montego Bay in Jamaica and Port au Prince in Haiti, using his company as sales agents. She was marketed under the 'Norwegian Caribbean Line' brand (often abbreviated as NCL) and was an immediate success.

Concurrently with the Enland–Sweden Line, Tor Line, Norske Københavnlinje and Sunward Car Ferries projects, Knud E. Hansen A/S also designed several smaller ferries. One was the 959 grt *Sydfyn*, built by the Flensburger Schiffbau-gesellschaft and delivered in August 1965 to Nordisk Færgefart for a route between Faaborg and Gelting. This linked Southern Fyn (hence the ferry's name) with Northern West Germany, just south of the Danish border with Jutland. Planned by Dag Rogne and styled by Tage Wandborg, the ship had a capacity for 500 passengers and 56 cars. Another was the *Ærøboen*, designed for Dampskibsselskabet Ærø and built by the Martin Jansen Werft at Leer. Measuring a mere 499 grt, she could, nonetheless, carry 400 passengers and no fewer than 32 cars. A third was the 299 grt *Marstal*, built by P. Høivolds Mekaniske Verksteder at Kristiansand in Norway in 1965 for the Sydfynske Dampskibsselskab's route from Marstal to Rudkøbing. This little single-screw ferry possessed most of the design elements of her larger cousins, but in heavily compressed form. Tage Wandborg emphasises that in small ferries such as this, maintaining the same proportional relationship of the hull and superstructure as in larger vessels was very important to achieving a pleasing and well-balanced appearance. By tapering the after decks downwards in a single sweeping curve, an illusion of greater length could be created. In 1967, a near-sister, the *Lohals*, was delivered from the same shipyard for the same owner.

In addition to his car ferry projects, Tage Wandborg designed two new passenger vessels for Ragnar Moltzau's Helsingør–Helsingborg route. As with previous 'Sundbusserne', the 138 grt *Sundbuss Henrik II* and *Sundbuss Pernille II* were ordered from Lindstøls Skibs og Båtbyggeri A/S in Risør in Norway. Completed in December 1964 and May 1965 respectively, each could accommodate 225 passengers, more than twice as many as the original 1958 'Sundbusserne'. This was achieved by having two decks of passenger saloons with sun-deck space to the rear. In styling the ships, Wandborg applied a profile similar to that of his many recent car ferry designs with a raked bow, a dummy funnel at the base of the forward mast and tapering after decks.

The *Koningin Juliana* as actually delivered, based on the design on her British Rail-owned operating mate, the *St George*; a little Wandborg styling is evident where the shell plating sweeps down below the aft sundecks. (Bruce Peter collection)

The Dutch-headquartered Stoomvaart Maatschappij Zeeland (SMZ), meanwhile, commissioned a design for a new day and overnight ferry for the Hook of Holland–Harwich route across the southern North Sea. Traditionally, this was a rail-connected service for foot passengers but neither SMZ nor British Rail could ignore the fact that demand from car owners and road hauliers was rising steeply and a recent upstart rival, North Sea Ferries, was all too happy to pander to motorists' needs. Tage Wandborg produced what he considered to be a suitable design for SMZ, based to a large extent upon his recent *Stena Germanica* and *København* projects. He recalls that the SMZ directors were charming older gentlemen with whom it was a pleasure to work, but equally their views about ship design were just as conservative as those of Jahre Line and Swedish Lloyd.

Instead of choosing Wandborg's solution, SMZ decided to build a ship derived from plans by British Rail's in-house naval architects Tony Rogan and Don Ripley for a

Top left: The *Peter Wessel* shortly after completion. (Bruce Peter collection)

Top right: The *Peter Wessel* berthed at Larvik. (Bruce Peter collection)

Left: The Helsingør-Helsingborg ferry *Ursula* at Helsingør. (Bruce Peter collection)

Left: The passenger vessel *Malmö*. (Bruce Peter collection)

Above: The Dragør-Limhamn ferry *Ophelia*. (Bruce Peter collection)

British-flag partner ferry, the *St George*. There was, of course, an obvious logic in having two similar vessels on the route. Consequently, Knud E. Hansen A/S was merely retained to modify the *St George*'s design according to SMZ's wishes and subsequently an order for the 6,682 grt vessel was placed with Cammell Laird of Birkenhead, which completed her in 1968 as the *Koningin Juliana*.

Wandborg also designed a new 2,291 grt ferry named the *Betula* for Linjebuss to operate between Helsingør and Helsingborg. Built by Jos. L. Meyer of Papenburg on the River Ems in West Germany, she was likewise delivered in 1968. Two sister ships, named the *Regula* and *Ursula*, were built by Meyer Werft in 1971 and 1973. Four Humboldt-Deutz diesels gave considerable redundancy, enabling service to be maintained even if one was out of use. Each vessel could carry 900 passengers and 105 cars – a ratio indicative of the great popularity among Swedes of short shopping trips to Denmark.

A concurrent project of which Wandborg was especially proud was the 991 grt *Malmö*, a small but stylish passenger excursion ship built by Husumer Schiffswerft at Husum in West Germany in 1969 for Centrumlinjen, which operated between Malmö and Copenhagen. She could carry 740 passengers and her two 6-cylinder MaK diesels gave her a 14-knot service speed.

Dag Rogne, meanwhile, had designed a new 3,100 grt *Peter Wessel* for Larvik-Frederikshavn Fergen, finally to replace the pioneering 1937-vintage ship of the same name. Ordered from Aalborg Værft, she was of similar dimensions and external appearance to the Kristiansand Dampskipsselskap's *Skagerak* and the *Christian IV* although, as she would be making both day and night crossings, there were many more cabins than on these ships. Her general arrangement therefore had more in common with those of the *Jens Kofoed* and *Visby* with cabins in the forward half of the main deck and to either side of the upper level of the car deck. By the time the *Peter Wessel* was delivered in May 1968, Knud E. Hansen A/S had produced many designs for substantially bigger ferries and soon Larvik-Frederikshavn Fergen were experiencing capacity problems with their new ship. Quite simply, they had misjudged the growth rate and so she was withdrawn in 1971, initially to be replaced by the chartered *København* and then by a third significantly larger, *Peter Wessel* (described below).

Rogne also was responsible for the 2,089 grt *Hamlet* and the *Ofelia*, which were ordered from two small West German shipyards, the Fr. Lürssen Werft in Bremen and the Krögerswerft at Rendsburg. They were intended for service between Helsingør and Helsingborg for an upstart operator, HH Linien, but prior to delivery, its owner was killed in a car crash. Even so, both were completed as planned, then laid up during the 1968 summer after which they were sold to Öresundsbolaget to link Dragør, Limhamn, Malmö and Copenhagen. Their design owed much to the *Scania*, *Stena Danica* and *Stena Nordica*. Accommodation was provided for 800 passengers and 85 cars. By 1970, there were at least a dozen ferries designed by Knud E. Hansen A/S shuttling back and forth across The Sound and just as many traversing the Kattegat.

In order to maintain such an output, Knud E. Hansen A/S' workforce was rapidly expanded. Tage Wandborg recalls that:

'By the mid-1960s, Knud E. Hansen A/S had grown to around 60 employees, half of whom were engineering specialists and the other half of whom dealt with planning, contract administration and clerical work to make the whole organisation operate effectively. The most senior naval architects had complimentary skills and so one could always get expert advice on particular aspects of a design from one's closest colleagues. Under Svend Aage Bertelsen, the good working atmosphere not only made the business productive but also reflected in the quality and innovation of our design work.'

In the second half of the 1960s, the permanent workforce consisted of three naval architects specialising in design; two specialising in the shaping and arrangement of hulls underwater; four dealing with calculations of speed, tonnage, stability and hydrodynamics; six draftsmen; four naval architects attending to outline, building and materials specifications; four working on the correct application of safety and classification regulations relating to insulation, fire subdivision, evacuation plans and escape routes; 10 naval architects and draftsmen in the steel department, producing construction drawings and specifications; five naval architects and engineers dealing with engine rooms, mechanical arrangements and all pumps, plumbing and pipework; two electrical engineers to plan wiring systems and to specify the required capacities and locations of generators and switchboards; four inspectors, charged with supervising and controlling all work during the building process; four naval architects specialising in port-related infrastructure, such as cranes, winches, rigging, gangways, ramps and ferry berths and, finally, 12 secretaries, accountants and general clerical staff.

In addition to these permanent employees, it was sometimes necessary to hire in extra temporary staff, usually draftsmen from Burmeister & Wain or from Orlogsværftet, who earned overtime by working for Knud E. Hansen A/S during evenings. Tage Wandborg observes that 'we never needed to advertise for work – clients came to us because of our reputation and we always tried to give the best possible assistance and advice.'

Top left: The Swedish Gulf Line cargo vessel *Andrew Salman* is seen in Gothenburg. A sister ship, the *Michael Salman*, was subsequently constructed. (Rickard Sahlsten collection)
Above: The Fred. Olsen cargo vessel *Brisk*. (Bruce Peter collection)
Left: The liquefied gas tanker *Janegaz*. (Bruce Peter collection)

Cargo ship projects

While Wandborg, Rogne and their colleagues were working hard to design a succession of ferries, Gerhard Erichs and Preben Agner continued to concentrate on designing cargo vessels and tankers of various sizes. The 1,400 dwt oil tanker *Irland* was designed by Erichs for Dansk-Fransk – the parent company of Juelsminde–Kalundborg Linien – and delivered by Helsingborgs Varv in 1964. Meanwhile, the 2,250 dwt *Rubicon* was constructed by Moss Verft & Dokk for the Norwegian company A/S Ramses and also completed in 1964. Thereafter, in 1966, the same yard delivered the *Arctic Propane*, a 2,691 grt liquid propane gas carrier for K/S Bulkship A/S of Tromsø. She was followed in 1967 by two near-sisters, the 2,863 grt *Gazania* for Odfjell Rederi of Bergen and the 2,759 grt *Janegaz* for Skib A/S Widan of Bergen. The *Imperial Acadia* was, in contrast, a 10,000 dwt tanker built in Port Weller in Canada for operation on the Great Lakes. General cargo vessel projects included the Finnboda-built *Stella*, a 500 grt paper carrier for Stockholms Rederi AB Svea, the 499 grt Fred. Olsen-owned *Brisk* and *Bastant* from Kristiansands Mekaniske Verksteder plus the Sölvesborg-built 2,600 dwt *Andrew Salman*. The 1,397 dwt *Freyfaxi* was a cargo vessel constructed by Aukra Bruk A/S in Norway to carry bags of cement on pallets from a factory in Akranes.

Agner's production of designs for coasters was prodigious; in 1961, he drew up a standard coaster type for Laivateollisuus Oy (literally 'Ship-industry Company') in Turku, Finland. It was established in 1945 by Finska Ångfartygs Aktiebolaget (FÅA), Rederi AB Atlanta and Rederi AB Oceanfart (both of which were closely related to FÅA) to build wooden sailings ships as war reparations to the Soviet Union. Laivateollisuus Oy was created with money paid out by the Finnish state in exchange for ships ceded to the Soviets as war reparations. The *Lokki*, *Kurki*, *Tiira*, *Sotka*, *Vikla*, *Alli* and *Tavi*, all names of sea birds in Finnish, were built for FÅA between 1961 and 1964 while Siljarederiet, in which FÅA owned a third of the shares, operated the *Floria*, also completed in 1964.

Three smaller coasters, the *Mercantic*, *Astrid Rarberg* and *Kleven*, plus a refrigerated cargo vessel called the *Snowman*, were built in Marstal on the island of Ærø in Southern Denmark while *La Bonita* was constructed by Jadewerft and the *Susan* by Husumer Werft, both in West Germany. Concurrently, Frederikshavn Værft & Flydedok A/S constructed the *Ebba Victor*, *Bellatrix* and *Poula Sinding* also for independent owners.

In the same period, the 550 grt coasters *Gitte Danielsen*, *Jens Rand*, *Hans Priess*, *Lone Krogh*, *Mogens Græsborg*, *Adda*, *Mette Pan*, *Kirvi*, *Sisu*, *Costas*, *Ditte Holmo*, *France*, *Pimpernel*, *Romeo*, *Lonni* and *Amely* were built at the Ørskov shipyard in Frederikshavn for a variety of mainly Danish private owners. They were part of a 27-strong series of near-identical sisters, 24 of which were built by Øreskov, while a further two, the *Kenitha* and *Tobitrader*, were delivered from Århus Flydedok. The *Cynthia Bres* was the only example of the type built by Westermøen Slipp at Mandal in Norway.

Agner also produced a design for a seven-strong series of small 2,100 dwt cargo vessels built by the various shipyards in the Netherlands for Otto Danielsen. These were the *Etly Danielsen* by Scheepswerf Hoogezand, the *Thea Danielsen* by Zaandamsche Scheepsbouw, the *Ketty Danielsen* by E. J. Smit & Zonen, the *Else Danielsen* by Scheepswerf Kerstholt, the *Laura Danielsen* by Scheepswerf

The liquefied gas carrier *Arctic Propane*. (Bruce Peter collection)

The coaster *Storesund*, one of many similarly-dimensioned vessels designed by Preben Agner between the early-1950s and the mid-1960s. (KNUD E. HANSEN Archive)

The Finnish-built coaster *Floria* in the livery of Silja Line. (Marko Stampehl collection)

The coaster *Beta*. (Museet for Søfart)

The Grimsby trawler *Saxon Onward*, one of several fishing vessels built to Knud E. Hansen A/S designs during the 1960s. (KNUD E. HANSEN Archive)

Another British-flagged KEH-designed trawler, the *Longset*, also registered in Grimsby. (KNUD E. HANSEN Archive)

Ferus Smith, the *Dorthe Danielsen* from Niestern Kerstolt and the Bijkers-built *Ulla Danielsen*. Finally, there was a further series of four for various owners constructed by E. J. Smit & Zonen, the *Anne Bøgelund*, *Eny Højsgaard*, *Inger Højsgaard* and *Ellen Helleskov*. Large trawlers were also planned for a British owner in Grimsby who was so pleased with Knud E. Hansen A/S' design that he coined the phrase 'a Hansen ship is a handsome ship'. As with Wandborg's ferry silhouettes, Agner's trawlers and coasters were distinguished by their harmoniously curvaceous forms.

Not all of Agner's designs were problem-free, however. In August 1961, the *Beta*, a new coaster built by Westermøen Slipp for De Danske Sukkerfabrikker was undergoing trials on a hot summer day when the captain turned the wheel hard and she gradually capsized. The reason was that, due to the warm weather, portholes in the aft hull were left open and so, when the vessel heeled sharply, these were submerged. Those onboard, including Agner and Svend A. Bertelsen, ending up having to jump overboard then scramble on to the upturned hull. Although the *Beta* was subsequently raised and repaired, for Knud E. Hansen A/S, the incident was very embarrassing.

The shipping revolution of the 1960s saw the beginning of the gradual replacement of general cargo ships with more efficient tonnage able to handle containers. A conventional cargo liner spent about half of her time in port, while the average crane could handle only between two and five tons. A nine-man gang of stevedores could shift around eight tons of cargo per hour with 20% of their time spent resting. Therefore, harbour expenses accounted for 70% of these vessels' operating costs. In contrast, containers offered a far faster and more secure means of transporting goods, but as a new container ship might cost eight times as much as a cargo liner, only the larger and wealthier shipping companies could afford them. Besides, in the latter 1960s, full containerisation had yet to spread beyond routes from the Americas to Europe and the Far East, meaning that elsewhere a substantial proportion of the world's goods was still carried on general cargo vessels.

In the second half of the 1960s, Knud E. Hansen A/S produced designs for the final generation of general cargo vessels, their output of freight-carrying ships thereafter being mainly roll-on, roll-off ferries.

Gerhard Erichs designed the 11,415 grt *Heering Susan* and *Heering Lotte* for the Heering Line, a family-owned company established in the mid-nineteenth century by Peter Heering, whose wider business interests famously included the manufacture of Cherry Heering brandy liqueur. Completed in 1966 and 1967 built by AG Weser of Bremerhaven in West Germany, as was typical of the majority of large cargo vessels planned by KEH, their superstructures were aft-located.

Next, Erichs designed the 25,046 dwt gearless bulk carrier *Normandiet* for Dansk-Fransk, which had a full automated engine room. The vessel was delivered from the Fujinagata shipyard in Osaka, Japan in May 1967. Of course, Knud E. Hansen A/S already had considerable experience in working with Japanese yards, having been involved in the construction of vessels for A. P. Møller and for the Iraqi Line in the country. The advent of jet air travel meant that it was far easier for shipping people, including naval architects, to travel worldwide to carry out negotiations and supervision work as necessary.

Erichs also produced a design for new 8,093 grt cargo liners, the *Kinshasa* and *Banana*, to modernise Danska–Fransk's Dafra Line service between North European ports and the Congo. These too were built at Fujinagata and delivered towards the end of 1967. A new development was the specification of a straight mid-body so that containers or large sections of tree trunk could easily be stowed around the hatch openings (hardwood for the Danish furniture industry was one of Dafra Line's key cargoes).

In 1967 Erik T. Møller produced an entirely new design for an approximately 23,000 dwt bulk carrier type for Haugesunds Mekaniske Verksted. Møller's design had more hull volume and far fewer curved plates than previous KEH-designed bulkers; the stern was a transom, the superstructure was flat-fronted and fore-square with none of the streamlining previously employed. These developments were very much in line with wider practices in designing of ships of this type in the latter-1960s. As well as bulk cargoes, the vessels were designed also to handle forestry products and so they were fitted with electric cranes set well above the hatch covers so as to be capable of loading timber on deck. Eight of these vessels were commissioned by Scottish Ship Management which, in recent years, had been ordering a large number of bulk carriers from various Norwegian shipyards and a further two were for the Norwegian owner Richard Amlie. The first of the class to enter service was Amlie's 14,508 grt *Vestland*, delivered in 1970. She was followed by eight for Scottish Ship Management – the *Baron*

Below: The Soviet-built Iraqi cargo liner *Basrah*.
(Bruce Peter collection)

Bottom: The *Babylon* was another example of the series.
(Bruce Peter collection)

Above images from top left: The cargo vessels *Heering Lotte*, *Banana* and *Kinshasa* and the bulk carrier *Normandiet*. (Bruce Peter collection and Museet for Søfart)

Right: The bulk carrier *Baron Wemyss* at the outfitting quay at the Haugesund shipyard. (Bruce Peter collection)

Left: The Haugesund-built geared bulk carrier *Sneland*. (Bruce Peter collection)

Bottom left: A stern-quarter view of the *Cape Grafton*. (Mick Lindsay collection)

Bottom right: The *Cape Grenville*, loaded with a consignment of timber. (Mick Lindsay collection)

Ardrossan (1970), *Cape Horn*, *Baron Inchcape*, *Cape Hawke*, *Cape Grafton* (all 1971), *Temple Inn*, *Baron Wemyss* (both 1972) and *Cape Grenville* (1973). In between, a further vessel for Amlie, the *Sneland*, was finished in 1972, meaning that, on average, the Haugesund yard produced three ships per annum (whereas only two of the previous design could be built each year).

Rather than a single slow-speed engine as was standard for diesel-powered bulkers, most unusually, twin 12-cylinder medium-speed V-diesels were specified, more in the manner of KEH-designed passenger ships of the same era such as the Caribbean cruise ferries *Starward* and *Freeport* (see below). The reason was that such machinery was much lighter and more compact, enabling 15% extra deadweight capacity to be freed up for the carriage of revenue-earning cargo. The idea was sound, but, unfortunately, Scottish Ship Management selected Ruston Paxman 12-cylinder diesels for its eight vessels. In service, they proved most unreliable and so, within only three years, all were replaced with Stork-Werkspoor units, involving expensive and time-consuming conversions. (It may be that Knud E. Hansen A/S suggested this marque as they were successfully installed on the ferry *Koningin Juliana*.) From the outset, the bulk carriers for Richard Amlie had Pielstick diesels which apparently proved very dependable; this was reflected in the vessels' unusually long 28-year lives, whereas most of the Scottish Ship Management-owned members of the class were scrapped before they even reached sixteen.

At the smaller end of the scale, Preben Agner spent the latter 1960s drawing up yet more coasters. The *Capella* and *Canopus* were built by Laivateollisuus Oy in Finland for the FÅA to larger dimensions than those of their earlier series. The *Elly*, *Lion* and *Hamlet* were constructed by Ørskov in Frederikshavn while the *Arnatindur*, *Christian Holm* and *Elizabeth Hentzer* were by Skála in the Faroe Islands and the *Gerda Rarberg* was built in Marstal. Ørskov also constructed the suction dredger *Ormen* and the trawler *Tine Gaj*, while Århus Flydedok built a 299 dwt tanker called the *Rønland*.

In May 1967, the *Biologen*, a small research vessel designed by Agner for the Danish Government suddenly capsized when on her maiden voyage off the island of Anholt in the Kattegat. Although the *Biologen*'s hull design was eventually found to have had an insufficient stability margin, the incident was fortunately an isolated one, although Agner must have been embarrassed by the sinking of another of his ships only six years after the coaster *Beta* had overturned.

In 1969, Iraqi Maritime Transport Co requested that Knud E. Hansen A/S modify a design prepared in the Soviet Union for further pair of substantially larger cargo vessels, each measuring around 10,500 grt, which had been ordered from the Kherson Shipyard. These had an engines-aft layout with a straight mid-body was chosen. Furthermore, while most existing general cargo vessels were notable for their prominent cargo derricks, electric cranes were fitted instead, plus only one heavy lift derrick, approximately amidships between hatches three and four. Working behind the Iron Curtain was a new experience for Knud E. Hansen A/S's naval architects – especially as Soviet approaches to construction and detailing were different from those favoured in most Western shipyards. The vessels were delivered as the *Baghdad* and the *Babylon* in 1971 and 1972 respectively. The shipyard subsequently built further examples of the type for other shipping companies in the Soviet sphere of influence.

Next, the Iraqis requested a cheap-to-build and operate 6,000 gt standard cargo ship design, and this project was allocated to a new member of Knud E. Hansen A/S' staff, Hans Kjærgaard who joined the company in 1969. Kjærgaard had begun his career in naval architecture in 1958, when, as a teenager, he became an apprentice at the Odense Staalskibsværft, owned by A.P. Møller. He attended evening classes at the local Teknikum, from which he graduated in 1965 aged only 24, the youngest student to complete his studies. Between 1965 and 1968, he served in the Danish Royal Engineers, then found employment in the United States, working at the Yordica ship model testing basin, which was very sophisticated and even used a computer for calculations. In 1969, he had a meeting with Gerhard Erichs to discuss the details of a ship hull undergoing testing at Yordica. Erichs asked Kjærgaard to join Knud E. Hansen A/S. Although his work for Yordica was interesting and at the leading edge of developments, he accepted Erichs' offer as, at Knud E. Hansen A/S, he would actually be able to design large modern ships, rather than merely working on issues of hull lines, stability and damage calculations, as was the case at Yordica. Nonetheless, at Knud E. Hansen A/S, Kjærgaard made damage stability and lines calculations for a great many projects.

Hans Kjærgaard took a couple of years to settle into KEH and to learn how the company functioned. He found that, at first, he was watched by his new colleagues who were equally

One of the numerous Yugoslav-built Iraqi pusher-tugs for the Tigris and Euphrates river system. (Hans Kjærgaard collection)

keen to find out how he went about designing and doing calculations. He found that all of them were of a slightly older generation and, unlike him, not computer literate. Indeed, he found that at Knud E. Hansen A/S, he hardly touched a computer during over 40 years of employment. Apart from the conservatism of a generation of naval architects whose training pre-dated the digital age, one practical reason for KEH to avoid computers in the 1970s and 1980s was that they were so big and heavy that they could not be moved and, as KEH staff travelled a lot and did much of their work 'on site' in shipyards around the world, they were arguably of limited practical use at that time.

Kjærgaard's economy cargo ship design for Iraq was an early example of what subsequently became a fairly standard worldwide approach to the planning of such vessels. Aesthetics were negated in favour of construction efficiency so as to use as many flat or single-rolled plates as possible, the hull volume being calculated to maximise the payload. Besides, ship owners in other less developed countries often needed to replace ageing World War 2 'standard' cargo ship types at a time when labour and materials costs were rising exponentially and so any changes to make vessels less expensive to construct were welcome. Subsequently, the economic tribulations caused by the 1973 Oil Crisis made the twin demands of cheapness and efficiency universal throughout the shipping world and tonnage which did not suit these criteria was dispatched prematurely to ship-breakers. The Oil Crisis was brought about by Arab oil-producing countries which were members of OPEC. They quadrupled the price per barrel of Gulf crude in protest against America's support for Israel in the Yom Kippur War. For the shipping industry in particular, fuel was a major cost and so many hitherto profitable operations suddenly became marginal, or lost money.

Certainly, Kjærgaard's cargo liner design for Iraq was hardly pretty, but it proved highly practical in everyday service. A relatively slender hull at the waterline widened quickly to give a substantial main deck, with steel hatch covers and five big electric cranes to handle containers and heavy general cargo for to Iraq's development of oil-related infrastructure.

In the early 1970s, Daimaru, a company representing Japanese shipyard interests in Iraq and elsewhere, became Knud E. Hansen A/S's trading partner in the project and the vessels themselves were to be built at the Shinhama shipyard. Kjærgaard recalls that:

'On the day that the contract was to be signed in Japan in front of Iraqi TV and the Japanese media, at the last moment, the Iraqi's chief negotiator told the shipyard's managing director that he would like a gift of school buses and company cars to be included in the contract for the first vessel. The managing director smiled and told the Iraqi representative that he would be delighted to assist. Then the Iraqi said that he wanted specifically Fiat buses and Volvo cars, at which point the shipyard's managing director exploded into a rage. Nonetheless, the contract was signed as planned, the vessels were built and the correct cars and buses were delivered to Basra, where the army immediately took them over for military use, as had been the Iraqis' intention all along.'

The first of the series of six vessels was delivered in 1972 as the *Al Waldid Al Saadi*. Further projects for Iraq consisted of the design of a floating dock at Ajnaden in 1970, a 35,000 dwt tanker named the *Rumalia* built in Spain by Asterillos Matagorda, and designs for tankers measuring 60,000 and 120,000 dwt. In 1974, plans for a large Iraqi Port Administration dredger, the

Above: The New Zealand-owned ro-ro *Wanaka*, one of a pair built in Hong Kong for service over the Cook Strait.
(Bruce Peter collection)

Right: The Thoresen-owned freight ferry *Viking IV*.
(Bruce Peter collection)

Al-Khalij Al-Arabi, were drawn up and the vessel was built by Orenstein & Koppel in Lübeck, West Germany. A further smaller dredger, the *Al Merbid*, meanwhile, was constructed by IHC Verschure in the Netherlands.

Next, the Iraqi government decided to develop the Tigris and Euphrates rivers as major domestic transport arteries. For Knud E. Hansen A/S, this ambitious project was the biggest contract attempted up to that time. For five years from 1974 onwards, Hans Kjærgaard worked on the scheme jointly with a newly-appointed colleague, Ole Olesen. Born in Frederikshavn in 1948, Olesen had first worked as an apprentice shipbuilder in Frederikshavn Skibsværft og Flydedok A/S, before moving to Helsingør to study at the Teknikum, from which he graduated in 1974.

Before design work commenced, Hans Kjærgaard worked with Iraqi engineers to survey the Tigris and Euphrates. Water depths, the width of locks and height restrictions due to overhead cables were taken into account in order to establish the parameters for the new river fleets of dredgers, tugs and barges. Due to variable water depths from season to season, they found that, if the tugs and barges were to operate all year round as intended, their draft would need to be limited.

Next, Kjærgaard designed trailer hopper dredgers to create and maintain navigable channels, followed by plans for a new type of pusher tug of which 64 examples were to be built, a fleet of dumb barges, two estuary tugs and eight survey vessels. In addition, new harbour installations in Baghdad and Basra were designed jointly with Iraqi engineers. To oversee these projects, over a three-year period from 1975 to 1978, Kjærgaard and Olesen spent nearly half of their time working in Baghdad and the other half in Yugoslavia, where the river craft were built. Kjærgaard recalls that the Iraqi authorities were very afraid of 'backshish' and many Iraqi and some foreign businessmen were jailed for giving or accepting bribes. In an attempt to clean up business practice, government officials would approach him in hotel foyers and in restaurants either offering or asking for bribes in relation to projects he was working on; the only thing to do was to refuse politely and explain that the law in Iraq was very clear about this not being acceptable.

The pusher tugs and barges were built in eight different Yugoslavian shipyards. As the Yugoslavs used pusher tugs and barges on the River Donau, they had considerable expertise in their design, construction and operation and they could even train Iraqis involved in the project.

Initially, Kjærgaard wanted to use a hydraulic system to couple the tugs and barges but instead chose the old-fashioned and simple solution of using ropes and winches as it required little maintenance and anybody could operate it without special training. As the River Tigris was muddy, another problem was cooling the tugs' engines. At first, the Iraqis asked for water-cooled engines to be fitted because they were already familiar with these, but Kjærgaard and his Yugoslav colleagues successfully dissuaded them, fearing that their cooling systems would quickly become choked. Instead, they selected air-cooled engines manufactured by Deutz which were based on the type fitted to German tanks in the Second World War. Jastram azimuthing rudder propellers were also specified, giving the tugs great manoeuvrability.

In addition to the new fleet of river craft, by the latter-1970s, the Iraqi Maritime Transport Co possessed 22 sea-going cargo vessels and tankers, nearly all of which were built according to Knud E. Hansen A/S designs. The lucrative relationship might have continued, but for a disastrous change at the very top of Iraq's political elite. In 1979 a coup within the Ba'ath party resulted in the Iraqi Presidency being seized by Saddam Hussein, a regional politician whose brutal approach to the wielding of power brought international notoriety. Soon, Saddam Hussein struck a barter deal in exchange for oil with Yugoslavia's Marshall Tito whereby all responsibility for designing and building ships for Iraq thereafter would go to Yugoslavian yards. Meanwhile, Yugoslavian universities and technical colleges would train Iraqis in naval architecture and other engineering disciplines. As it turned out, the early years of Saddam Hussein's presidency marked the beginning of the end of the development of Iraq's national infrastructure and a desire instead to build up its military so as to menace its neighbours. Indeed, through three major wars, two involving the United States of America plus European allies, nearly all that had been achieved since the 1950s by way of river and sea transport infrastructure was destroyed.

In the period from the mid-1970s until the early 1980s, the oil-rich Middle East proved a lucrative area of activity for Knud E. Hansen A/S, which was forced to diversify from its established business of designing ships into other areas during the difficult years in the wake of the 1973 Oil Crisis. Apart from the many projects for Iraq, a new temporary harbour extension for Jeddah in Saudi Arabia was designed. Saudi was using its newly found wealth to import goods in unprecedented amounts, so much in fact that the existing Jeddah port facility was suffering severe congestion problems and vessels were delayed. The Norwegian shipping entrepreneur, Knut Kloster, had business connections with the Saudi Royal Family and he brought the problems in Jeddah to the attention of Svend A. Bertelsen and subsequently acted as an intermediary between Knud E. Hansen A/S and the Saudi Transport Ministry to help them quickly to find a solution.

Kloster's own answer to Jeddah's problems was to acquire second-hand landing craft from Canada and, using crews of stevedores from South Korea, to load cargo from vessels anchored off Jeddah on to these. Knud E. Hansen A/S was to help build a temporary unloading berth for the landing craft and adjacent storage facilities for cargoes. They bought a large inflatable building second-hand from a tennis club in Odense and sent it to Saudi Arabia in a chartered Mercandia cargo ship, also carrying other supplies from Denmark for the temporary port project. According to Hans Kjærgaard, the money earned and connections made by Kloster assisting the Saudis in Jeddah helped him subsequently to buy from a Saudi Arabian entrepreneur, Akkram Ojjeh, the trans-Atlantic liner *France*, which Knud E. Hansen A/S then converted into Kloster's Norwegian Caribbean Line cruise ship, the *Norway* (see below). Kjærgaard also notes that, while the temporary port in Jeddah was intended to handle general cargo, it was actually used mainly to import via Saudi Arabia munitions to Iraq for use in the war with Iran.

A further temporary harbour project for Saudi Arabia involved Ole Olesen working in Japan for a year in 1978. This time, the client was the Saudi Ministry of Housing, which wanted five temporary berths for cargo vessels to enable an increased importation of building materials for housing projects. Olesen's solution was to design floating pontoons, each measuring approximately 180 by 60 metres, which could be linked together in lines of three to enable offloading to take place. The pontoons were built in Japanese shipyards and while they were under construction, in Saudi Arabia other related shoreside infrastructure was put in place, including storage facilities and even a village for workers, which included a mosque. After a few years, however, the Saudi government invested in a large and sophisticated new port for Jeddah, which permanently solved its capacity problems.

The first ro-ro freight ferries

In the early 1960s, Knud E. Hansen A/S first produced speculative designs for smallish bow- and stern-loading roll-on, roll-off freighters with aft-located superstructures. An early customer was DFDS, for whom KEH's Gunnar Toft Madsen carried out initial studies for vessels to carry Danish agricultural exports across the North Sea to the United Kingdom. DFDS subsequently used this research as the basis for their own cargo ferry designs, built at Helsingør. Thereafter, Dag Rogne was Knud E. Hansen A/S' leading designer of freight-carrying ro-ro vessels.

Those designed in the ensuing decades followed one or other of two basic layout patterns. Some had aft-located superstructures, while others had their superstucture near the bow but machinery towards the stern with uptakes routed through side-casings. Each solution had particular advantages and disadvantages. By placing the machinery and superstructure at the stern, the entire mid- and fore-body was available for freight, but this tended to ride high in unloaded condition. A superstructure-forward and machinery-aft solution gave a more balanced hull, but possibly used space slightly less optimally and also made a vessel more complex to lengthen as there was more pipework and cabling to cut through.

The first order placed for a KEH-designed ro-ro freighter was by Thoresen Car Ferries, which required a dedicated truck-carrying vessel to complement its existing trio of 'Viking' passenger and car ferries on the English Channel. The 1,152 grt *Viking IV* was built by Trosvik Verksted A/S in Norway.

Norwegian Caribbean Line's *Starward* is seen at Miami in the late-1960s with her stern visor open to enable the loading of freight and ship's stores. (Bruce Peter collection)

KNUD E. HANSEN • 80 YEARS **93**

Top left and top right: The Tropicana Garden on the *Starward*, viewed from ahead and astern and showing the two open tiers of deck overlooking the swimming pool. (Bruce Peter collection)

Centre left and right: A hotel-like suite on Boat Deck and the mid-ships lounge on the *Skyward*. (Bruce Peter collection)
Bottom: The *Skyward* at Nassau, berthed with other cruise ships converted from liners of a slightly older generation. (Bruce Peter collection)

94 KNUD E. HANSEN • 80 YEARS

Freight is loaded aboard the *Starward* at Miami in the late-1960s.
(Bruce Peter collection)

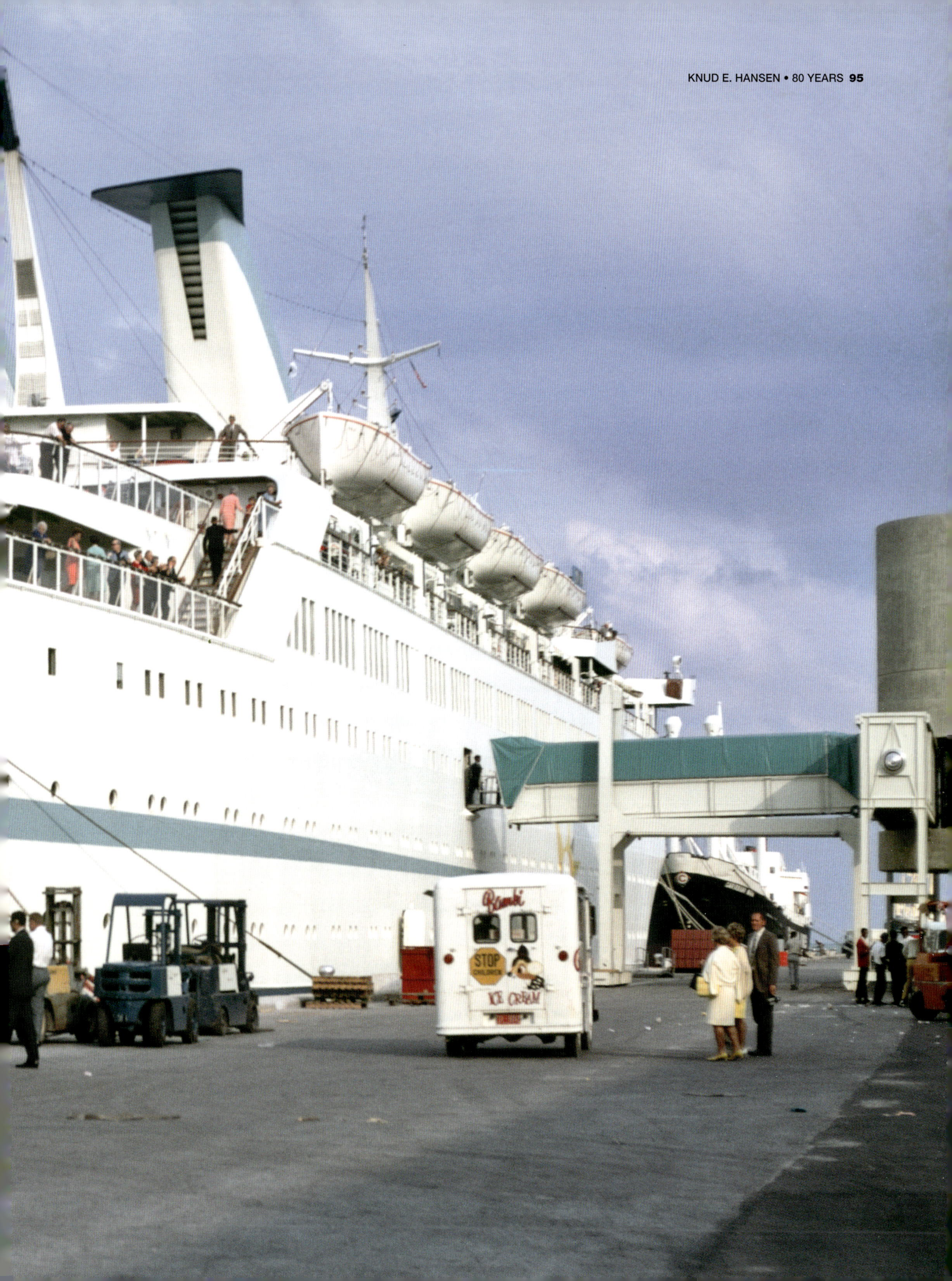
Bambi
STOP
ICE CREAM

96 KNUD E. HANSEN • 80 YEARS

Top left: The launch of the *Freeport* at Lübeck on 20 April 1968. (Tage Wandborg collection)
Top right: The *Freeport*'s aft dining saloon. (Bruce Peter collection)
Centre: The *Freeport* on her builder's trials; in her day, she was one of the world's biggest and best-appointed ferries. (Bruce Peter collection)
Bottom left: The bright and informal café-bar, located aft on the *Freeport*'s Boat Deck. (Bruce Peter collection)
Bottom right: The conference suite, amidships on Bridge Deck; note the Arne Jacobsen 'Swan' chairs. (Bruce Peter collection)

The Bolero *and the* Massalia *were two out of three ferries built in France to plans derived from those of the* Freeport.
(Bruce Peter collection)

Her superstructure was forward-located with machinery aft, the vehicle decks providing 480 lane metres for trucks and trailers – an impressive capacity considering her relatively compact dimensions of 92 by 17.4 metres. This was possible because the forward half of her tank top deck was a clear space into which freight trailers could be lowered by elevator. This solution subsequently became commonplace on nearly all ro-ro freighters.

While the *Viking IV* was nearing completion, Knud E. Hansen A/S was contacted by the Union Steamship Company in New Zealand (a subsidiary of the London-headquartered P&O Group) to assist in the detailed design and stability calculations for two new freight ferries, the 2,769 grt *Wanaka* and *Hawea*, to be built by the Taikoo Dockyard & Engineering Company of Hong Kong. These vessels were mainly the work of P&O's in-house naval architecture department and their layout was inspired by the fleet of the Atlantic Steam Navigation Company, a well-known British ro-ro ferry operator. As with ASN's ferries, the superstructure was forward with the engine room amidships, meaning that there was no possibility of using the tank top level for additional freight lane-metreage. The *Wanaka* and *Hawea* were, however, exceptionally solid vessels, designed to withstand the treacherous Cook Strait between New Zealand's North and South Islands.

From cruise ferry to cruise ship

In Miami, meanwhile, Knut Kloster and Ted Arison's Norwegian Caribbean Line had decided that more ships were needed to cope with the expansion of the Caribbean cruise market. Tage Wandborg was therefore asked to plan two substantial and highly innovative 12,940 grt vessels specially tailored for this trade and geared to the tastes of American passengers. As well as cruise passengers, the first of the new vessels had a freight deck to carry trailers from Miami to The Bahamas and Jamaica but the design of the second was modified as a pure cruise ship with additional cabins instead. Built by AG Weser Seebeckwerft in Bremerhaven, the construction processes were somewhat unusual as the vessels were built in two halves which were joined together in dry dock. First to be finished was the *Starward*, assembled in only 12 months and delivered in November 1968.

She could carry 540 passengers, all berthed in en suite cabins, and 220 cars, loaded through the stern which had a special lifting visor covering the ramp to continue the lines of the hull so that while at sea, she looked more a passenger liner than the passenger and trailer ferry she actually was. Two 16-cylinder 8,690 bhp MAN V-diesels, chosen for their high power output and relatively low height, provided a 21-knot speed. Twin funnels were located aft of amidships, ahead of which there was a sheltered lido area with a three-storey glazed sun lounge. Developed from the 'skybars' on earlier Knud E. Hansen A/S-designed ferries, the Tropicana Garden, as it was known, was a remarkable shipboard environment with two balconies accessed by a spiral staircase.

The car and freight deck ran down the middle of the hull with outside cabins on each side and more cabins on main deck above. To save time and money, the builder developed an innovative prefabrication technique to assemble the shower and toilet cubicles as complete units, prefacing the widespread use of modular construction for ship interiors during the ensuing decade.

The *Starward* was constructed and outfitted in accordance with American 'Method 1' fire protection standards. These specified the use of non-combustible materials throughout the passenger and crew accommodation. In Scandinavia, it was

An artist's impression, showing how the cruise ship Copenhagen was initially intended to look, again showing considerable similarity to the Freeport.
(Bruce Peter collection)

The innovative expedition cruise ship *Linblad Explorer*. (Bruce Peter collection)

more common to use the British approach, 'Method 2', in which non-fire-retardant finishes could be utilised in conjunction with a sprinkler system. Thus, a lot of laminate, aluminium and glass fibre were used for wall and ceiling finishes as well as for furniture, giving a light and fresh ambience more like that of a modern hotel.

For Norwegian Caribbean Line, the *Starward* was a notable success and the subsequent delivery of her near-sister, the Skyward, in 1969 brought Kloster's investment in the Miami cruise business to over $100 million. Without a trailer deck, she had berths for 750 cruise passengers. Later, in the mid-1970s, the *Starward* was stripped of her vehicle-carrying capacity and the space was used for additional cabins and for a cinema/theatre called 'The Four Vikings'. These were installed gradually while she remained in service using prefabricated components.

A further key vessel in the Miami cruise-ferry boom of the latter 1960s was the 10,448 grt *Freeport*, built by Orenstein & Koppel in Lübeck and delivered in 1968 to US Freight of New York and the Bahamas Development Corporation. She was intended to sail as a ferry-come-cruise ship to bring trailers, containers on flatbeds and passengers from Miami to Freeport on Grand Bahama Island.

In terms of overall dimensions and layout, the *Freeport* was broadly similar to the *Starward*. Forward of her engine room, an extra freight deck at tank top level was accessed by a scissors-lift. As with the *Starward*, her mid-body had no sheer but her decks were angled upwards at the bow. A large single funnel was located aft of amidships and featured a 'flying saucer'-shaped smoke deflector, placed at an angle near the summit. Given that Wandborg admired Italian passenger ship aesthetics, the funnel on the then-recently-rebuilt liner *Angelina Lauro* may have inspired this solution.

Because she was built for a short-duration shuttle service she had a wider range of public rooms than on the *Starward*, spread over two decks; these were the work of French designers, Pierre and François Lalonde. Her total capacity was 812 passengers and 144 cars – impressive, given that all passengers were berthed in *en suite* accommodation. The *Freeport*'s, Atop the superstructure, there was a solarium, sheltered from headwinds by tinted Perspex screens (similar features had been installed on earlier KEH-designed ferries, such as the *Kattegat* and *Stena Germanica*).

The Freeport's design was subsequently adopted by the Dubigeon-Normandie shipyard at Nantes for a series of three similar ferries – the *Eagle*, *Massalia* and *Bolero* – ordered by a variety of owners between 1969 and 1971 for deployment on lengthy overnight routes in southern Europe and Canada. Knud E. Hansen A/S already had a relationship with the yard, having carried out design work for the SNCF car ferry *Villandry* in 1964. These vessels established Dubigeon-Normandie as an important builder of ferries and, during the 1970s, a number of well-known vessels were constructed there.

The 13,750 gt cruise ship *Copenhagen* had many commonalities with the *Freeport* and was likewise the work of Tage Wandborg, who designed her immediately after completing drawings for the latter in 1967. She differed, however, in not having any vehicle decks. Ordered by a newly created Danish concern, K/S Nordline A/S, she was intended for European cruising based in the Danish capital. Nordline actually consisted of 850 investors who, encouraged by a tax break, intended to enter the

The innovative expedition cruise ship *Linblad Explorer*.
(Bruce Peter collection)

cruise business with no fewer than four newly-built ships. Early publicity material suggested that the first of these would be named *Prins Henrik af Danmark* in honour of the Danish Prince Consort, but this idea was later abandoned.

After dithering over how to proceed, eventually in 1970 Nordline placed an order with the long-established British shipyard of Vickers in Barrow-in-Furness. Indeed, the *Copenhagen* was the last passenger ship to be built there. Before she could be finished, however, her owners got into a dispute with the yard over escalating costs, leading to the cancellation of the contract. After some time elapsed, the partially completed vessel was towed to Wallsend on the River Tyne where she was fitted out by Swan, Hunter & Wigham Richardson at Vickers' expense. The Tyne yard had recently completed the Norwegian-America liner *Vistafjord* and was doubtless anxious to find similar outfitting work to keep its skilled employees occupied. Having been fully finished, the *Copenhagen* returned to Barrow, where she was laid up, smartly painted in full Nordline livery. Eventually, the vessel was sold to Soviet owners, the Black Sea Steamship Company, for whom she finally entered service in 1975 as the *Odessa*.

In the eight years between the *Copenhagen* being designed and belatedly entering service as the *Odessa*, Knud E. Hansen A/S became established as the leading designers of a new generation of purpose-built cruise ships for the American and worldwide markets. Shortly after finishing drawings for the *Starward*, *Skyward*, *Freeport* and *Copenhagen* in 1967, Tage Wandborg designed the 2,841 gt *Lindblad Explorer*, arguably the world's first purpose-built expedition cruise ship. She was delivered two years later from Nystads Varv AB in Finland to a Norwegian company, managed by Leif Usterud-Svendsen of Oslo. The *Lindblad Explorer* had an ice-strengthened hull and so was capable of sailing among the ice floes of Antarctica, carrying only 118 adventurous passengers. The segregation of her hull into watertight compartments extended above bulkhead deck level and into her superstructure. Fuel tanks were arranged along the centre line within cofferdams well inboard of her sides and machinery spaces were contained between additional longitudinal watertight bulkheads.

Although she had a number of hair-raising scrapes, among the most serious being a grounding at La Plaza Point in the Antarctic in 1972, which necessitated a full evacuation, she was deemed a success and she opened up a new frontier in the cruise business. From 1992, she operated as the Liberian-registered *Explorer* until November 2007 when she struck submerged ice in the South Atlantic. Fortunately, her passengers and crew were evacuated before she heeled over and sank.

Between designing the *Linblad Explorer* and her being built, a modified version of her hull design was supplied to Svendborg Skibsværft in Denmark for a new 2,097 grt coastal passenger ship for Greenland. Named the *Disko*, she entered service in 1968 ahead of the building and completion of the *Linblad Explorer*. Although the *Disko*'s dimensions were similar, she was a little shorter, due to having a truncated aft-body finishing in a flat transom stern. She survives today as an expedition cruise ship, operating mainly in the Barents Sea and named the *Polaris*.

Xxxxxxx Xxxxxx *Linblad Explorer*.
(Bruce Peter collection)

The Scandinavian second generation of ferries

A view of Gothenburg harbour in 1969, showing the recently-introduced *Stena Danica* sailing inward from Denmark. (Bruce Peter collection)

Right: The *Gedser* of 1968 is seen traversing the southern Baltic in calm conditions. (Jan Vinther Christensen collection)

Below left: An aerial view of the *Stena Danica* at sea. (Bruce Peter collection)

Below right: The *Gustav Vasa*. (Werft Nobiskrug Rendsburg)

Above left: The *Stena Danica*'s 'Dansk Lillian' restaurant, designed by Robert Tillberg. (Bruce Peter collection)

Above right: The restaurant on the *Gustav Vasa*, occupying the forward third of her superstructure on the saloon deck. (Werft Nobiskrug Rendsburg)

Left: The *Prins Oberon*. (Bruce Peter collection)

The Nils Dacke, which had a larger superstructure and funnel than the Gustav Wasa. (Werft Nobiskrug Rendsburg)

In Scandinavia, traffic volumes on short ferry crossings grew to such an extent that the early-1960s generation of Knud E. Hansen A/S-designed vessels soon struggled to keep pace with demand. Moreover, labour rates were also increasing and so, by the latter 1960s, operators typically sought to replace four smaller 'first generation' ferries with two that were substantially bigger and so, one by one, Knud E. Hansen A/S' existing clients returned to request designs for these vessels. Indeed, during the five-year period between 1968 and 1973, a prodigious output of plans for ferries was maintained. That year, however, the Oil Crisis brought growth to a shuddering halt throughout the Western World.

The 'second generation' were generally broader and longer than their predecessors with more lanes for cars and trucks across the beam of their hulls. Vertical services typically were routed through a slim off-centre casing, with four car lanes to port and three to starboard. Above, an extra deck of superstructure was sandwiched between the hull and upper deck. This could either be fitted out with public rooms or with cabins, depending on the duration of the crossing, or it could even be left clear as an extra car deck on services where vehicular traffic was a major source of revenue. Typically, such vessels were fitted with twin engines (usually with 12 cylinders each) rather than four smaller units coupled in pairs, as specified for many earlier vessels. The development of compact, reliable and relatively powerful diesels for ferries had advanced considerably during the 1960s, particularly in West Germany, where MAN and Pielstick became market leaders. The *Stena Germanica* of 1967 pioneered their use and also greatly influenced subsequent vessels' exterior styling; in this regard, the *Freeport* was also highly influential.

Ragnar Moltzau's 4,614 grt *Gedser* of 1968, sailing between Gedser and Travemünde, was arguably the first of this new generation. Built by the Schiffbau-Gesellschaft Unterweser AG in Bremerhaven, she could carry 1,200 passengers and 225 cars, a large increase in vehicle capacity, in particular, over the 1963-built ferry of the same name which she replaced. Both decks of her superstructure contained public rooms with particular prominence being given to a commodious tax-free shop. This was amidships next to the entrance hall, with the bar and lounge located fore and aft and the restaurant, galley and cafeteria on the deck above.

As Schiffbau-Gesellschaft Unterweser AG had excess steel in stock and a gap in its order book, it additionally built at cost price a 'Sundbuss' passenger ferry, the 114 grt *Sundbuss Baronen*, for Moltzau's Helsingør–Helsingborg route; she entered service in 1969.

The *Gedser* was followed in 1969 by the broadly similar though somewhat longer 5,537 grt *Stena Danica* from the AG Weser Seebeckwerft in Bremerhaven for Stena Line's Gothenburg–Frederikshavn route. At that time, the shipyard had an empty order book and was, therefore, prepared to build the ferry at close to cost price. The *Stena Danica*'s slight extra length made a positive difference and she was the most elegant-looking ferries of her era. Her sleek, powerful lines made her a stirring sight

104 KNUD E. HANSEN • 80 YEARS

Right: The spectacular side-way launching of the *Prince of Fundy* at the Unterweser shipyard in Bremerhaven on 9 February 1970. (Anders Bergenek collection)

Far right: The *Prince of Fundy* arrives for the first time at Yarmouth in Nova Scotia. (Anders Bergenek collection)

The *Saint Patrick*, dressed overall with signal flags on her maiden voyage between Rosslare and Le Havre in June 1973.

The restaurant on the *Saint Patrick*, occupying the forward section of her superstructure and affording both panoramic views ahead and the most pronounced sea motion in rough weather. (Bruce Peter collection)

An early-1970s Moltzau Line brochure in German with the *Travemünde* illustrated on the cover. (Bruce Peter collection)

Above: The *Prince of Fundy* is seen leaving Portland in Maine. (Anders Bergenek collection)

Below: The *Kalle III*, operating between Juelsminde and Kalundborg in Denmark. (Jan Vinther Christensen collection)

Left: The Tuborghavn-Landskrona ferry *Svea Scarlett*. (Bruce Peter collection)

Above: The *Bastø V* is prepared for handing over at the Moss Rosenberg shipyard on 30 April 1973. (Bruce Peter collection)

Above: The *Terje Vigen* is seen at Aarhus. (Bruce Peter collection)

Right: The *Bastø V* is seen when briefly in service across the Oslofjord in the mid-1970s. (Bruce Peter collection)

Left: A stern-quarter view of the *Terje Vigen* at Oslo. (Bruce Peter collection)

Below: The Grenå-Hundested ferry *Kattegat*. (Bruce Peter collection)

106 KNUD E. HANSEN • 80 YEARS

Top: The newly-delivered *Stena Olympica* at Gothenburg. (Rickard Sahlsten collection)

Upper left: The forward lounge on the *Stena Olympica*, designed by Rolf Carlsson. (Bruce Peter collection)

Left: The cafeteria on the *Stena Danica*. (Bruce Peter collection)

Above: The shop on the *Stena Olympica* with over-the-counter service. (Bruce Peter collection)

Above right: The *Stena Jutlandica* is seen leaving Gothenburg. (Rickard Sahlsten collection)

A stern-quarter view of the *Stena Danica* at Frederikshavn. (Bruce Peter collection)

motoring through Gothenburg Harbour and she established Stena as an increasingly dominant force on the short route from Sweden to Denmark.

Inboard, the *Stena Danica* was outstandingly well-appointed, Stena once again having employed Robert Tillberg to design her interiors. Tage Wandborg specified an entirely fireproof construction in line with the US 'Method 1' protocols followed in designing the Miami-based *Freeport*, *Starward* and *Skyward*. Therefore, Tillberg was unable to use any wood veneer for bulkhead finishes and, instead, brightly-coloured laminates were selected, giving the *Stena Danica* a very fresh ambience. As with the *Stena Germanica*, two 16-cylinder MAN diesels were installed, giving an impressive 22.5-knot service speed.

Following the *Stena Danica*, Tage Wandborg became occupied with the design of new cruise ships and so most of Knud E. Hansen A/S' subsequent ferry projects were coordinated by Dag Rogne. Wandborg did, however, continue to provide designs for his long-standing clients Stockholms Rederi AB Svea and Rederi AB Gotland.

The latter 1960s and early 1970s were a golden era for Swedish ferry companies in particular as they benefited from tax incentives to invest in new tonnage. For example, in 1970 Lion Ferry introduced the 7,993 grt *Prins Oberon*, built by the Werft Nobiskrug at Rendsburg, on the Harwich–Bremerhaven route. As she was expected to meet large waves and stormy seas, especially during winter gales, a relatively slim and well-flared bow was designed. For security, there was no door and, instead, vehicles were loaded and discharged via a stern ramp only. The *Prins Oberon* could accommodate 1,040 passengers, 702 of whom were berthed, and 238 cars. Her twin Pielstick diesels gave a speed of 22 knots, making her a relatively fast ship and therefore ideal for North Sea conditions.

Subsequently, Werft Nobiskrug constructed two further ferries based upon the *Prins Oberon*'s design. The 7,457 grt *Gustav Vasa* was delivered to Lion Ferry in 1973 for use by Öresundsbolaget on their comparatively sheltered route from Malmö to Travemünde. Thus, the ship had a blunter bow construction with a visor and ramp, fewer cabin berths relative to her overall capacity (only 594) but more space for cars (238). The third near-sister of *Prins Oberon*, the 7,927 grt *Nils Dacke*, was delivered to Öresundsbolaget in 1975. She had a slightly longer and broader hull and a more extensive superstructure to give a higher berthed capacity of 768, without reducing the payload of cars. Both of these ferries had four Stork-Werkspoor diesels, chosen for their ability to use a heavier (and cheaper) grade of marine diesel, which had to be heated up before being burned in the engines. As a result, when the *Gustav Vasa* had first entered service, she caused consternation among the Swedish seafaring unions as her crew's quarters, below the car deck and atop the fuel tanks, was found to be hot and claustrophobic. As a result of these complaints, the crew cabins in this area were omitted on the *Nils Dacke* and, instead, all crew were accommodated on bridge deck, bringing about a significant improvement in their living and working conditions.

108 KNUD E. HANSEN • 80 YEARS

Right: The *Visby* and the *Gotland* together at sea; note that whereas the *Visby* has an aft docking bridge, the *Gotland* has a swimming pool in her aft deck, perhaps indicating an intention that she might be chartered for winter tropical cruises. (Bruce Peter collection)

Right: The *Gotland*'s forward lounge. (Bruce Peter collection)

Far right: Part of the *Gotland*'s observation lounge, located above the bridge, contained reclining seats. (Bruce Peter collection)

Bottom left: A standard cabin. (Bruce Peter collection)

Bottom right: The cafeteria on the *Gotland*. (Bruce Peter collection)

A stern-quarter view of the *Gotland*. (Bruce Peter collection)

A further Knud E. Hansen A/S-designed newbuilding for Lion Ferry, the 5,464 grt *Prince of Fundy*, was ordered from the Schiffbau-Gesellschaft Unterweser AG in Bremerhaven because Werft Nobiskrug had no spare capacity due to so many other ferries already taking shape there. As with the *Prins Oberon*, she entered service in 1970, though on a new North American service from Yarmouth in Nova Scotia to Portland in Maine – a sphere of operation very different from Lion Ferry's existing Southern Baltic and North Sea territories. The plan was to bring American holidaymakers to Nova Scotia and, as Lion Ferry signed a 10-year deal to work the route, the Nova Scotia government gave them five years' free use of new port facilities at Yarmouth.

The *Prince of Fundy*'s passenger accommodation was designed in accordance with US 'Method 1' specifications. Her two Pielstick 12-cylinder diesels gave a 20-knot service speed and so the crossing each way took 10 hours, meaning that it was also possible for passengers to make return trips as 22-hour cruises. During the summer, the route was such a success that Lion Ferry quickly sought another vessel to provide morning and evening departures in both directions, but in winter the *Prince of Fundy* had to battle through extreme weather conditions. These Atlantic storms took their toll on the ship's structure, which began to crack around the window openings. Although the *Prince of Fundy* was fitted with a Knud E. Hansen A/S-designed stabilising tank, she had no fin stabilisers, meaning that she pitched, rolled and corkscrewed her way through the big Atlantic swells.

In 1973, Schiffbau-Gesellschaft Unterweser AG delivered the *Saint Patrick*, a near-sister to the *Prince of Fundy*, to the Irish Continental Line, a company set up jointly by Lion Ferry and Irish business interests, for a service from the Irish Republic to Le Havre in France. This vessel had smaller saloon deck windows than her older sister specifically to avoid cracking problems and she was also fitted with fin stabilisers.

Simultaneously, the yard also built three KEH-designed daytime ferries of comparable design, but with an upper car garage space at main deck level where the *Prince of Fundy* and the *Saint Patrick* had a majority of their cabins. These were the 3,999 grt *Travemünde* of 1971 for Ragnar Moltzau's Gedser–Travemünde service and the 4,371 grt sisters *Djursland II* and the *Kalle III* of 1974 for Jydsk Færgefart, which resulted from the combining of the Danish domestic Juelsminde–Kalundborg and Grenaa–Hundested operations. With potentially three car decks (when the platform decks were lowered), each could carry over 300 cars and up to 1,500 passengers.

The 2,957 grt *Svea Scarlett*, designed in 1969 by Tage Wandborg for Skandinavisk Linjetrafik's busy route from Landskrona to Tuborghavn and delivered in 1971 from Meyer-Werft at Papenburg had somewhat more compact dimensions than these, yet she was the biggest ferry yet to operate across The Sound with space for 800 passengers plus 95 cars. Her single streamlined funnel amidships and relatively long hull were treated in a manner similar to the DSB Rødby–Puttgarten car and train ferry *Danmark*, completed at Helsingør in 1968, her blue paintwork sweeping up to the forepeak, which had a whaleback form.

Dag Rogne, meanwhile, designed the 5,731 grt *Terje Viken* for was Da-No Linjen, owned by an Oslo-based ferry entrepreneur called Jens C. Hagen who since the early 1960s had offered a ferry service linking Oslo and Frederikshavn. In 1969, Hagen decided to begin a second route to Århus for which purpose the *Terje Vigen* was delivered in 1972 from the Chantiers du Havre shipyard in France. Hagen failed to raise sufficient money to make the required final payment to the builder and so the vessel was actually delivered to a German investment group, Skan-Fähre K/G and was managed by the shipping company J. Reinecke on Da-No Linjen's behalf, flying the German flag. Aesthetically, her design borrowed several details from the Norwegian Caribbean Line's cruise ferry *Starward*, including twin streamlined exhaust uptakes aft and an air conditioning plant below the front mast, shaped to echo the *Starward*'s Tropicana Garden.

Svend A. Bertelsen coordinated the design of two new 3,960 grt ferries for Jydsk Færgefart, the *Kattegat* and the *Lasse II*, which were built by Helsingør Skibsværft and delivered in 1972 and used between Grenaa and Hundested and from Juelsminde to Kalundborg. Meanwhile, yet another KEH client to receive new ferries was Rederi A/S Alpha, which operated the Moss–Horten route across the Oslofjord in Norway. Whereas its existing fleet consisted of double-ended ferries, the new vessels were intended to open an international service across the mouth of the Oslofjord from Tønsberg in Norway to Strömstad in Sweden as this offered the potential to sell tax-free goods.

Dag Rogne produced a design for a pair of 2,997 grt ferries, each capable of transporting 500 passengers and 120 cars. The first of these, the *Bastø V*, was delivered in April 1973 from the Moss Rosenberg Verft. The 1973 Oil Crisis caused traffic volumes to be disappointing and so the route was quickly closed down. Her sister ship, the *Bastø VI*, was therefore offered for sale while still under construction. A ready buyer was found in the Scottish nationalised shipping company, Caledonian MacBrayne for use on the exposed and often stormy crossing from Ullapool to Stornoway in the Outer Hebrides. During construction and outfitting, various alterations were carried out to comply with British regulations and, most importantly, the ship was fitted with fin stabilisers and cabin berths for 16 passengers. Delivered to Caledonian MacBrayne in 1974 as the *Suilven*, she was an outstanding success and thereafter she shuttled back and forth across The Minch for over 20 years.

Ferries from Yugoslavia

As shipbuilding costs in Northern Europe escalated, some more imaginative Scandinavian ferry operators discovered that by building elsewhere it was possible to commission ferries for almost half the cost of construction in North European shipyards.

In the latter 1960s Rederi AB Gotland began discussions with Knud E. Hansen A/s for a substantially larger 'second generation' ferries, measuring 6,665 grt and capable of making both day and night crossings. For Rederi AB Gotland, ordering two such vessels, each more than three times as big as her predecessor, was a substantial financial undertaking. Another Baltic ferry operator, Viking Line, had recently introduced new ferries built in Yugoslavia and each reputedly cost half as much as equivalents from West German or Scandinavian shipyards would have done. Rederi AB Gotland's managing director, Eric D. Nilsson, therefore decided to emulate this approach, entering into negotiations with the Brodogradiliste Jozo Lozovina Mosor in Trogir, a yard that had never previously built a modern passenger vessel of any kind.

Between the commencement of development work on Rederi AB Gotland's new ferries and their delivery, Stena Line's equally money-conscious owner, Sten A. Olsson, found out from Nilsson how cheap Yugoslavian-built ferries were and reasoned that he could buy four there for the cost of two from a North European yard. (Olsson had approached AG Weser Seebeckwerft with a view to them building a sister to the *Stena Danica* but, as the yard now had a full order book, its management was disinterested in constructing another ferry without including a substantial profit margin, which Stena refused to pay.) As a result, Olsson ordered two daytime ferries from Trogir for his Gothenburg–Frederikshavn route (the 6,333 grt *Stena Danica* (III) and *Stena Jutlandica*) and two 7,125 grt overnight vessels from Kraljevica to operate between Gothenburg and Kiel, the Stena *Olympica* and the Stena *Scandinavica*. (The former was so named as to commemorate the 1972 Munich Olympic Games.) Stena also bought some shares in Rederi AB Gotland to help finance its Yugoslavian newbuildings.

At a glance, all four Stena ferries appeared practically identical but the daytime vessels had wider hulls to carry eight rows of cars or six lanes of trucks and an additional upper garage, filling the superstructure's main deck, whereas the overnight Gothenburg–Kiel ships had cabins in the same space. Furthermore, their narrower hulls contained only seven vehicle lanes, with the casing located off-centre, just like on Rederi AB Gotland's forthcoming *Visby* and *Gotland*.

While the new Stena ferries were all fitted with twin 18-cylinder Swedish-made Lindholmen-Pielstick diesels, those for Rederi AB Gotland followed an approach tried on other recent Swedish ferries – such as Silja Line's *Botnia* and Sessanlinjen's *Prinsessan Christina* – in having multiple compact medium-speed engines, enabling the speed to be varied depending on the season and demand for crossings. Six Nohab-Polar V-diesels, connected in groups of three via gearboxes to each of the propeller shafts were chosen. Using all six, four single crossings could be made in each 24-hour period at speeds of over 20 knots.

Stena's new Gothenburg–Kiel ferries could each carry 1,500 passengers, 825 of whom were berthed, and 250 cars, whereas those for the Gothenburg–Frederikshavn route could transport 1,800 passengers and up to 425 cars. While Stena's Kiel vessels had significant numbers of cabins below their vehicle decks, those for Rederi AB Gotland had all 379 berths on their main and boat decks, with the remainder of the passengers accommodated in reclining seats which filled the 'skybars' above their navigation bridges.

When Knud E. Hansen A/S' naval architects had first visited Trogir to commence discussions with the yard's representatives on behalf of Rederi AB Gotland, they had found that almost nobody could speak fluent English and that, furthermore, the technical language of car ferry design was new to everyone there. While steel construction progressed well, it became clear that outfitting the ships to the required standard would be too much of a challenge. Therefore, Tage Wandborg, who was in charge of the project, approached a contact of his in West Germany, Horst Warneke, who owned HW Metalbau, a sheet metal company that worked to a very precise quality. Together, they developed a modular system for the entire interior, which Warneke manufactured to within a millimetre tolerance for assembly without further machining or adjustment. Rederi AB Gotland provided money to buy the necessary machine tools to carry out this job. The complete interiors were exported to Trogir in containers for installation on the ships, carefully wrapped in silk paper for protection. Hans Kjærgaard recalls:

'When Warneke visited Yugoslavia to see for himself how the outfitting of the *Visby* was progressing, he discovered that the interior components his company had so carefully made and packaged were being chucked onto carts hauled by donkeys to be brought on board the ferry for installation. When he saw this, Warneke's face turned red and he had to be physically restrained from intervening by colleagues.'

Although the precision of tolerances in the ferries' steelwork was less exacting than the prefabricated

Drawings of the *Gotland*/*Visby* showing their layout, circulation and vehicle access arrangements. (KNUD E. HANSEN Archive)

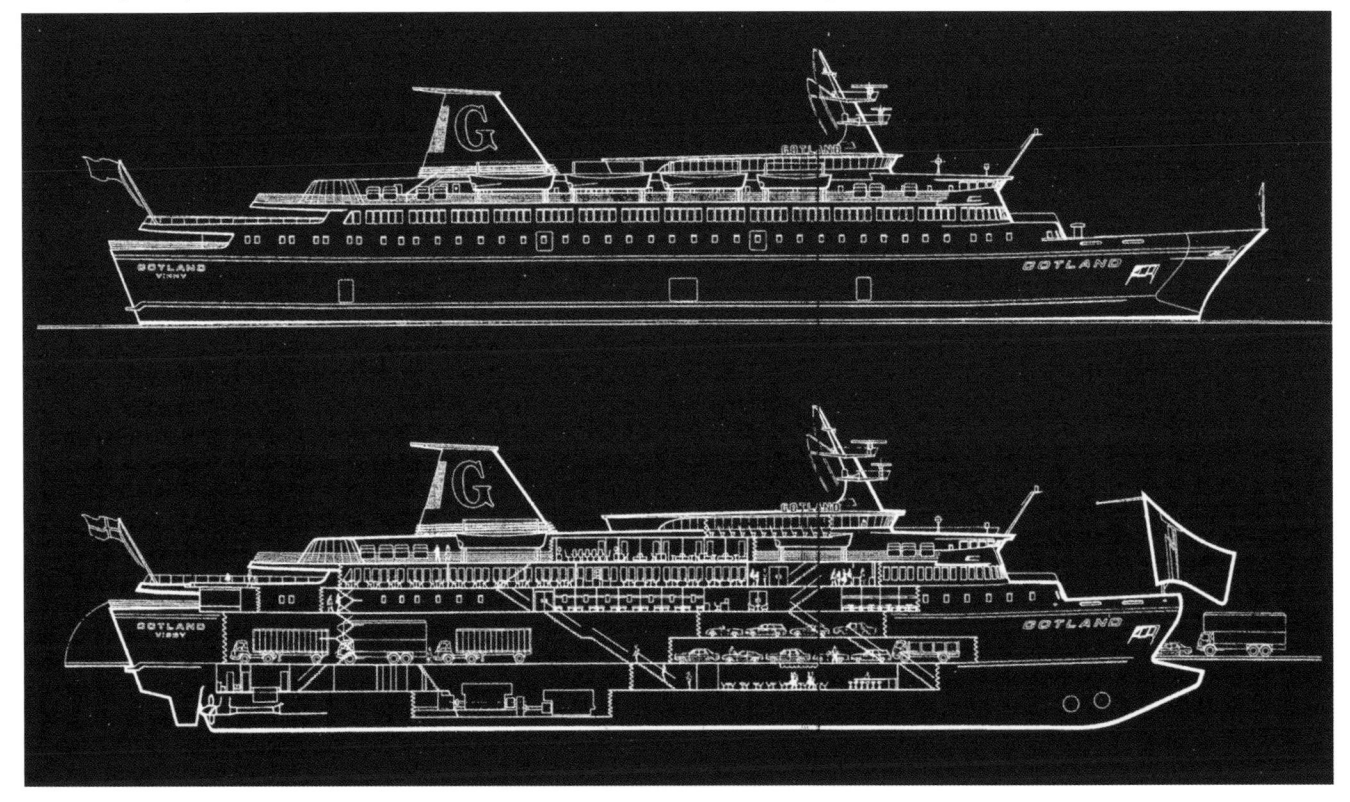

112 KNUD E. HANSEN • 80 YEARS

Right: The Larvik-Frederikshavn ferry *Peter Wessel*.
(Bruce Peter collection)

Below: The Viking Line Baltic ferry *Aurella*. (Viking Line)

interiors, the result was very successful and, thereafter, the use of prefabricated modules to fit out passenger ships came to be standard practice throughout the shipbuilding industry.

Inboard, the décor was highly colourful with several shades of orange predominating and modern Swedish designer furniture throughout. A bar and discotheque were located beneath the car deck, forward of the engine room and well away from any of the passenger cabin areas. In all of the public rooms, Wandborg made use of decorative metal screens to divide the spaces into more intimate sections; these were inspired by similar screens he had seen in the London Hilton's top-floor restaurant.

The *Stena Olympica* and the *Stena Scandinavica*, concurrently under construction at Kraljevica, had interiors crafted 'in situ' by the shipyard's joiners, who had garnered experience with this type of work when earlier on building ferries for Viking Line.

All six ferries were notably handsome with flared bow profiles and big red funnels with 'flying saucer' smoke deflectors at their summits. Each ship had extensive teak-planked sun-decks, giving summer daytime crossings a cruise-style atmosphere. While the *Visby* was under construction, however, Rederi AB Gotland requested that the *Gotland*'s design should be changed sufficiently to make her suitable for cruising as well as ferry work. Thus, while the *Visby* had an aft docking bridge, the *Gotland* was given more extensive sun-decks and even an outdoor swimming pool, just like the one on the *Freeport*. A reason for this change may have been that during the initial stages of the *Gotland*'s construction, her owner was negotiating with Finnlines with a view to chartering her out for winter cruises but no final agreement was achieved.

The six Yugoslavian-built ferries were delivered over two years from June 1972 onwards. Tage Wandborg recalls that, while the first Stena vessel, the *Stena Olympica*, had a smooth entry into service, the sea trials of Rederi AB Gotland's *Visby* in October 1972 revealed an unexpected problem:

'For reasons that I simply couldn't begin to comprehend, the *Visby* had the most dreadful shudders towards the stern. Nobody could understand why, until we dry-docked the ship and discovered that on one of the propellers, two blades were different from all of the others. What had happened was that a couple of the *Visby*'s blades had mistakenly been swapped with those from a cargo ship being completed at the same time. As the cargo ship had already been delivered, we had to carry out some delicate negotiations to get the blades swapped around but, once this happened, she performed like a dream and there were no more significant problems.'

On the Central Baltic ferry routes between Sweden and Finland, the lure of tax-free shopping had led to an exponential growth in the number of ferries in service. By the early 1970s, the two leading

The newly-completed *Tor Britannia* at Lübeck. (ShipPax Archive)

ferry consortia, Silja Line and Viking Line, each of which was owned by three different ship owners, had taken delivery of numerous ferries in the 3–5,000 gt range. Rising fuel prices and increasing labour costs in Sweden and Finland brought about an urgent need for rationalisation and so one of the three owners of Viking Line, SF Line of Mariehamn, decided to order a single substantially larger ferry, capable of doing the work of two existing vessels. In particular, the company's managing director, Gunnar Eklund, was intrigued by the latest Knud E. Hansen A/S-designed ferries on which an extra upper car deck provided space for almost twice as many cars. Eklund, therefore, contacted the firm to seek assistance in developing a suitable design for a similarly capacious ferry for Viking Line operation. Eklund and his Technical Inspector, Kaj Jansson, observed, however, that recent KEH-designed vessels' hulls tended to be optimised for speed rather than deadweight capacity and requested a hull solution with fuller lines. The result of this work was a ferry design not only accommodating 420 cars (a capacity similar to the Yugoslavian-built *Stena Danica* and *Stena Jutlandica*) but also with cabin berths for 330 out of a total passenger capacity of 1,500. Some of these were adjacent to the upper car deck while others were below the main vehicle deck, ahead of the machinery spaces.

The 7,210 grt *Aurella* was built by the J.J. Sietas shipyard in Hamburg and delivered in 1973. She proved highly effective, much to the consternation of Eklund's partners in the Viking Line consortium. On the other hand, her economy-of-scale design allowed Viking Line to lower its fares while increasingly offsetting reduced ticket prices by generating larger amounts of revenue from passengers eating, drinking and shopping in her roomier onboard facilities. The forward-facing restaurant and cafeteria, stacked one above the other, were particularly attractive features, perpetuated in subsequent Viking Line tonnage.

On the Kattegat, meanwhile, Larvik-Frederikshavn Fergen's 1968-built *Peter Wessel* had proved to be much too small to cope with the growth in traffic between Denmark and Norway and so a new *Peter Wessel*, designed by Dag Rogne, was ordered from the Ateliers & Chantiers du Havre of Le Havre, France, for delivery in time for the 1973 summer season. Measuring 6,801 grt and with accommodation for 1,500 passengers and 270 cars, she was twice the size of her immediate precursor and she was much better able to cope with traffic on the busy Kattegat crossing. During the summer, she sailed on an intensive schedule with three crossings a day and so four 8-cylinder Werkspoor diesels were installed to give a service speed of over 20 knots with reserves of power to compensate for weather delays.

In 1972, Knud E. Hansen A/S were asked by the owner of Tor Line, Sweden's Salénrederiena, to produce a design for a very large, fast and luxurious 'second generation' ferry type for the routes from Gothenburg to Immingham, Felixstowe and Amsterdam. In 1967, Salénrederiena had bought Tor Line from its original founders, Trans-Oil and Rex. Salén's Chairman, Christer Salén, evidently regarded the project as being particularly prestigious.

Initial design work was coordinated by Dag Rogne. As Immingham on the Humber Estuary was to be one of the ports of call, the breadth was constricted by the size of the tidal lock there and so, to compensate, a hull measuring over 182 metres in length was proposed. To maintain Tor Line's desired 26-knot maximum speed, very fine lines and a powerful set of four 12-cylinder Pielstick PC3 diesels was specified, geared in pairs to each propeller shaft and altogether generating 45,600 bhp to enable Gothenburg–Felixstowe crossings to be made in around 22 hours. The vehicle deck could accommodate up to 420 cars and was arranged around a narrow centre casing, cars entering via one of two wide stern doors and exiting either via a hatch in the bow quarter or by making a U-turn around

A stern-quarter view of the *Tor Scandinavia*.
(Bruce Peter collection)

The Sundbuss Erasmus. (Bruce Peter collection)

the casing to drive off aft on its other side. The superstructure layout, however, was similar to the Freeport with a cabin deck and public rooms filling the aft two-thirds of the two decks above, with more cabins filling their forward sections. Berths were provided for all 1,507 passengers. As with the Nils Dacke, great attention was paid to the comfort of the crew, who were all accommodated on the two uppermost decks. Forward of the funnel was an outdoor lido area with sheltering glass screens.

Once Dag Rogne and his colleagues had produced the basic design, however, they ceased to be involved in the project, all subsequent development being carried out by Tor Line's technical director, Lars Wikander, who appointed an ex-Swedish Lloyd engineer, Thomas Wigforss, as Project Manager. Two ferries, the Tor Britannia and Tor Scandinavia, were ordered from the Lübecker Flenderwerke for delivery in 1975 and 1976 and they exhibited a mixture of Knud E. Hansen A/S design traits – such as the tiered after decks, reminiscent of the recent Peter Wessel – and Tor Line's own ideas. On the original Knud E. Hansen A/S basic design the boat deck promenade continued unbroken around the front of the superstructure but there Wikander added extra blocks of cabins. Furthermore, it was discovered that, in order to fit silencers to the engines, it would be necessary greatly to increase the height of the funnel. Unfortunately, the extra top hamper added through these changes somewhat reduced the ships' deadweight capacities. Nonetheless, they proved highly successful in North Sea service.

At the smaller end of the ferry size scale, Knud E. Hansen A/S produced a design for three new Sundbuss passenger ferries for Ragnar Moltzau's Helsingør–Helsingborg route; these were the 191 grt Sundbuss Erasmus, Sundbuss Magdelone and Sundbuss Jeppe which were built by Lindstøls Skips og Båtbyggeri in Risør, Norway and delivered between 1971 and 1973. A small car ferry, the 399 grt Ærø-pilen was built by Husumer Schiffswerft of Husum for the Danish operator, Øernes Dampskibsselskab, to link Søby and Faaborg.

The Ærø-Pilen. (Jan Vinther Christiansen collection)

An elevation drawing of the Tor Britannia, showing a far smaller funnel than in the built version and also an open forward boat deck where, as built, additional cabins were located instead. (Bruce Peter collection)

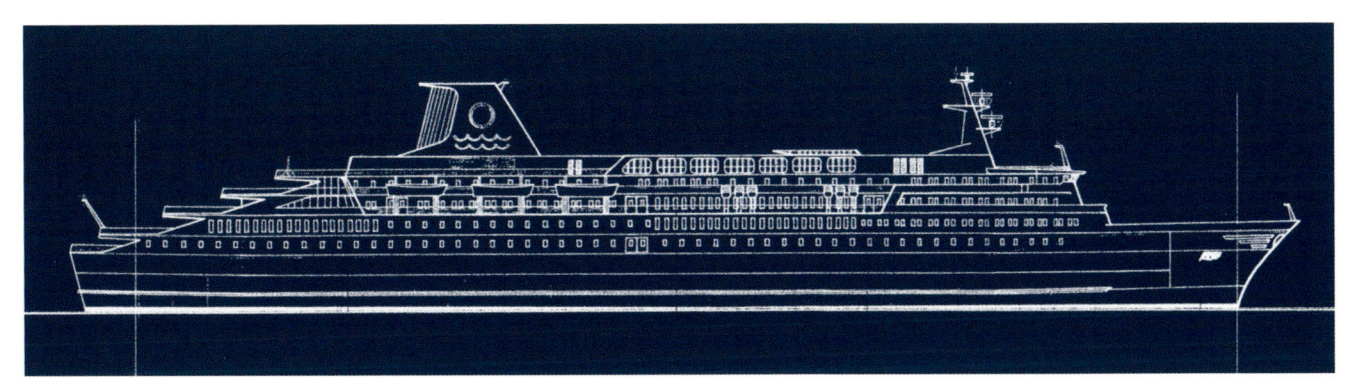

The new cruise ships

The bows of the *Skyward* and the *Song of Norway* – two of the many Knud E. Hansen A/S-designed Caribbean cruise ships introduced in the late-1960s and early-1970s. (Bruce Peter collection)

118 KNUD E. HANSEN • 80 YEARS

Above: The *Song of Norway* is seen off Miami. (Bruce Peter collection)

Left: The *Song of Norway*, berthed in Miami in a view showing her extensive sun decks and 'Viking Crown Lounge' on the funnel. (Bruce Peter collection)

Right: 'The King and I' restaurant on the *Song of Norway*. (Bruce Peter collection)
Below: The 'Merry Widow' lounge on the *Sun Viking*. (Bruce Peter collection)
Bottom right: A deck scene on the *Nordic Prince* with passengers sunbathing; note that the deck is covered in Astroturf. (Bruce Peter collection)

The Nordic Prince.
(Bruce Peter collection)

The great success of Norwegian Caribbean Line led other Norwegian ship owners, normally associated mainly with the liner trades, also to enter the cruise industry from Miami.

In the late 1960s, an American hotel owner called Edwin Stephan based in Wisconsin, met directors of the ship brokerage arm of Fearnley & Eger. Evidently, they were impressed with his proposal as they then contacted another Norwegian shipping company, I.M. Skaugen, to lead a joint venture, but when it turned out that a minimum of two vessels was needed, Anders Wilhelmsen agreed to join. Later, it was decided that a third vessel would be needed and so Skaugen asked Gotaas-Larsen to join in the venture. The shipping activities of these firms were widespread and diverse. For example, Skaugen was principally an operator of cargo liners and bulk carriers (some of which were designed by Knud E. Hansen A/S). Wilhelmsen too operated cargo liners but was diversifying as an operator of roll-on, roll-off and container ships, as well as support services for the developing North Sea oil and gas industries. Gotaas-Larsen, primarily a tanker operator, had also been active in the emigrant trade and had for some time been represented in the Miami cruise business through its Eastern Steamship Lines subsidiary. In 1968, these companies jointly established Royal Caribbean Cruise Line. Gotaas-Larsen, with its expertise in cruise the Caribbean cruise industry, assumed overall responsibility for the development of the new fleet of three purpose-built vessels, employing Knud E. Hansen A/S to assist in developing a suitable basic design. Of the potential builders, Wärtsilä in Helsinki appeared particularly enthusiastic and it too submitted a design proposal to the Norwegian owners. Consequently, its directors were asked to attend a meeting in Copenhagen with representatives of Knud E. Hansen A/S. Alas, Wärtsilä's team failed to see eye-to-eye with those from Knud E. Hansen A/S, each side refusing to acknowledge any superior attributes in the other's design proposals. Indeed, an unseemly brawl was only narrowly averted by Anders Wilhelmsen's shipbroker, who quickly suggested that the potential combatants should all go for dinner and drinks in the Tivoli amusement park.

Wärtsilä tendered successfully to build all three members of the new Royal Caribbean fleet at their Helsinki shipyard. The final design emerged as a hybrid of elements proposed by Wärtsilä's drawing office with others put forward by Knud E. Hansen A/S and other still by Martin Hallen, plus various architecture and interior design consultants. Measuring 18,346 gt and accommodating 714 passengers each, they

The Sun Viking.
(Bruce Peter collection)

Top left and right: The *Sea Venture* is seen leaving New York. (Bruce Peter collection)

Above left: The *Cunard Adventurer*, showing her 'drooping' bow design. (Bruce Peter collection)

Above right: A stern-quarter view of the *Cunard Ambassador*. (Bruce Peter collection)

Left: The *Sunward II*, following rebuilding by NCL to eradicate as much evidence as possible of James Gardiner's original styling; even the forepeak has been straightened. (Bruce Peter collection)

were to be named the *Song of Norway*, *Nordic Prince* and *Sun Viking*. Despite being nearly twice the size of NCL's the *Starward* and *Skyward*, their passenger numbers were about the same, indicating bigger average cabin sizes and a lower density of accommodation overall as Royal Caribbean sought to position itself slightly upmarket of NCL.

Propulsion was by four Wärtsilä-Sulzer diesel engines of a recently-developed design, coupled in pairs to each propeller shaft; just as on ferries, a four-engine solution gave a greater ability to vary speed depending on the length of voyage from one port to the next and to provide better redundancy, enabling one or more to be shut down for maintenance while at sea. Together, they enabled a 20.5-knot service speed to be easily maintained. Henceforth, similar four-engine solutions became more-or-less a standard throughout the cruise industry.

Royal Caribbean felt a strong need for an up-to-date, yet distinctive exterior design identity to make its vessels immediately recognisable and easy to differentiate from those of NCL and other operators. The initiator of their strikingly distinctive and innovative exterior styling was a youthful Finnish industrial designer, Heikki Sorvali, who was employed by Wärtsilä Turku Shipyard to produce conceptual designs for futuristic passenger ship exteriors. Sorvali's initial sketches and models contained many of the essential elements of the rather futuristic-looking overall silhouette eventually realised. As the vessels were not expected regularly to meet high waves, it was decided that a very pronounced 'clipper'-shaped bow profile would be attractive to passengers, perhaps reminding them of the romance of the days of sail. Near the summit of the funnel casing, a protruding cocktail lounge was proposed. Sorvali's design proposal was worked on further by the Norwegian modernist architect Geir Grung who had previously styled the superstructure of Anders Wilhelmsen's Japanese-built oil tanker the *Wilstar*, which had entered service in 1967. For the cruise ships, Grung added glazed shelter screens around the lido decks and restyled the cocktail bar on the funnel, making it resemble a circular concrete observation room he had previously designed for visitors to a hydroelectric power station in Røldal in Norway. Thereafter, it became known as the 'Viking Crown Lounge.'

In terms of internal planning, the vessels had a similar circulation pattern to the *Skyward*, with two aisles along the length of the public room decks reflected in the cabin deck corridors and transverse lobbies containing the stairwells and lift shafts in between. On the cabin decks, the inside cabins were built in blocks across the hull between these main end-to-end corridors. The interiors were designed in compliance with American 'Method 1' fire prevention standards, making much use of laminates, glass fibre mouldings and enamelled aluminium. The majority of the interior design was by Mogens Hammer while some public rooms were by the Finnish interior designer Vuokko Laakso. The colour palettes were bright and the spaces were accented by wide ranges of specially-commissioned artworks. Public rooms were named and themed after famous musicals (the 'Can Can Show Lounge', the 'King and I Restaurant' and so on). Externally, there were large expanses of sun-deck with spacious lido areas extending over the sides aft of the funnel and between it and the mast. According to Tage Wandborg:

> 'The design values of these cruise ships were totally different from the older liners and ferries. Externally, passengers expected to see sleek, white, even yacht-like silhouettes as the exteriors of cruise ships need to engender the kind of feel-good factor one gets when driving in a beautiful

The *Southward*, showing her nested lifeboats which enabled a full-width lido area above. (Bruce Peter collection)

sports car or lounging on a big yacht. It is vital for a cruise line's success for passengers to perceive that its ship is the best looking in port. Inside, however, a completely different philosophy governs the design. Unlike liner or ferry travel, cruising is about relaxation, nostalgia and, possibly, over-indulgence. Thus, to be successful, cruise ship interiors require to be filled with what might be called 'eye-candy' to at least distract or, ideally, to captivate and enchant the passengers.'

The *Song of Norway* was delivered in October 1970, the *Nordic Prince* following in July 1971. The third example of the class, named the *Sun Viking* was completed in November 1972 to a modified design with 882 berths. Externally, at the suggestion of Tage Wandborg, she was distinguished from her otherwise identical sisters by her bow plating which was carried up an extra deck, thus giving a more imposing forward profile.

Concurrently with the Royal Caribbean projects, Knud E. Hansen A/S also were involved in the basic design of two further cruise ships for a different consortium of Norwegian ship owners, Øivind Lorentzen and Fearnley & Eger, which joined forces to develop a Bermuda-based subsidiary, Flagship Cruises, to operate the ships.

The 19,903 grt *Sea Venture* and *Island Venture* were built by the Rheinstahl Nordseewerke shipyard at Emden, West Germany. The yard consulted Knud E. Hansen A/S during the early design stage in the winter of 1967–68 to assist in the preparation of the general arrangement. Svend A. Bertelsen coordinated this work in collaboration with Jan Erik Wahl, Øivind Lorentzen's technical manager. Almost from the outset, the Swedish interior designer Robert Tillberg was involved in the project's development. (He was selected on account of his acclaimed contributions to the Swedish American liner *Kungsholm*.) The intention was to use the vessels on cruises from New York to Bermuda in summer, with Caribbean and Mexican itineraries in the winter months. In order to fit the quay in Bermuda Harbour, they were rather short at only 168.76 metres (compared with the 238.44 metres of Home Line's 1966-built *Oceanic*, another famous New York-based cruise ship of approximately the same era). An unfortunate consequence was their inability to ride more than one Atlantic wave at a time and so they tended to pitch in anything more than a moderate sea.

Another consequence of their dual North Atlantic and tropical spheres of operation was the fitment of a retractable glazed roof over the lido so that it could be fully-enclosed in poor weather. (This was no doubt inspired by the success of a similar feature on the *Oceanic*.) Forward of this, there was an observation lounge and cocktail bar above the bridge. All the other entertainment spaces were arranged in open plan on a single deck, connected by a side arcade with large picture windows, while the dining

The *Spirit of London*, as completed to P&O's modified design. (Bruce Peter collection)

room was three decks lower in the hull, perhaps another concession to the possibility of encountering Atlantic storms.

The space was structurally adventurous as there were no supporting columns for the decks above and instead these were held aloft by the longitudinal cabin corridors, which were constructed as box girders, and by deep lateral beams which spanned the entire width of the ship. The most impressive space, though, was the double-height purser's square. Its dramatic centrepiece was a wrap-around white marble panel, weighing seven tons, adorned by an abstract metal artwork made by students of the Oslo College of Art. Unfortunately, such weighty fixtures and fittings made the ship top heavy and the situation was only solved by removing some of the teak covering from the topmost external decks and by fitting counterweights into the bottom of the hull. By the time that the interior fixtures and fittings were chosen, Knud E. Hansen A/S were no longer involved in the project, the vessels' detailed design instead being by Øivind Lorentzen's technical department and the shipyard.

The *Sea Venture* and *Island Venture* were introduced in 1971, the former wholly owned by Øivind Lorentzen while the *Island Venture* belonged to Fearnley & Eger, whose management developed grave misgivings about the Flagship Cruises project, believing that Lorentzen's insistence on sailing from New York to Bermuda, rather than from sunny Floridan ports to the Caribbean was misguided. Shortly after the *Island Venture* was delivered, therefore, Fearnley & Eger chartered her to P&O to boost their newly-acquired Princess Cruises fleet and they subsequently bought the vessel, renaming her *Island Princess*.

P&O was not the only long-established British liner company to enter the North American cruise business in the early 1970s; Britain's other major liner operator, Cunard, also broke into this lucrative

Top left: A late-1960s artist's impression of a cruise ship for Wärtsilä, showing a mix of the yard's typical design features and those of Knud E. Hansen. Elements of this initial study subsequently fed into the vessels built in Helsinki for Royal Caribbean and Royal Viking Line.
(Bruce Peter collection)

Top right: A slightly later artist's impression of a cruise ship for Det Bergenske Dampskibs-Selskab; after further development work, this concept was used for the three Royal Viking Line vessels.
(Bruce Peter collection)

Above: The completed *Royal Viking Star* at the commencement of what was to prove a lengthy and highly successful career.
(Bruce Peter collection)

Interiors of the *Golden Odyssey*, designed by Tage Wandborg with abstract bulkhead decorations by the Greek artist (and interior designer), Michael Katzourakis. (Bruce Peter collection)

The *Golden Odyssey* is seen leaving Vancouver. (Bruce Peter collection)

market and likewise purchased new tonnage built to Knud E. Hansen A/S designs. The *Cunard Ambassador* and *Cunard Adventurer* had been ordered by a Texan entrepreneur called Steedman Hinckley, who was chairman of Overseas National Airways for an experimental fly and cruise operation in the Caribbean. Such a concept was certainly ahead of its time and, at first, the idea had been to build two clipper-type sailing ships, each with three masts. These were drawn up and an order was placed with the Rotterdam Drydock Company. The steel was delivered and cutting commenced to form the hull sections, but before work could proceed further, the owner had a change of heart. Construction stopped abruptly when it was decided instead to build two larger, but more conventional, cruise ships without sails. This brought about the unusual situation of the shipyard invoking penalty clauses in the contract for delays against Overseas National Airways.

Meanwhile, the bemused naval architects at Knud E. Hansen A/S were set to work again, under Tage Wandborg's direction, to produce a new design, measuring 14,160 grt and accommodating 831 passengers. To style the exterior, Hinckley employed the well-known British industrial designer James Gardner, who had recently styled the exterior of the Cunard flagship, the *Queen Elizabeth 2*. Tage Wandborg recalls that, while he and Gardner got on well on a personal level,

'It was clear that Gardner didn't really understand ships and the way that the shapes of a superstructure have consequences for its behaviour in different weather conditions. He had very clear ideas about how these vessels should look and I simply didn't agree with him. To me, his designs were neither logical, nor were they coming from any kind of inheritance of naval architectural practice, so far as I could see. But he had the client's ear.'

One vessel was ordered from the Rotterdam Drydock Company and the other from Machinefabriek en Scheepswerf van P. Smit Jr, also of Rotterdam. When the first was nearing readiness for launching, however, Overseas National Airways got into temporary financial difficulties and sold both hulls to Cunard, which was only too happy to expand its American cruising operations with new and economical motor ships.

The *Cunard Ambassador* and *Cunard Adventurer* were delivered in 1971 and 1972 but the former

The expedition cruise ship *World Discoverer*. (Bruce Peter collection)

had only a very short career as a cruise ship. In September 1974, she was damaged by fire while en route from Miami to New Orleans and the wreck was sold to Danish owners, C. Clausen, for conversion by Knud E. Hansen A/S into a sheep carrier named the *Linda Clausen*. (It will be remembered that many years previously, in 1943–45, KEH designed the tramp steamer *Linda Clausen* for the same company.)

The Cunard Adventurer was sold in 1977 to Norwegian Caribbean Line, who sent her to Bremerhaven for a radical refit which transformed her into the *Sunward II* for three and four day trips from Miami to the Bahamas. Tage Wandborg was delighted finally to get his way with regard to the vessel's external appearance as nearly all of James Gardiner's design elements were replaced.

Following on from the great success of its *Starward* and *Skyward*, late in 1968, Norwegian Caribbean Line's chairman, Knut Kloster, informed Knud E. Hansen A/S that orders were shortly going to be placed for an additional pair of cruise ships to be named the *Southward* and the *Seaward*, based upon the *Skyward*'s design. The lowest bid for their construction was from an Italian shipyard, the Cantieri Navali del Tirreno e Riuniti of Riva Trigoso, near Genoa. Since designing the *Skyward*, however, Tage Wandborg's had developed new ideas and so he persuaded Kloster to allow him to re-work the plans so as to produce larger and more sophisticated 16,607 grt cruise ships. By then, there was very little time before construction was due to begin. To supervise the project, Wandborg booked himself in to a hotel nearby, where he set up a small design office so he could work closely with the shipyard's technical staff. He recalls that:

'I worked in my hotel room, which had a balcony overlooking the Ligurian coast. I spread my paper out on the floor. My patio door was opened and the warm sunshine and sea air filled the room. It was the most inspiring setting one could imagine in which to design ships. Within hours, I had developed the forms of the new ships. I have a great love of Italy and much respect for Italian design. As a young man, I regarded Nicolò Costanzi as my great hero. He not only revolutionised hull design and hydrodynamics through his rigorous research, but he was also an artist and a great aesthete. He was, in fact, a father figure and an architect whose sculptural methods, innovation and aesthetic judgement I admired. His most outstanding ship, in my opinion, was the *Oceanic* of 1965, a big, powerful hull upon which there sat a low, streamlined superstructure. There was a wrap-around promenade at main deck level with the lifeboats recessed above it. With the machinery located aft, this layout meant that the top of the superstructure could be entirely given over to sun-deck space, with several swimming pools and glazed screens on either side, making a spacious, sheltered sun trap. It was the ideal model for a modern cruise ship.'

Wandborg followed Costanzi's example, stowing the lifeboats at main deck level and creating a wrap-around promenade deck on which passengers could enjoy strolling. The tapering line of the glass screens, which sheltered the sun-deck, was continued in the shape of the after decks, making a bold yet harmonious composition. Another felicitous effect of this layout was that it was possible to gain extra height for the dining room, which was located between the lifeboats at main deck level, and for the main lounge, directly above. The latter had a sunken floor in the centre with raised wings above the lifeboat recesses on either side, ensuring that all passengers had a reasonable view of the stage and dance floor. Wandborg furthermore recalls that:

'The shipyard was traditional with very grand, genteel and dignified old directors in beautifully cut Milanese suits and with immaculate shoes who supervised the work from their office windows. As a result, I had to do a lot of on-the-spot retraining to help the shipyard foremen and staff to make an imaginative leap to the new possibilities for *Southward* and *Seaward*.'

At Riva Trigoso, ships were usually launched in a nearly completed state but, because the yard was busy, the *Southward* took to the water somewhat earlier and was completed at a wharf in Genoa. She entered service in December 1971 but work on the *Seaward* was abandoned when industrial unrest at the shipyard increased her price by more than 50%. By the time the Italian government intervened by nationalising the yard, NCL had lost interest. Instead, the unfinished hull was sold to P&O for operation in American waters and completed as the *Spirit of London*.

In order to ensure that the *Spirit of London* had a family resemblance to P&O's other recent passenger ships (such as the *Canberra* and the *Arcadia*), their own naval architecture department designed for her a single tall and tapered buff funnel, but otherwise she was externally identical to the *Southward*.

While the *Southward* and the abortive *Seaward* projects were under construction in 1972, Knut Kloster and Knud E. Hansen A/S developed plans for a cruise ship of around 20,000 grt which would have had a conventional bow, aft of which the hull would divided into a catamaran design. One advantage was a gain in stability while another was that the vessel could be unusually wide, enabling enough space for facilities more akin to those of a beach resort hotel or shopping mall. On the other hand, a catamaran hulled vessel would be significantly more expensive to build than a conventional single-hulled design.

The project, which was code-named 'Elysian,' never progressed beyond the planning stages, however, and it was not until the 1980s that NCL was in a position to introduce larger tonnage.

Following on from the consortia of Norwegian ship owners who formed Royal Caribbean Cruise Line and Flagship Cruises, another three established Norwegian ship owners formed the Royal Viking Line. Whereas NCL, RCCL and Flagship typically operated short cruises of no more than a week's duration, Royal Viking ambitiously planned to provide lengthy and expensive worldwide itineraries.

The origins of the Royal Viking Line can be traced back to 1967 when the directors of Det Bergenske Dampskipsselskap (for whose company the then-young Knud E. Hansen had drawn up the Venus in 1931) began to explore the idea of running a cruise-ferry service between Key West in Florida and Vera Cruz in Mexico. Slightly later on, in 1968, the company considered the formation of a new American-based cruise subsidiary and in 1969 a contract was signed with Wärtsilä's Helsinki shipyard for the construction of a 21,847 grt cruise ship with delivery planned for 1972. Wärtsilä and Knud E. Hansen A/S collaborated to produce a suitable design, following their in the end successful joint work for Royal Caribbean. As the intention was to operate worldwide itineraries, Cunard's *Queen Elizabeth 2* provided an obvious design precedent with regard to the vessel's layout and appearance and the intention was that she would be named *Stella Polaris*.

Shortly after, Bergenske was approached by two other Norwegian shipping companies, Det Nordenfjeldske Dampskipsselskap and A.F. Klaveness & Co as they too wished to explore the possibility of ordering similar vessels and perhaps operating them jointly with Bergenske. Both Bergenske and Nordenfjeldske had long cooperated in the Hurtigruten service, an essential local lifeline to the isolated communities along Norway's west coast, but Klaveness was new to the passenger market. Each partner would contribute one ship and in the autumn of 1970, the three founded the Royal Viking Line.

Within similar hull dimensions to the recent Royal Caribbean trio and with an extra deck of superstructure, only 536 passengers were carried (in comparison with the 882 of RCCL's *Sun Viking*). The majority of the interior design work was carried out by the Norwegian designer Finn Nilsson in conjunction with the Oslo-based architect F.S. Platou. As the Royal Viking fleet was designed for long cruises, cabins were large and many had their own sitting areas.

The first of the three new cruise ships, the *Royal Viking Star*, was delivered in June 1972 The remaining two vessels arrived in 1973, the *Royal Viking Sky* being introduced in July and the *Royal Viking Sea* entering service in December.

Having been inspired by the *Queen Elizabeth 2*'s layout when designing the Royal Vikings and having also recently designed the *Cunard Ambassador* and *Cunard Adventurer*, in 1972 Knud E. Hansen A/S received a request from Cunard to carry out rebuilding work on the three-year-old *QE2*. Recently, Cunard had experienced a hostile take-over by Trafalgar House, an upstart construction and property group whose directors were determined to maximise profits by refitting the vessel with additional cabin berths and by converting public rooms space into more lucrative uses, such as by installing additional shops plus a casino.

Tage Wandborg was put in charge of the project and sent to London with two colleagues, where they were accommodated by Cunard in the Hilton Hotel in Park Lane. Hans Kjærgaard, accompanying Wandborg, recalls what happened during their stay at the Hilton:

> 'Because the hotel was fully booked, Tage was given the bridal suite, where we assembled to discuss and prepare drawings for the *QE2* conversion before an important meeting with Cunard's technical staff. Tage telephoned room service and asked for a bottle of champagne, three glasses and also a screwdriver. At first, the waiter thought that he was asking for the cocktail of that name, but what he really wanted was a plain old screwdriver, which he used to remove the bathroom door from its hinges, then to take the handle and lock off the door. He then poured the champagne and laid the door across the backs of two chairs to use as a drawing board.
>
> The Hilton had a restaurant and nightclub on the topmost floor where we spent the evening. The dance band and other guests were very curious to see Tage carefully examining the construction of the metal decorative screens around the bandstand, but he was completely oblivious to everyone's stares and later he used such screens in the interiors of many of his ferry and cruise ship designs.'

The most striking change to the *QE2* proposed by Wandborg was the construction of a group of new penthouse cabins with private balconies atop her superstructure, replacing what had been a little used games deck in a sheltered well behind the bridge structure. These were carefully formed and prefabricated in aluminium alloy to minimise the additional weight and to avoid spoiling the ship's sleek silhouette any more than strictly necessary. Although a very few passenger ships dating back to the 1920s had cabins with private verandahs, in terms of design and manufacture, these new top deck

The *Cunard Princess* is seen leaving New York in the late-1970s. (Bruce Peter collection)

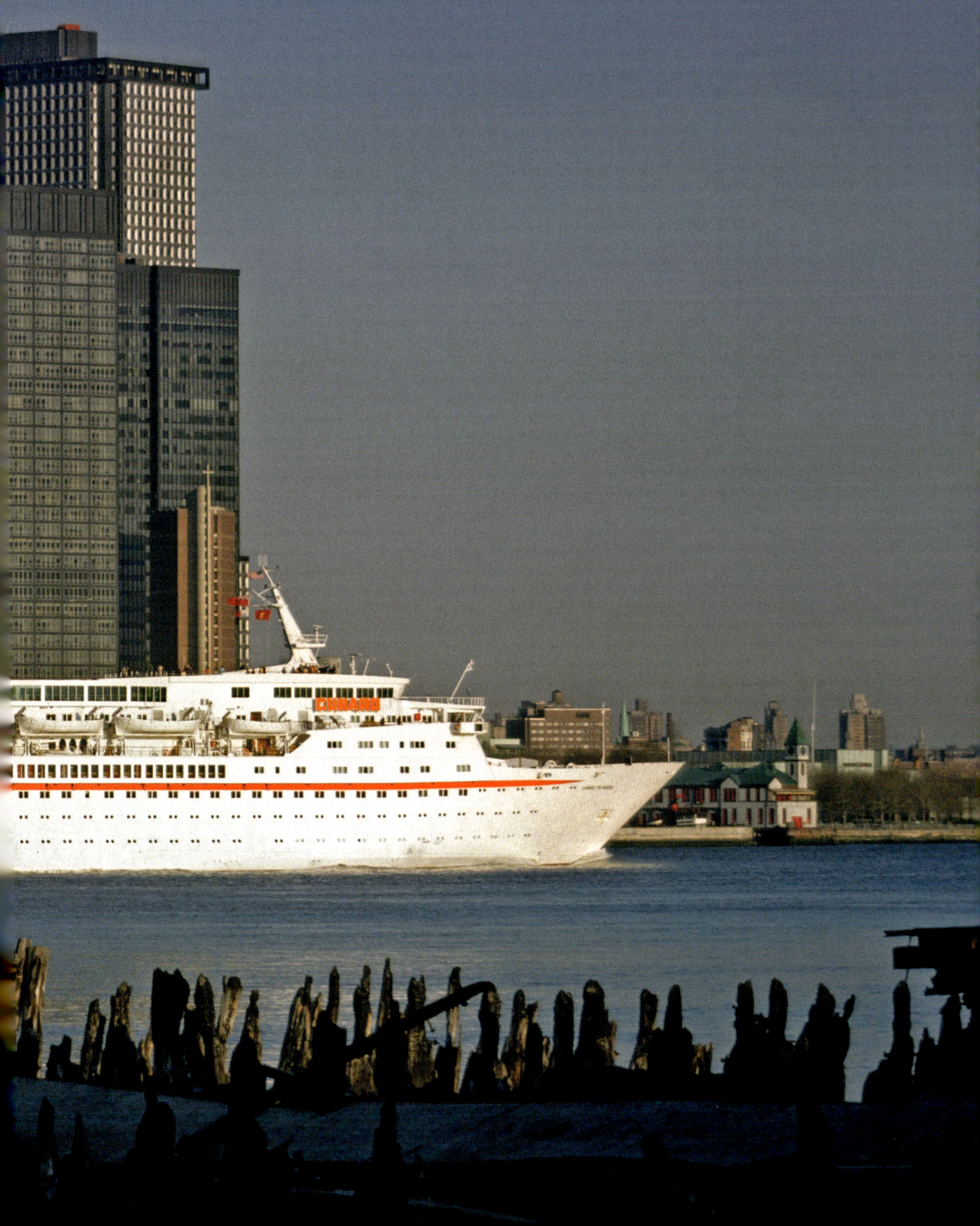

An aerial view of the Burmeister & Wain shipyard in Copenhagen with the *Cunard Countess* under construction in one of the building docks, adjacent to a bulk carrier. (Museet for Søfart)

The *Cunard Princess* off New York. (Bruce Peter collection)

penthouses were the first of their kind on any ship. Not surprisingly, they became the *QE2*'s most exclusive and sought-after accommodation and they were highly profitable for Cunard.

At the beginning of 1972, Hans Kjærgaard produced his first ever cruise ship design, a 3,153 grt expedition vessel for a Danish company, Bewa Line A/S, who then sold shares in her to 550 private investors. The building contract was awarded to the Schiffbau-Gesellschaft Unterweser in Bremerhaven and the ship was launched on schedule in December 1973 as the *Bewa Discoverer*. Accommodating only 152 passengers, she was compact but robust, having an ice-strengthened hull.

In the latter 1960s and 1970s, Greek ship owners entered the cruise industry with enthusiasm, but their fleets consisted almost exclusively of converted ships, some of which had been built as ocean liners and others of which had been ingeniously fashioned out of cargo ships, ferries and day excursion boats. The 6,757 grt *Golden Odyssey*, completed in 1974 by Helsingør Skibsværft for Royal Cruise Line, owned by Pericles Panagopoulos was, in fact, the first brand new and purpose-built Greek-owned cruise ship, intended to carry a jumbo-jet load of American passengers on Mediterranean itineraries. The aim of Royal Cruise Line was to emulate the approach of Royal Caribbean as closely as possible, albeit initially on a smaller scale. The task of producing a general arrangement was allocated to Hans Kjærgaard who spent eight months working closely with Panagopoulos to refine the scheme. Kjærgaard recalls that:

'Panagopoulos ensured that every last corner was effectively utilised to optimise revenues. If he spotted a large linen cupboard, he wanted it to become a two-berth cabin. Having extensive personal experience as a manager of cruise ships, he had an intuitive sense for how people occupied space onboard these vessels and so I learned a lot from him.'

Once Panagopoulos signed a contract to build the *Golden Odyssey*, Tage Wandborg took over, making further revisions to improve the passenger flow, styling the exterior and assisting with the interior design. In terms of layout and aesthetics, she had much in common with the *Sea Venture* while her interior design involved a Greek artist called Michael Katzourakis, who chose colour schemes, selected furniture and decorated the bulkheads with abstract murals. Subsequently, he went on to design further ship interiors for Panagopoulos and eventually set up his own specialist passenger ship interior design firm, AMK Design, based in Athens.

As we shall see, following the *Golden Odyssey*'s success, Pericles Panagopoulos was to remain one of Knud E. Hansen A/S' most loyal clients. Tage Wandborg recalls:

'Panagopoulos and his organisation were superb clients as they had very good ideas about how cruise ships should be arranged. Projects initiated by them took a long time to gestate and often never progressed to actually building a ship, but they were always a pleasure to be involved in. They approached Knud E. Hansen A/S on many occasions to have cruise ship concepts prepared and then refined and this work did indeed result in the building of a couple of outstanding vessels.'

The final cruise ships planned before the Oil Crisis put a temporary stop to the industry's expansion were acquired by Cunard to replace their *Cunard Ambassador* (which had been destroyed by fire) and *Cunard Adventurer* in the still relatively buoyant Caribbean cruise market. The new vessels were actually to have been two of eight identical sister ships. MGM, the well-known film and entertainment conglomerate, was to have owned the other six, but its management had a last minute change of heart about entering the cruise business and they never were built. The eight ships were to have been positioned throughout the world – the Caribbean, the Mediterranean, even the Indian Ocean and the South Pacific – for what was expected to be a boom in long distance air-sea cruising. The plan was to build the ships at the Burmeister & Wain shipyard in Denmark and then to outfit and complete them at the Industrie Navali Merchaniche Affine shipyard at La Spezia in Italy.

The 17.496 grt *Cunard Countess* was delivered in the summer of 1976 but the *Cunard Princess*, which was originally to have been named the Cunard Conquest, was delayed by a shipyard fire in April 1976, and was not introduced until March 1977. According to Hans Kjærgaard, who coordinated the design effort with Svend A. Bertelsen:

'These ships were 3,000 tonnes larger than the previous ships we designed for Cunard and they were some 16 metres longer, which gave them superior sea-keeping qualities. The hull design was unusual as the topsides tapered outwards towards the waterline, increasing stability and lessening the rolling motion. Four relatively small B&W diesels gave a top speed of well over 20 knots and the combination of a fast hull profile with a curving transom stern to give rigidity aft and a low streamlined superstructure was very effective.'

When Princess Grace of Monaco (formerly the film star Grace Kelly) named the *Cunard Princess* at New York's newly renovated Passenger Ship Terminal, Cunard's Chairman, Victor Matthews declared that the new vessel would be 'the last cruise ship'. Within two years, however, the building of new ships as large as 40,000 grt had begun, but alas Cunard failed to order any further vessels.

Ro-ro freight ferries

The *Dana Maxima* at Grimsby. (Bruce Peter collection)

134 KNUD E. HANSEN • 80 YEARS

Top left: One of the lifting side cargo access doors on the *Laurentian Forest*. (Jack Brown collection)

Top right: One of the *Laurentian Forest*'s cargo spaces with retractable platform decks lowered. (Jack Brown collection)

Centre left: British MG-B cars for export on the *Laurentian Forest*. (Jack Brown collection)

Centre right: One of the mobile scissors lifts on the *Laurentian Forest*. (Jack Brown collection)

Right: The *Laurentian Forest*, nearing completion, with her bow-quarter access door open. (Jack Brown collection)

From the latter 1960s onwards, Knud E. Hansen A/S received a succession of commissions to design freight ferries for several of the leading Northern European ferry operators. Many of these projects were handled by Dag Rogne, who became KEH's leading expert in designing vessels of this type.

In 1969, an innovative car carrier was designed for the long-established Swedish liner operator Olof Wallenius, which at that time was diversifying away from traditional 'deep sea' scheduled services for general cargo and into the lucrative specialised niche of transporting new cars overseas. At first, Wallenius experimented by converting existing cargo vessels, removing their cranes and inserting new decks in the holds on which cars could be parked. KEH designed a stern-loading car carrier with an aft-located superstructure measuring 2,885 grt. Ordered from the Finnboda Varv in Stockholm and delivered in 1970, she was named the *Mignon*, following Wallenius' tradition of giving vessels operatic names. A single-screw vessel, she had 900 lane metres for cars, involving the use of retractable hanging decks. As car ownership grew throughout the Western World and as greater numbers of cars came to be imported from Japan and elsewhere in the Far East, Wallenius' business expanded greatly and so the *Mignon* was quickly displaced by far larger car carriers.

In late-1970, Knud E. Hansen A/S was commissioned by the Federal Commerce & Navigation Ltd of Montreal to design two unusually complicated paper and car carriers, the 16,284 gt *Laurentian Forest* and *Avon Forest*, for trans-Atlantic service between ports on the St. Lawrence River in Canada and Avonmouth in the UK. The vessels were built with a subsidy by Port Weller Dry Dock Ltd.

Westbound, large rolls of paper would be shipped on pallets on three internal decks, whereas eastbound, British-made cars would be carried on seven decks with four mezzanine decks lowered between the three paper decks. As the entire mezzanine deck, ramp and lift installation needed to be relatively light in weight so as not to reduce the vessels' deadweight capacity, the use of conventional ferry-type steel platforms, raised and lowered by hydraulic equipment, was impossible. In addition, the vessels needed to operate independently of specialist shore-based infrastructure and so large ship-to-shore ramps that could be adjusted to offset to offset tide, trim and sinkage were essential. The heavy but easily damaged paper rolls, were moved on large pallets by straddle-carriers, which dropped the pallets on cargo elevators serving the lower decks, from where the individual rolls were picked up by forklift trucks for stowage. Once cleared, the empty pallets were returned to the main deck level from which the straddle-carriers took them ashore.

One of Federal Commerce & Navigation Ltd's directors, Jim Murray, knew an old school comrade from Glasgow, Jack Brown, whose family had run the Greenock shipyard of George Brown (Marine) Ltd, which many years previously had built the Knud E. Hansen-designed cargo coaster *Teddy* (described above). By the 1970s, Brown's company was specialising in the manufacture and supply of bespoke ro-ro cargo-handling equipment under the 'Cargospeed' brand. At a meeting at Knud E. Hansen A/S' office in Copenhagen, Cargospeed was commissioned to design and fabricate the extensive specialist cargo-handling system which formed a core part of the vessels' design. This task required close cooperation with KEH, the ship owner and builder.

A stern-quarter view of the *Laurentian Forest*.
(Jack Brown collection)

136　KNUD E. HANSEN • 80 YEARS

Top left: The Helsingborg-Travemünde freight ferry *Svealand*. (Bruce Peter collection)

Top right: The *Stena Timer* was one of a series built by Stena for the charter market. (Bruce Peter collection)

Above left: The Gedser-Travemünde ferry *Falster*. (Jan Vinther Christensen collection)

Above right: The ro-pax (freight, cars and passenger) ferry *Gedser*. (Bruce Peter collection)

Right: The *Mercandian Exporter II*, one of a series built for chartering. (Museet for Søfart)

Bottom: The *Scandinavia*, which had been ordered by Moltzau for the Gedser-Travemünde route but which was sold during construction to of Rederi AB Nordö. In 1976, she was lengthened with the insertion of a new mid-body section, as shown here. (Bruce Peter collection)

The Norwegian *Admiral Atlantic*, one of a class of three intended for 'deep sea' liner service. Note that her funnel casing overhangs the hull so as to free up additional space within.
(Bruce Peter collection)

The superstructure and engine room, containing two 9,000 bhp Pielstick diesels, were aft-located and the extensive forward-facing weather deck was mostly occupied with vehicle deck ventilation plant, deck islands containing elevator machinery and other technical equipment (all cargo was stowed below deck). To bring paper rolls on board, Cargospeed designed and manufactured two three-part ramp systems for each vessel, one located forward on the starboard side of the hull and the other aft on the same side. These comprised athwartships ship-to-shore ramps, connected to self-levelling platforms, from which long fore-and-aft ramps linked to the main deck. The platforms were raised and lowered by an ingenious hydraulic drive systems.

Rather than leaving the ramps exposed, breaking the line of the shell plating at the bow and stern, shell doors were required to give added protection from high Atlantic waves. These were envisaged by Knud E. Hansen A/S staff as side-hinging, but Cargospeed proposed instead upward lifting doors, the exteriors shaped to continue the vessels' hull form without interruption so as not to catch the waves. As the classification society Lloyd's of London was concerned that the large forward door opening in the hull would reduce the vessels' longitudinal strength, a substantial steel reinforcement beam was fabricated over the forecastle deck above to compensate for the door aperture.

Designing the four hoistable car deck levels was a major project in itself. To save weight, their steel frames were covered with panels of very strong industrial plywood. To save additional weight and expense, instead of hydraulic raising and lowering, mobile scissors lifts were be moved on the steel decks to beneath each panel needing moving. The total car capacity with all decks in use was 2,250 cars.

Delivered in 1972 and 1973 respectively, the *Laurentian Forest* and *Avon Forest* were from a technical point of view highly successful and they received extensive coverage in the shipping professional journals. In the late-1980s, both vessels were sold to the US Military Sealift Command, becoming the *Cap Lobos* and *Cap Lambert*; at the time of writing, they remain in commission.

Another long-lived Knud E. Hansen A/S-designed ro-ro freight ferry of the same period was the 3,987 grt *Svealand*, delivered in 1972 from Helsingør Skibsværft for the Stockholms Rederi AB Svea-owned Trave Line service between Malmö and Travemünde. Her superstructure was forward-located with an enclosed shelter deck astern and a centreline casing. Inboard there were 600 lane metres for trucks.

At around the same time, Larvik-Frederikshavn Fergen commissioned a 2,793 grt ro-ro freighter designed by KEH for its route from Norway to Denmark. Built by Kristiansands Mekaniske Verksteder in Norway, the intention was that she

The *Duke of Yorkshire*.
(Bruce Peter collection)

Top left: The DFDS freighter *Dana Hafnia* (ex *Dana Gloria*) was intended for North Sea service but frequently chartered for 'deep sea' liner operation. (Bruce Peter collection)

Top right: The Japanese-built *Dana Maxima* of DFDS had a hull form optimised to fit the tidal lock at Grimsby. (Bruce Peter collection)

would be named *Cort Adeler* but prior to delivery in 1974, the effects of the Oil Crisis caused Larvik-Frederikshavn Fergen to charter her out to Norfolk Line, an expanding North Sea operator of ro-ro freight vessels for whom she entered service between Scheveningen and Middlesbrough as the *Duke of Yorkshire*. In terms of overall layout, she was quite similar to the *Svealand*, albeit with her exhausts routed through side-casings, rather than one in the centre. Her capacity was 590 lane metres.

In the early 1970s, Stena Line became an important Knud E. Hansen A/S client for freight as well as passenger and car ferries. Sten A. Olsson found chartering ships to other operators a very lucrative business area in which to be involved and so, during the 1970s, he built up a growing fleet of flexible and effective ro-ro freighters for the charter market. Hans Kjærgaard recalls:

'The ferries designed for the majority of operators in the 1970s were so tightly optimised that one couldn't add even 50 tons of extra weight without hitting the damage stability margin. Some Danish domestic ferries were even built according to inland waterway rules. Stena, however, was different. Typically, they'd request that we design the cheapest possible freight ferry, but with a margin for an additional 1,000 tons of top weight. From the mid-1970s onwards, Stena always requested big margins so that their vessels could be modified or converted at a later date, or so that they could carry special cargoes, such as railway vehicles, whenever a charterer required.'

In the early 1970s, Knud E. Hansen A/S designed for Stena a series of six similar approximately 3,450 grt freight ferries, three of which were constructed by the J.J. Sietas shipyard in Hamburg with a further trio being ordered shortly thereafter from the Österreische Shiffswerften AG Linz-Korneuburg on the River Danube near Vienna. Both yards already had close relationships with Knud E. Hansen A/S as Sietas had previously built the KEH-designed Viking Line ferry *Aurella*, while Österreische Shiffswerften had constructed the Iraqi floating crane *Al Miqdad*.

In terms of layout and dimensions, the new Stena freighters followed the precedent set by the *Svealand*, albeit powered by twin Kloeckner-Humboldt V-diesels and having only the forward third of the shelter deck enclosed, beneath the forward-located superstructure. The use of V-diesels for freighters of this type enabled a relatively high service speed (around 18.5 knots) while maintaining a compact machinery space.

The first of Stena's new freighters were completed by Sietas in 1974–75 as the *Bison* and *Buffalo*, reflecting that, upon delivery, they were to be taken over by the P&O Group for its Irish Sea ro-ro freight routes. The third Sietas-built example also was used by the P&O Group, initially operating as the *Union Melbourne* under charter to the Union Steamship Company of New Zealand, which already ran the *Wanaka* and *Hawea* across the Cook Strait.

The decision to build three of the freighters in Austria was soon regretted, however. Due to the shallow depth of the River Danube, it was decided to build the hulls and superstructures separately and to fit these together at Galatz in Romania, to which the hulls were towed and the superstructures brought on barges. In the spring of 1976, however, melt water collapsed a road bridge across the Danube, blocking the river and delaying the tow of the hull of the first vessel, the *Stena Tender* until summer. It was particularly hot and dry, meaning that the river was low, causing it to ground en route. Meanwhile, Stena had already decided to lengthen the vessel to meet the needs of a charterer and had signed a contract for this work to be carried out by Werft Nobiskrug in West Germany. By the time the superstructure was added in Galatz, however, heavy rain had caused the Danube to swell to the extent that there was now insufficient clearance beneath a bridge at Novostad in Yugoslavia and so the *Stena Tender* was trapped there for six months until the Danube's waters receded again. Eventually, the vessel was indeed towed to Werft Nobiskrug's yard at Rendsburg where she was cut in half and a new midship section was inserted before she finally entered service. The other Austrian-built examples

Top left: An artist's impression of the innovative Stena 'Searunner' class, built in South Korea. (Anders Bergenek collection)

Top right: The *Atlantic Project*, one of two 'Searunners' chartered by Stena to Atlantic Container Line and fitted with sponsons. (Bruce Peter collection)

Centre left: The *Stena Freighter*, one of several 'Searunners' to have served a variety of routes within Stena's own network. (Ferry Publications Library)

Centre right: The *Baltic Ferry*, a 'Searunner' equipped with an enclosed shelter deck and modular passenger accommodation at Felixstowe with another example of the class, the *Doric Ferry*, to the rear. (Bruce Peter collection)

Left: The Rederi AB Gotland freighter *Gute* was in many respects a miniature version of the 'Searunner' type. Here, she is seen in Visby in lengthened condition. (Bruce Peter)

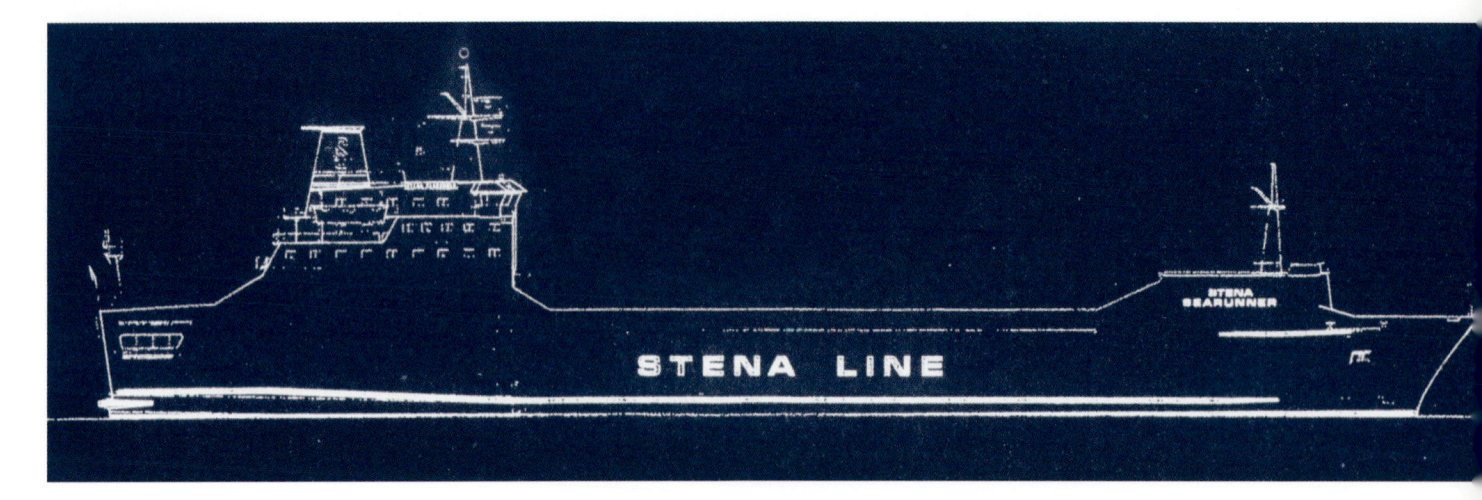

An elevation drawing of the *Stena Searunner*. (KNUD E. HANSEN Archive)

were the *Stena Timer* and *Stena Topper*, both of which were delivered in 1977.

In 1972, Ragnar Moltzau ordered two new Knud E. Hansen A/S-designed ro-ro freighters to provide additional capacity on their Gedser–Travemünde route. These 1,682 grt vessels were built by Trondheims Mekaniske Verksteder in Norway with delivery expected in the 1974–75 period. In terms of overall layout, these vessels were much like the *Cort Adeler/Duke of Yorkshire*. An innovation by Dag Rogne was to place the exhaust uptakes half way through the shell plating, reducing their impingement into the hull to no more than the breadth of a single staircase and thereby freeing up more

The staff of Knud E. Hansen A/S at the company's 40th anniversary party in 1977.
(Niels Fisker-Andersen collection)

A rare photograph of the unfortunate *Zenobia*, which sank in the Mediterranean off Cyprus following a failure of the computers controlling her bilge pumps. (ShipPax archive)

The small BP-owned liquid petroleum gas carrier *Danish Arrow*. (Hans Kjærgaard collection)

space for trucks. Aft, the ramp accessing the upper vehicle deck overhung the stern.

Between placing orders and the vessels' delivery, however, Moltzau changed its plans, also in response to the Oil Crisis, wishing to replace four ferries (two carrying passengers and cars, plus two dedicated freighters) with a single passenger vessel plus a far larger 4,998 grt combined freight and passenger ferry. This too was designed by Knud E. Hansen A/S and ordered in 1974 from the Schichau-Unterweser shipyard in Bremerhaven with delivery expected in 1976. Meanwhile, the two freighters under construction in Trondheim were sold to the Swedish Rederi AB Nordö, the pair being chartered briefly to their original owner for Gedser–Travemünde service as the *Scandinavia* and *Falster* in 1974 and 1975 respectively.

While the new ro-pax ferry for the Gedser–Travemünde route was under construction in Bremerhaven, Moltzau decided to sell the entire operation, which was reconstituted as Gedser–Travemünde Ruten A/S and it was to this new company that the ferry was delivered in 1976 as the *Gedser*.

Dag Rogne's solution of partially locating casings outboard of the superstructure was reprised in three bright turquoise-painted ro-ro freighters designed for a new subsidiary of Larvik-Frederikshavn Fergen and built by the Ishikawajima Shipyard in Tokyo, Japan, with delivery in 1977. The 2,574 grt *Admiral Caribe*, *Admiral Atlantic* and *Admiral Pacific* were to operate on a 'deep sea' ro-ro liner service linking North European ports with North Africa and the Middle East. Each not only had a capacity of 1,187 lane metres, but also could transport 282 20-foot containers, crane-loaded onto an open shelter deck.

A similar design approach was used for a series of eight 1,599 grt freighters ordered by the Danish ship owner Per Henriksen's Mercandia Rederi from Frederikshavn Værft & Flydedok A/S ærft for operation under charter both on short-duration ferry crossings and longer-haul liner services. The design of these, too, involved Dag Rogne. Constructed in the 1978–85 period, the *Dana Atlas*, *Mercandian Carrier II*, *Mercandian Exporter II*, *Mercandinan Importer III*, *Mercandian Merchant II*, *Mercandian Transporter II*, *Mercandian Supplier II* and *Mercandian Trader II* all served numerous operators and worldwide spheres of operation.

At the same time, Rogne was involved in designing two large new freighters for DFDS' North Sea routes. It happened that a former KEH employee, John Kristiansen had joined DFDS' Technical Department in 1970. As DFDS struggled with the effects of the Oil Crisis after 1973, their own naval architecture staff was greatly reduced and so they began instead to use KEH whenever they required a new ship to be designed, or an existing vessel converted. The *Dana Futura* and *Dana Gloria* were 5,991 grt vessels designed primarily to transport refrigerated trucks bringing Danish agricultural exports to the UK – for which they required many reefer plugs – and manufactured goods in the opposite direction. In addition, they could carry around 400 20-foot containers on deck, loaded by their own gantry crane. Fast, powerful vessels, their twin Burmeister & Wain 18-cylinder diesels, enabled speeds of up to 22.5 knots to be maintained. Unfortunately, DFDS specified them with larger dimensions than the tidal lock accessing its man UK freight port, Grimsby, could accommodate, meaning that their usefulness was limited and soon after entering service in 1975 and 1976 they were chartered out for operation elsewhere, including in the deep-sea liner trades between the USA and the Middle East.

Following a change of management, DFDS subsequently ordered another freighter – the 4,928 grt, 2,160-lane-metre *Dana Maxima* – which Knud E. Hansen A/S was also involved in designing. Built in Japan by the Hitachi Shipbuilding & Engineering Company at Nagasu, she was designed specifically for service between Esbjerg and Grimsby and was the maximum size possible to fit through the tidal lock there (141.5 x 20.6 metres). Her hull had a particularly bluff bow configuration, the underwater lines being enhanced by a pronounced bulbous forefoot. In addition, space was saved by the use of lifts, rather than fixed internal ramps to move trailers between decks and this made her slower to load

Bottom left: The Shell tanker *Felipes*. (Mick Lindsay collection)

Bottom right: The *Flammulina* at Southampton. (Mick Lindsay collection)

The *Axel Mærsk*, one of a series of six container ships delivered to A.P. Møller bt Blohm & Voss for Maersk Line service, had hull lines designed by Knud E. Hansen A/S. In this photograph, the vessel has been slightly lengthened amidships. (Bruce Peter collection)

Seen off San Francisco, the *Charlotte Mærsk* was one of seven general cargo liners rebuilt with new cellular fore-bodies with design input from Knud E. Hansen A/S. (Andrew Kilk)

An aerial view of the *Clara Mærsk*, another of the same series, following the fitment of the new container-carrying fore-body, actually slightly wider than the original hull.
(Bruce Peter collection)

and unload. This did not matter in any case because she needed to spend 12 hours in Grimsby as she could only arrive and depart during each high tide.

In the mid-1970s, the idea that ships could be designed from the outset with the possibility of future enlargement was a novel one, and, as we have seen, Stena Line's ro-ro freight ferry division were the pioneers of this concept. In autumn 1974, Stena began working with Dag Rogne on a new freight ferry type with both engines and superstructure towards the stern. With such an arrangement, their mid-body could subsequently be cut in two more easily for lengthening without disturbing the machinery spaces. The new design was known as the 'Searunner' class and no less than 11 examples were ordered in two batches from Hyundai Shipbuilding & Heavy Industry at Ulsan in South Korea for delivery between 1977 and 1978. This was the first occasion that ferries for a European ship owner were built in Korea and Hyundai impressed both Stena's technical staff and the KEH naval architects with its very efficient organisation.

Measuring 5,463 grt, the 'Searunners' could accommodate 1,650 lane metres of freight. Propulsion was by twin 12-cylinder Pielstick V-diesels, giving an had an 18-knot service speed. They were also one of several Knud E. Hansen A/S ro-ro designs from the mid-1970s onwards to have twin-skeg hulls whereby instead of protruding from the hull's underside, each of the propeller shafts was encased in a steel housing extending from the hull all the way to the screw. Twin-skeg hulls were developed by Svend A. Bertelsen and Poul Erik Rasmussen who spent over six years working to refine the idea through numerous tank tests. Because they increased the amount of underwater hull volume, they had the potential to significantly enhance a vessel's deadweight capacity while reducing proneness to cavitation. On the other hand, as more steelwork was required and welding involved, a twin-skeg aft body was also more expensive to fabricate. Furthermore, if not very carefully designed, it could induce an increase in drag at certain speeds and might also have a negative effect on damage stability.

Upon delivery, the third and fourth Searunners were chartered by Stena to Atlantic Container Line for whom they operated for over three years as the *Atlantic Prosper* and *Atlantic Project* in trans-Atlantic liner service between Northern European and North American ports, a very demanding duty requiring vessels of outstanding robustness. Later, in 1982, another Searunner, the P&O-operated *Elk* was chartered to the British Ministry of Defence to bring military supplies to the South Atlantic during the Falklands War, her successful naval deployment again showing the Searunner type's capabilities.

In the early 1980s, several Searunners were lengthened and fitted with enclosed shelterdecks to expand their lane metres, while side and aft 'duck tail' sponsons were fitted to increase deadweight capacities. Dag Rogne recalls how the idea for 'duck tail' sponsons emerged:

'During lunch time, my colleagues and I often took our sandwiches to the Churchill Park near our offices in Bredegade, where we fed crumbs to the ducks in the ponds around an impressive sculpture of Gefion. I noticed that when a duck wants to paddle quickly, it pushes its tail feathers down into the water to increase the length of its body at and below the waterline. This was how I got the idea of making so-called 'duck tail sponsons' on ferries. The idea was that the hull would project out beyond the stern to give a longer, sleeker, form in the water and, thus, to save fuel. When this was combined with our special twin-skeg stern design, which enhanced the effectiveness of the propellers, and a long, torpedo-shaped bulbous bow, the result was very efficient indeed …'

Three examples of the Searunner class were even given passenger accommodation in prefabricated modules on top of their enclosed shelterdecks. The design was an immediate and enduring success and several examples remain in service today, over 35 years after they were initially planned.

Rederi AB Gotland' 1,594 grt *Gute*, also designed by Rogne, was conceptually a miniature version of the Stena 'Searunner' class. Built by Falkenbergs Varv and delivered in 1979, she was a stern-loading ro-ro freighter with an aft-located superstructure and an open shelter deck for the carriage of freight and dangerous goods from Nynäshamn and Oskarshamn to Visby. A very useful and reliable vessel, she was subsequently lengthened and spent parts of her long and diverse career under charter to other operators.

The same cannot be said of the *Zenobia*, which was the first of three 10,528 grt sisters designed for Rederi AB Nordö and built in 1979–80 by Kockums Varv in Malmö for a ro-ro liner service through the Eastern Mediterranean from Volos in Greece to Tartous in Syria. Propelled by twin Sulzer diesels located aft of amidships, giving a 21-knot service speed, the vessels could each carry 175 trailers, while well-appointed accommodation for the officers and crew and also 140 passengers was provided in a fairly tall forward-located superstructure.

The pumps adjusting the trim tanks were computer controlled but, unfortunately, on an early voyage, this automated management system malfunctioned on the *Zenobia* when en route along the Cypriot coast, causing the vessel to heel over and sink in shallow water. She was never recovered and has since become a diving attraction, regarded by connoisseurs as being among the best in the world.

Fortunately, her two sisters, the *Ariadne* and *Scandinavia*, operated successfully and were subsequently radically rebuilt as passenger and freight vessels for service on the Dover Strait (though Knud E. Hansen A/S was not involved in this project).

Towards the end of Knud E. Hansen A/S's relationship with Iraq, a commission was received to design three ro-ro freight and container ships which were to be built in Helsingør. Named the *Al Zahraa*, *Khawla* and *Balgees*, these vessels were highly controversial in Denmark as they were obviously designed to carry military equipment and, by the time they were completed in 1983, Iraq and Iran were at war, meaning that they could not be delivered. Yet, as Hans Kjærgaard observes, in the 1970s, all ro-ros designed by KEH were planned for alternative military use as, for European ship owners, NATO charters were lucrative earners during the Cold War with the Soviet Union. Thus, in terms of deck strength, capacity and range, there was no difference between a KEH-designed ro-ro for the Iraqi government and one for DFDS or Stena Line.

Tankers, bulkers and container ships

During the 1970s, Knud E. Hansen A/S continued to design tankers and bulk carriers and also became involved in developing container ships. At the beginning of the decade Erik T. Møller designed two 31,500 dwt tankers, the *Mobil Engineer* and *Mobil Navigator*, for the Mobil Tankers Co of New York, which were built in Haugesund and delivered in 1973. The same builder subsequently constructed a series of nine 32,400 dwt tankers for Norwegian, Dutch and British tanker operating subsidiaries of Shell. These were the *Fjordshell* (1974), *Fulgur*, *Felania*, *Fusus*, *Felipes* (all 1975), *Ficus*, *Flammulina*, *Fossarina* and *Fossarus* (all 1976). Meanwhile, Hans Kjærgaard designed the *Danish Arrow* and *Danish Dart*, 499 dwt liquid petroleum gas carriers for the Danish subsidiary of British Petroleum; these were built in Svendborg and delivered in 1976. Kjærgaard was proud of these vessels which he felt displayed a particularly elegant simplicity of line.

In contrast, the *Colon Brown* was a comparatively large 26,556 dwt bulk carrier designed by Erik T. Møller and completed in 1974 in Sasebo, Japan, for Ole Skaarup, a New York-based Danish shipping entrepreneur. In the 1950s he had pioneered the development of self-unloading bulk carriers to carry gypsum from Halifax in Nova Scotia to American East Coast ports. Additionally, Møller was responsible for the 32,265 dwt bulk carrier *Libra*, built by Finnboda Varv in Stockholm, which entered service in 1975, the 35,630 dwt *Federal Schelde* and her sisters *Federal St Lawrence* and *Federal Rhine*, delivered in 1977–79 from Hyundai in South Korea for service between the Great Lakes and Europe, and the 14,116 dwt Haugesund-built geared general cargo vessels *Pollux* and *Patria*, which also were completed in 1977.

Meanwhile, in 1974, Poul Erik Rasmussen was approached by the Blohm & Voss shipyard in Hamburg to refine the lines for a series of six new A-class container ships for A.P. Møller's trans-Pacific service from the United States Eastern Seaboard, via the Panama Canal, to the Far East. These vessels were designed jointly by A.P. Møller's Container Ship Development Division, led by Jens J. Kappel, Captain Troels Dilling, who was in overall charge of A.P. Møller's Technical Department, and Hans Langenberg, the Senior Naval Architect at Blohm & Voss. In total A.P. Møller wanted nine A-class ships and so the order was split between Blohm & Voss and Lübecker Flenderwerke, which built the remaining three vessels. Because the two builders were also rivals, they refused to cooperate in sharing lines plans and so, although all of the A-class had similar characteristics in terms of overall dimensions, speed and capacity, they had different hull configurations.

Through careful planning to optimise the hull volume, it was feasible to achieve a capacity of 1,600 TEU in vessels each measuring only around 27,000 gt and with dimensions of 210.75 x 30.56 metres. The intention was to maintain a fairly high service speed of around 24 knots and, therefore, so to avoid burning an unacceptably large amount of fuel, it was important to reduce drag as much as possible. To achieve this aim, the hull was configured with an unusually slender aft body, the lines of which were very similar to those at the bow. The first A-class container ship, the *Adrian Mærsk*, was delivered by Blohm & Voss August 1975 and placed in service that September. Her five sisters, the *Albert Mærsk*, *Anna Mærsk*, *Arthur Mærsk*, *Axel Mærsk* and *Anders Mærsk*, followed thereafter.

In the early 1980s, A.P. Møller decided also to containerise their route from the USA to the Middle East and so in 1980–81 their seven C-class cargo liners, dating from the latter 1960s, were comprehensively rebuilt by Hitachi Zosen in Japan and, once again, Knud E. Hansen A/S were involved in designing the conversion. Each vessel was cut in two just ahead of the superstructure and fitted with a new cellular forward section, slightly wider than the original hulls had been (29.7 metres versus 25 metres). To further maximise capacity, the forward mooring deck was very small and the container stacks began immediately behind a breakwater. The wheelhouse was raised by one deck, allowing containers to be loaded four-deep on the hatch covers. After rebuilding, each vessel could carry 1,222 containers,

Cruise ship conversions

The newly-converted *Norway*, ex-*France*, at New York – the world's biggest cruise ship in the early-1980s. (Bruce Peter collection)

The Port Line refrigerated cargo vessel *Port Melbourne* in her original condition.
(Bruce Peter collection)

Following the 1973 Oil Crisis, Knud E. Hansen A/S found that, suddenly, orders for new cruise ships and ferries dried up. Many schemes were proposed, none of which were built. Even so, cruise operators approached the company to supervise conversions of existing vessels and this was found to be another lucrative area in which to be involved. While Norwegian cruise entrepreneurs preferred newly-built tonnage, Greeks operators tended to convert existing vessels. Partly, this was because the country was under military rule at that time and it was difficult to raise enough finance to buy new passenger ships, which were comparatively expensive. Greek conversions – usually carried out by small shipyards located along the coast between Piraeus, Keratsini, Perama and Elefsis – were often highly ingenious.

The final generation of 1950s British combination passenger-cargo liners, in particular, offered excellent conversion opportunities. For starters, they were designed to be capable of carrying the deadweight of a full cargo, and so building additional superstructure fore and aft was unlikely to cause stability problems. Secondly, they were often extremely robust vessels and, thirdly, they were

The *Danae*, ex *Port Melbourne*, following rebuilding in Greece.
(Bruce Peter collection)

comparatively inexpensive as they were being replaced by container ships and often were available for not much more than scrap value. In addition, passenger-cargo vessels tended to have twin-screw diesel propulsion, also perfect for a modern cruise vessel.

In 1974, a Greek shipping magnate called John C. Karras bought two such vessels, the *Port Sydney* and the *Port Melbourne*, which had been built respectively by Swan, Hunter & Wigham Richardson in Newcastle and by Harland & Wolff in Belfast in 1955 for Port Line's services from London to New Zealand and Australian ports. At first, Karras planned to convert them to side-loading car ferries and it was with this in mind that he first contacted Knud E. Hansen A/S. Karras then changed his mind and requested instead that they be transformed into modern luxury cruise ships with air-conditioned accommodation for a little over 500 passengers. This task was undertaken by Tage Wandborg.

Each rebuild took two years to complete at a shipyard at Chalkis, near to Rafina. The centre part of the existing superstructure was maintained up to promenade deck level and extensive new accommodation was added fore and aft. Most public rooms were located on one deck with the galley forward, serving a large dining saloon amidships, and there was a multi-purpose main lounge towards the stern. The cabins were notably commodious and there were even six with private balconies. Renamed the *Daphne* and the *Danae*, they were completed in 1975 and 1977 respectively and came to be regarded as among the finest in the Greek cruising fleet.

The conversion of *France* to *Norway*

By the latter-1970s, Norwegian Caribbean Line's fleet was fully booked for months ahead and the company therefore had no option but to turn away trade. NCL's senior management reasoned that, one way or another, it would be necessary to add an additional, significantly larger vessel to its fleet. Tage Wandborg of Knud E. Hansen A/S proposed various designs but NCL failed to raise sufficient capital to build any of them. The next best option would be to buy then radically convert an out-of-work trans-Atlantic liner and, after NCL's technical staff had inspected a number of such vessels, they decided that the former French line flagship, the *France*, would be the best option. Constructed by the Chantiers de l'Atlantique at St. Nazaire with the help of a massive government subsidy and introduced in 1961 on the Le Havre–New York route, the *France* had been President Charles de Gaulle's *grand projet* – a spectacular and very chic showcase of all that was best in French technology, design and decoration. A quadruple-screw, steam turbine-powered vessel, she measured 1,035 feet in length – the longest liner in the world. Viewed externally, she had been designed to impress with a dramatic, tapering whaleback bow and two massive funnels, topped with giant wings to throw smoke away from her sides.

Having agreed to buy the vessel, Knut Kloster contacted Tage Wandborg, giving him three weeks to produce an outline conversion plan. To do so, he set up a design office on board, from where a team from Knud E. Hansen A/S worked for the next 14 months. Their proposal involved 'opening up' the largely enclosed superstructure to the sun with new lido decks and all segregations between First and Tourist Class removed. By converting the enclosed promenade decks into 'main streets', not only would passenger circulation be improved but also new retail opportunities could be created, generating additional revenue. Meanwhile, passenger capacity would be increased through the installation of additional cabins. Furthermore, the vessel would be made more fuel economic through the elimination of half her boiler capacity by closing the forward of her two engine rooms with the removal of the outer pair of her four propeller shafts. As a trans-Atlantic liner, it was necessary to maintain speeds of around 28 knots, but as a cruise ship, only half that speed would be acceptable. As the *France* was deep-drafted and required the assistance of tugs when manoeuvring in port, the solution was installing three lateral thrusters in the bow plus two in the stern, enabling her to turn within her own length in the port of Miami without any help from tugs. To bring passengers ashore at the various Caribbean islands, Wandborg's ingenious proposal was to store two landing craft, each for 450 persons, on the foredeck.[161] Knut Kloster appointed the well-known New York-based interior designer Angelo Donghia to work alongside Wandborg to make the ship's interiors more appealing to American passengers going on tropical cruises.

The *France* was towed to the Hapag-Lloyd shipyard in Bremerhaven which estimated the cost of the conversion at 42 million dollars. Wandborg recalls with enthusiasm that:

> 'There now started a most thrilling cooperation between a ship owner and his naval architect. Seemingly, each day I came up with new ideas and Knut Kloster did the same. All of this added to the cost and, in the end, the project came in at a total 100 million dollars. However, the result was outstanding.'

As the project gathered momentum, a greater number of naval architects and engineers was required to develop and to draw up the conversion plans in detail. Indeed, for nearly a year, over half of Knud E. Hansen A/S's workforce was involved, working under Wandborg's direction. Indeed, it became the company's largest project to date. Hans Kjærgaard recalls:

150 KNUD E. HANSEN • 80 YEARS

Top left: The magnificent *France* catches evening sunlight as she heads down the Solent in this mid-1960s scene. (Bruce Peter collection)
Top right: The newly-converted *Norway* at speed in the English Channel. (Ambrose Greenway collection)
Upper centre left: A stern-quarter view of the *Norway* in the Hudson River at New York. (Bruce Peter collection)
Lower centre left: A close-up view of the *Norway*'s forward superstructure, showing part of one of the new ship-to-shore tenders mounted on her bow. (Bruce Peter collection)
Bottom left: The *Norway* at Southampton, floodlit at night: shortly, she left for Miami and her second career as the Caribbean's largest cruise ship by far. (Bruce Peter collection)
Bottom right: The Leeward Dining Room on the *Norway* following conversion from the 'Rive Gauche' (Tourist Class) facility on the *France*. (Bruce Peter collection)

Far left: A model of the proposed *Phoenix World City* undergoes trials in a wave test tank: in this early iteration, she has four superstructure blocks. (Tage Wandborg collection)

Far left lower: A subsequent rendering of the *Phoenix World City*, reduced to only three blocks of superstructure. (Tage Wandborg collection)

Left: A rendering of the docking bay at the stern of the *Phoenix World City*, showing how ship-to-shore tenders would enter the vessel. (Tage Wandborg collection)

'I was one of three naval architects from Knud E. Hansen A/S working full-time for 11 months on the conversion under Tage Wandborg's direction. The day I arrived, one of our people was evaluating some steel construction towards the stern. He used a drill to find out how thick some deck plating was, but the drill bit broke. Another five drill bits also broke. Having looked more closely at the original detail construction drawings, which were labelled in French, he realised that he was actually trying to drill into the foundation for an anti-aircraft gun, as the France had been designed also to serve as an armed troopship in time of war. The gun foundation was made of special hardened steel, two inches thick.

One day Knut Kloster arrived with around 20 wealthy Americans to show them around the ship, which looked a real mess as there was building work taking place everywhere. Tage took the party around the ship, through rooms filled with scrap, dangling wires and pipes, telling them of his visions for how the completed *Norway* would look. They were all riveted by what he said. If he had been hired to sell sand in the Sahara, I think he would have succeeded …'

For Wandborg and his colleagues, the conversion meant long and stressful working hours, as he recalls:

'When you convert a ship, it is much more complicated than designing a new one because you never know for sure what you are going to find when the next wall or ceiling panel is removed. I spent every working day in my office on board, dealing with queues of workmen who had found problems needing solving immediately. After they went home, I then had to begin work on the drawings I had actually intended to prepare and often I did not finish until three in the morning. One day, I caught a glimpse of myself in a mirror and barely recognised the reflection I saw. The work took its toll, but the result justified all of the effort expended.'

The *Norway*'s arrival in Miami in June 1980 marked the beginning of a new epoch for the cruise industry. Because her mainly American passengers were used to constant entertainment while on vacation and, sailing from Floridan ports, they would have been familiar with such theme parks as Disneyland at Orlando, NCL placed great emphasis on hiring famous entertainers to perform on board. Whereas the earlier NCL ships were relatively small and thus offered only a limited choice of entertainment and activities, the sheer size of the *Norway* opened up a world of new possibilities. She was a floating resort with a theatre big enough to stage Broadway musicals and she had a vast range of sports facilities. The project's total cost of 130 million dollars was only half the price of a somewhat smaller newly-built cruise ship. According to Tage Wandborg:

'The conversion was one of the most rewarding projects of my entire career. Apart from the joy and professional pride of having returned one of the great liners of all time back to life and to profitable service, it cemented my friendship with Knut Kloster and its successful outcome freed up our imaginations. In terms of cruise ship design, there was a significant paradigm shift. After designing ferry-derived vessels of up to 16,000 gt, we suddenly felt, with the *Norway* about to enter service, that anything might be possible.'

While the *Norway* conversion had been under way, Knut Kloster had initiated a project for a giant purpose-built Caribbean cruise ship, code-named 'G-6' and measuring over 250,000 gt. At first he worked with a youthful Norwegian designer, Petter Yran, who had been trained as an architect but had been inspired to draw speculative designs for futuristic cruise ship concepts in the early-1970s. Later in the decade, Yran was briefly employed by Knud E. Hansen A/S, where the initial project development for G-6 was carried out.[169] When the *Norway* entered service, Tage Wandborg took over the project which was henceforth known as 'Phoenix World City.' Kloster's original idea had been to use an oil tanker hull as a 'platform' for the vessel, but he was persuaded by Wandborg that converting a tanker would be impossible and that a wholly purpose-built solution would be necessary. Wandborg's design had four apartment blocks on top of a gigantic hull with a marina built into the stern in which to dock four 'day cruisers'. Every passenger would have a spacious hotel-like stateroom with a private balcony looking forward, to the sides or astern. Unfortunately, an unresolved problem was to work out a way to raise enough finance to pay for the construction. A few years later, another version was proposed, this time with three apartment blocks, but this was not built either.

Subsequently, in 1988, Wandborg's colleagues Steen Nielsen and Hans Kjærgaard produced a design for an even larger apartment cruise vessel of around 400,000 gt, with a single continuous apartment block zig-zagging on top of a hull for an Indian shipping tycoon called Ravi Tikkoo. Tikkoo planned to build the ship, code-named the 'Ultimate Dream', at the Harland and Wolff shipyard in Belfast, Northern Ireland. The project progressed to the stage of ordering steel to enable the keel to be laid. British Government subsidies were not forthcoming, however, and so Ravi Tikkoo had second thoughts about progressing with construction.

Even although neither the Phoenix World City nor the Ultimate Dream projects came to fruition, Knud E. Hansen A/S had demonstrated that cruise ships of over 100,000 gt with balconies for thousands of guests were feasible and, by the late-1990s such vessels did indeed begin to appear, albeit designed by others.

Back in 1987, NCL's rival, Royal Caribbean Cruise Line, introduced the first very large purpose-built cruise ship, the *Sovereign of the Seas*, and so the *Norway* was temporarily knocked from her 'top spot' as the world's biggest cruise liner. However, in 1991 she returned to Germany where, at Lloyd Werft in Bremerhaven, a massive refit was carried out during which two extra decks designed by Tage Wandborg were added to her accommodation. These spoiled her sleek lines but, for the time being, made her the world's biggest cruise ship once again at 76,049 gt, as well as making her more profitable for NCL.

Tage Wandborg retired from Knud E. Hansen A/S in 1991, after which he continued to collaborate

Left: The dinner excursion ship *Star of Detroit* nears completion at Chesapeake Shipbuilding Corporation's yard. (Hans Kjærgaard collection)

Bottom left: The upper dining saloon on the *Star of Detroit*. (Hans Kjærgaard collection)

Below: A stern-quarter view of the *Star of Detroit*. (Hans Kjærgaard collection)

privately with Knut Kloster on further futuristic cruise ship concepts.

In 1983, Knud E. Hansen A/S designed a further significant cruise ship conversion, this time for Italy's Costa Line, which bought the 1964-vintage 27,900 grt former Lloyd Triestino Trieste–Sydney express liner *Guglielmo Marconi* for rebuilding as the *Costa Riviera*. To carry out the $50 million project, KEH collaborated with Costa's Italian architects, Studio de Jorio. At Genoa's Mariotti shipyard, the vessel's turbines were de-rated for an economical 17-knot service speed, rather than the 27 knots she could reach in liner service, and her superstructure was extended fore and aft over what had been cargo holds to enable new cabins and public rooms to be created. Indeed, a major part of the rebuilding work involved reconfiguring Tourist Class cabins without private facilities into larger rooms suitable for American cruise passengers. Meanwhile, the funnel was encased with wings and grills, designed by Studio de Jorio, to give what was hoped would be a more 'futuristic' appearance. In November 1985, the *Costa Riviera* left Genoa for Fort Lauderdale, where she began her new, and very successful, career as a Caribbean cruise ship.

American river cruise ships

Attending a passenger shipping conference in the USA in the early 1980s, Svend A. Bertelsen had met an American millionaire business entrepreneur called John P. McGoff, whose Star Line Corporation ran dinner cruise ships in Chicago, Cleveland and Florida. In addition, McGoff owned the Panax Corporation, a publisher of local newspapers, and had a close relationship with the controversial South African government of B.J. Vorster, who was forced to resign as Prime Minister when it was revealed that he and McGoff were clandestinely attempting to buy the Washington Star and Sacramento Union.

Unexpectedly, McGoff later appeared in Copenhagen to request from Knud E. Hansen A/S a design for a river cruise ship, the *Star of Detroit*, for his Starlite Cruises company to carry approximately 650 guests on luncheon and dinner cruises from Hart Plaza in Downtown Detroit. The project was allocated to Hans Kjærgaard, who was sent to Salisbury in Maryland to oversee the vessel's construction by Chesapeake Shipbuilding Corporation. Kjærgaard knew little of American inland waterway regulations and found these not to be based on any discernable logic but rather were the result of negotiations and compromises over many decades.

Kjærgaard designed a vessel measuring just below 100 grt with four decks, the lowest of which contained the machinery space with twin General Motors Detroit diesels supplying power to the same type of Jastram azimuthing propellers as had been used successfully on the Iraqi pusher-tug fleet. Ahead of this was the galley, providing food to passengers dining while enjoying panoramic views on

St Thomas in the Virgin Islands with the *Costa Riviera* berthed to the right of the *Nordic Prince* of Royal Caribbean and the *Celebration* of Carnival Cruise Line. Knud E. Hansen A/S was involved in designing all three vessels. (Bruce Peter collection)

154 KNUD E. HANSEN • 80 YEARS

Above left: Carnival Cruise Lines' first purpose-built 'fun ship', the *Tropicale*. (Andrew Kilk)

Right: The second Carnival 'fun ship', the *Holiday*, was the first of a series of three near-sisters. (Andrew Kilk)

Bottom: The *Royal Princess*, with nested lifeboats and suites with balconies above. (Andrew Kilk)

the two decks above. While the *Star of Detroit* was being built, Chesapeake Shipbuilding Corporation went bankrupt, but Kjærgaard was relieved to discover that American Chapter 11 bankruptcy law applied and so construction could continue as planned. Meanwhile, Kjærgaard was lavishly entertained by McGoff. He recalls that:

'One day, he called and said 'pack a tie and a dark suit, I'm sending my private jet to collect you. I was flown to Detroit, where I was transferred to his helicopter to continue to his mansion near Lancing. There, he was hosting a fund-raising dinner for the Republican Party, attended by former President Gerald Ford. His 32 guests paid out a total of four million dollars that day.'

The *Star of Detroit* was completed in 1984. Thereafter, Chesapeake Shipbuilding built two further examples of Kjærgaard's design for World Yacht, a subsidiary of the Circle Line in New York; these were the *Duchess* and the *Princess*, built to carry tourists round Manhattan Island.

The 1980s cruise generation

The advent of the *Norway* in 1980 heralded the beginning of a new round of orders for purpose-built cruise ships of unprecedented size and sophistication. As in the latter 1960s, Knud E. Hansen A/S was heavily involved in the design of three of the most significant of these projects, the *Tropicale*, *Holiday* and *Royal Princess*. The first two of these represented a new type of large cruise ship for mass-market cruising from Miami. Their owner, Carnival Cruise Line, was established in 1972 by Ted Arison, who hitherto had been Knut Kloster's business partner in Norwegian Caribbean Line. Kloster and Arison's approaches to business ethics were very different and so the two had parted ways unamicably. Thereafter, Arison effectively applied the principles of Fordism, meaning economy of scale and standardisation of infrastructure, to lower the price of his Carnival cruises so as to appeal to an expanded demographic who previously could not have afforded to go cruising. By the early 1980s, Carnival was in a position to build anew. Having been rebuffed by several well-known European passenger shipbuilders, the company eventually placed an order with Aalborg Værft for the 36,674 grt *Tropicale*. Knud E. Hansen A/S was called in to carry out large portions of the vessel's detailed design.

The *Tropicale* followed ferry design precedents with straight hull lines and the superstructure extending well forward and aft. Five decks were given over entirely to cabins, which were unusually large given the relatively inexpensive cost of Carnival cruises. Decoratively, the vessel was very much in the style of Las Vegas or South Miami Beach resort hotels, her interiors being the work of the Miami-based designer Joe Farcus, a protégé of the well-known hotel designer, Morris Lapidus. Farcus, incidentally, also designed the distinctive winged funnel, which thereafter became a Carnival trademark.

So pleased was Carnival with the *Tropicale* that, immediately after her delivery, they began work with Aalborg Værft and Knud E. Hansen A/S on a further, considerably larger version. The 46.052 grt *Holiday* was delivered in 1985, the biggest vessel ever built by Aalborg Værft. The yard's location was actually rather constricted, meaning that the vessel's hull and superstructure required to be constructed in two sections, which were fitted together in a floating dock.

In terms of design, the *Tropicale* and *Holiday* were actually most innovative from a sociological perspective in that they succeeded in making cruising more affordable than hitherto. In terms of layout and propulsion, they were rather conservative in comparison with a third significant cruise ship in which Knud E. Hansen A/S also was involved, the *Royal Princess*. The concept for her design originated in the drawing office of Wärtsilä's Helsinki shipyard where the company's Project Manager, Kai Levander, enjoyed great success in attracting ship owners to build new and innovative passenger vessels.

The Baltic 22-hour cruise ship *Birka Princess* operated daily between Stockholm and Mariehamn.
(Bruce Peter collection)

Levander was a highly perceptive and imaginative naval architect who devised 'ships of tomorrow' by examining and addressing changing lifestyle and economic trends. One such potential client for a new cruise ship for the American market was P&O's Princess Cruises. Levander's plan was that this vessel should only have outside cabins and that an unprecedented proportion of these would have private balconies. He proposed a 'hotel block' superstructure containing only cabins with the lifeboats recessed on each side and public rooms in the upper decks of the hull. So intrigued were P&O's directors by Levander's economic arguments in favour of this design – outside cabins would sell for around 25% more than insides – that a contract was signed for a 1,200-passenger, approximately 45,000 grt vessel with delivery scheduled for October 1984.

Knud E. Hansen A/S' naval architects were called upon to work closely with Wärtsilä and with P&O's in-house naval architecture subsidiary, Three Quays, on the *Royal Princess*' design. Indeed, Holger Terpet and Hans Kjærgaard each spent the best part of a year in Wärtsilä's Helsinki drawing office. Their long sojourn in the Finnish capital led one of Wärtsilä's managers only half-jokingly to tell a P&O representative that Terpet was now working for his company. Terpet's response was 'No, actually I'm working for the ship'. A great deal of intensive detailed work was carried out to optimise the cabin and public room arrangements while tank tests in Copenhagen and Trondheim helped to refine the hull lines for maximum efficiency at the liner's required 18-knot service speed (her maximum was 22 knots). Four 8-cylinder medium-speed diesel engines were installed, coupled in pairs via gearboxes to each propeller shaft. Under normal operational conditions, only two engines, one on each shaft, would be in operation, giving excellent fuel economy.

The *Royal Princess* was arguably the most innovative and influential cruise ship of her era. Indeed, her design was subsequently perpetuated in the 1989-delivered 48,621 grt *Crystal Harmony*. Designed entirely by Knud E. Hansen A/S, she was built by Mitsubishi Heavy Industries in Nagasaki, Japan for Crystal Cruises, a newly-established upmarket subsidiary of the famous Japanese shipping line Nippon Yusen Kaisha.

Following the *Royal Princess* collaboration with Wärtsilä, Knud E. Hansen A/S next worked jointly with the Jos. L. Meyer Werft at Papenburg in West Germany and its client, Home Lines, on the design of a new 42,092 gt cruise ship to be named the *Homeric* for operation mainly from New York. She was broadly similar in terms of layout and propulsion to the *Tropicale* and *Holiday*, albeit with forward and aft superstructure arrangements more reminiscent of *Royal Princess*. Winning the contract to build the *Homeric* represented Meyer Werft's first move into the cruise ship construction business which has since become their speciality.

The 21,484 gt Baltic cruise ship *Birka Princess* was a smaller cousin of the *Tropicale*, *Holiday* and *Homeric* and shared their horizontal layout with cabins below and public rooms above, albeit with a hull configuration closer in form to the most recent Scandinavian jumbo ferry tonnage. She was built specifically for 22-hour tax-free shopping cruises from Stockholm to Mariehamn in the Åland Islands, a trade in which Birka Line had operated since the early 1970s using second-hand tonnage. Knud E. Hansen A/S provided the basic design for the *Birka Princess*, which was delivered by the Valmet shipyard in Helsinki in 1986. KEH had collaborated with this builder many years before in the design of the Danish-owned cargo liner *Inge Toft*. The *Birka Princess* had generous accommodation for 1,100 passengers, all berthed, but only a small side-loading car deck with space for 80 vehicles was provided to allow passengers to park on board.

During the latter 1970s and early 1980s, Pericles Panagopoulos, the Greek owner of the Royal Cruise Line, had been one of Knud E. Hansen A/S' best clients. When he returned from Iraq in 1978, Hans Kjærgaard was sent to Piraeus to work with Panagopoulos on a design for a new vessel. This work lasted for over 11 months, but no vessel was actually built as a result. For Knud E. Hansen A/S, this was lucrative and rather enjoyable as Panagopoulos and his technical staff were knowledgeable clients and pleasurable working partners.

Rather than building anew, Panagopoulos instead bought Home Lines' cruise ship *Doric*, the former Israeli Zim Line trans-Atlantic flagship *Shalom* built by Chantiers de l'Atlantique at St Nazaire in France in 1964. An extensive conversion to the cruise ship *Royal Odyssey* took place Perama in 1981–82. As Tage Wandborg recalls:

> 'I surveyed the *Doric* for Panagopoulos and found her to be a fine vessel, although when she pitched in a head sea, there was a strange shuddering which at first I could not explain. When she was dry-docked in Perama, it was found that the stem of her bow was not exactly straight and, remarkably, this was actually the result of a collision she had suffered when, brand new as the *Shalom*, she collided with an oil tanker on the Hudson River. The repairs carried out were less than perfect and so, ever since, she had sailed with this misalignment.'

The opportunity was thus taken fit a new bulbous bow designed by Poul Erik Rasmussen and this was tested on a model of the vessel's hull at the Vienna Model Basin in 1981. For aesthetic reasons, a

The Wärtsilä-built 'yacht' cruise ship *Sea Goddess I*. (Bruce Peter collection)

Right: The *Crystal Harmony*, with an even higher proportion of suites with balconies than on the *Royal Princess*. (Bruce Peter collection)

Bottom left: The *Homeric* is seen leaving New York. (Bruce Peter collection)

Bottom right: Seen in Copenhagen, the *Royal Odyssey* was converted in Greece from the *Doric* (ex *Shalom*). (Ambrose Greenway)

158 KNUD E. HANSEN • 80 YEARS

The *Crown Odyssey* is seen in the Solent off Southampton. (Mick Lindsay)

Interiors of the *Crown Odyssey*, below left to right, her observation lounge, dining room, indoor swimming pool and above, atrium; all were decorated in a rather glitzy manner, typical of their era. (Attica Group)

A stern-quarter view of the *Crown Odyssey*. (Bruce Peter collection)

more impressive funnel than her existing twin uptakes was fitted, while inboard, the Greek artist and interior designer, Michael Katzourakis, devised entirely new interiors. At the shipyard, Hans Kjærgaard supervised the project's progress. Costis Stamboulelis, recently appointed as Royal Cruise Line's Technical Manager, recalls:

> 'The conversion of the *Royal Odyssey* was a tremendous task which was carried out jointly by the owner and various contractors, rather than by one shipyard which would have been so much easier. The owner was responsible for purchasing all materials, dividing the work according to the capacity of local contractors, making all subcontracts, reclassifying and re-flagging the vessel, supervising all work – design, construction and commissioning. When all was finished successfully, Mr Panagopoulos confessed that, in future, he would only commission new buildings.'

In 1983 Panagopoulos again approached Knud E. Hansen A/S to plan a new cruise ship, the *Crown Odyssey*. As with the *Crystal Harmony*, the reference for her overall design and layout was the *Royal Princess*. Measuring 34,242 gt, the *Crown Odyssey* was somewhat smaller than P&O and Crystal Cruises' vessels, but she was superbly appointed and with a very high level of fit, finish and detailing, characteristics both of Panagopoulos' method of working and of Meyer Werft's very progressive approach to ship construction. According to Costis Stamboulelis:

> 'At first, it seemed that the order for *Crown Odyssey* would most likely be placed with Aalborg Værft but, after negotiations broke down, Meyer Werft was the next option and so a contract was signed in April 1985. I will never forget Tage Wandborg's first presentation to three engineers from Meyer Werft. In those days, nearly everyone smoked in the office and Tage was standing on one side of the conference table describing the layout of the public rooms – 'aft lounge, relaxed atmosphere, afternoon tea, pre-dinner cocktails, champagne, etc.' While doing this, he was smoking continuously, pulling slim Henry Winterman cigarillos from a metal box, taking one or two puffs and then putting it out and pulling another one from the box. All this was done with very theatrical movements of his hands. The German engineers were listening to him while following the cigarillo ritual with their eyes. When they went back to the yard and submitted their quotation, Mr Panagopoulos rejected it because it was too low. "It is obvious," he told them, "that you have not understood what we want." Mr Panagopoulos held Tage Wandborg in very high esteem. He had kept everything Tage had drawn for him during the construction of the earlier *Golden Odyssey* in a leather bound book which he still cherishes like treasure.
>
> When construction of the *Crown Odyssey* began, Meyer Werft's new enclosed building dock was anything but completed. In fact, the dock and the *Crown Odyssey* in it were built simultaneously. I believe that for the yard, it was a big test and one it passed successfully, thereby gaining a very good reputation for constructing high quality cruise ships. On our recommendation, Holger Terpet was invited by the yard to assist in the detail design and did so in a most effective way knowing very well the peculiarities of the layout and our own requirements. Holger, whose office I visited many times, had the habit of singing while working on his drawing desk – especially when he was pleased with his drawings, but as soon as he would start singing (obviously very loudly) you would hear big bangs of all other office doors getting violently shut. Holger seemed oblivious to the fact that nobody else could stand his singing.
>
> KEH's office in Bredegade was rather special to visit. The building was magnificent with a grand staircase in the hallway and high ceilings with ornate plasterwork. In each room above the door, there were red, yellow and green colour lights, which were flashed on in combination by the secretary at the switchboard when there was a phone call for someone. Every staff member had their own colour code so as to know when to pick up the phone. Across the street was Café Petersburg, a well-known restaurant serving open sandwiches, marinated herring and other delicious things, so whenever I visited KEH on business, I also went there with Holger and his colleagues.'

From the early 1990s onwards, the cruise industry experienced a decade of rapid expansion and consolidation, during which the many small operators either were merged or taken over by the larger ones. By the end of this process, the industry was reduced to two giant conglomerates, Royal Caribbean International and Carnival Corporation, each of whom owned several subsidiary brands. Knud E. Hansen A/S had been heavily involved in designing each of the two giant operators' initial vessels, but now the owners were sufficiently large to have their own extensive in-house technical departments and so consultant naval architects such as Knud E. Hansen A/S were no longer required to assist in project development processes. As a result, the *Crown Odyssey* was the last large new cruise ship for which KEH provided an overall design package. After only four years, however, Panagopoulos sold Royal Cruise Line to Kloster Cruise, the owner of NCL, as part of the industry's consolidation process. Her tonnage in the 30,000 gt range was considered substantial at the time of her delivery but now most new cruise ships are four, five or even six times her size.

Iraqi presidential yachts

In 1980, Knud E. Hansen A/S designed two presidential yachts for Iraq. One was a 2,200 grt river yacht for use on the Tigris to be named *Qidissiyat Al Saddam* and the other was a 4,800 grt sea-going yacht, more like a small cruise liner, named *Al-Mansur*. Helsingør bid for both projects, but only won the river yacht with a low bid. When the yard's managing director, Flemming Bredmose, went to Iraq to negotiate, he found that two Danes, Hans Kjærgaard and Franklin Petersen from Knud E. Hansen A/S, were representing its government. Wärtsilä won the order for the sea-going *Al-Mansur* and Ole Olesen oversaw her construction, living in Finland during the process, while Steen Nielsen was involved with the *Qidissiyat Al Saddam* in Helsingør.

In appearance, the *Al-Mansur* was a beautiful vessel and she shared a family resemblance with the earlier cruise ship *Golden Odyssey*. Tage Wandborg, who was responsible for both vessels' exterior styling, recalls that:

> 'The *Al-Mansur* was built amid great secrecy and was beautifully outfitted with the interiors elements being designed in Islamic style by London-based Arab architects and many of the decorative elements, such as intricate carvings and quotations from the Koran, were specially manufactured by expert craftsmen. The public rooms occupied one deck with a small atrium amidships and a glazed dome overhead, a unique design feature at that time.'

More conventionally, the *Al-Mansur* offered twin two-room state suites and 12 double guest cabins, as well as numerous staff and crew cabins for her total complement of about 300 persons. Delivered in 1983, the vessel actually saw little use as Saddam Hussein's government in Iraq became ever more paranoid and isolated. Sadly, the ship was destroyed in the Shatt al Arab Waterway near Basra in April 2003 by American bombing during the Iraq War.

For Wärtsilä, winning the contract to build *Al-Mansur* had far-reaching positive consequences as shortly thereafter the yard was invited to design in-house, then build the first of a number of so-called 'yacht cruise ships', small passenger vessels able to offer discerning passengers an exclusive atmosphere, such as one would find on a large motor yacht. The design of the first such vessels, the Norwegian-owned *Sea Goddess I* and *Sea Goddess II* also involved Hans Kjærgaard of Knud E. Hansen A/S.

The Iraqi presidential yacht *Al-Mansur* undergoing trials in the Baltic. (Bruce Peter collection)

KNUD E. HANSEN • 80 YEARS **161**

Left: The view aft from the base of the *Al-Mansur*'s mast. (Tage Wandborg collection)

Below left: A sitting room on the *Al-Mansur*. (Tage Wandborg collection)

Below right: A lounge space on the *Al-Mansur*. (Tage Wandborg collection)

Bottom left: The private bathroom of the Presidential Suite on the *Al-Mansur*. (Tage Wandborg collection)

Bottom right: One of the suites on the *Al-Mansur*, somewhat in the manner of Western cruise ship interiors of the same era. (Tage Wandborg collection)

Unbuilt projects

For every new ship built to a Knud E. Hansen A/S design, there were others which, for one reason or another, failed to progress beyond the idea stage. A shipping line's directors might have a board meeting, during which one would ring to Knud E. Hansen A/S to request a basic outline design for a ship to serve a possible new route under discussion – 'and could we have this within the next twenty-four hours, please.' Consequently, the work would be allocated and a potentially suitable layout would be produced. Sometimes, a project went no further than this most primitive stage of development, other times it went as far as the ordering of steel before the owner changed their mind. Whichever was the case, the drawing archives of Knud E. Hansen A/S contain numerous schemes for unbuilt ships of many types. Of course, the ferry and cruise ship 'what ifs' are amongst the most intriguing as they often vaguely resemble other vessels that actually were built.

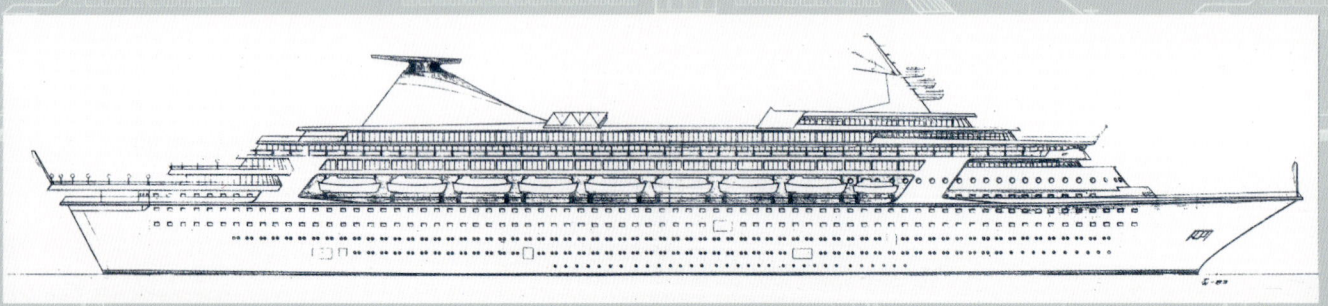

Right and below: An artist's rendering and an elevation drawing of a proposed 'second generation' cruise ship for Norwegian Caribbean Line from the early-1980s. As with the *Phoenix World City* project, there was a docking bay at the stern for ship-to-shore tenders. (Tage Wandborg collection and KNUD E. HANSEN Archive)

KNUD E. HANSEN • 80 YEARS **163**

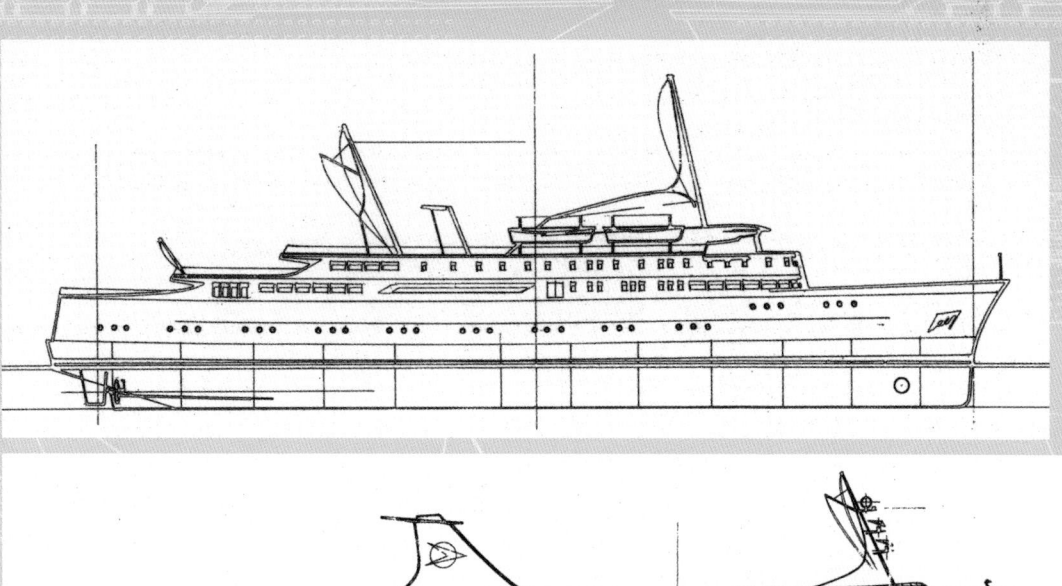

Left: A 1962 proposal for an overnight ferry.
(KNUD E. HANSEN Archive)

Below: A 1969 design for a cruise ship for an unspecified American owner. (KNUD E. HANSEN Archive)

Centre: A remarkably advanced 1969 scheme for a cruise ship, featuring nested lifeboats.
(KNUD E. HANSEN Archive)

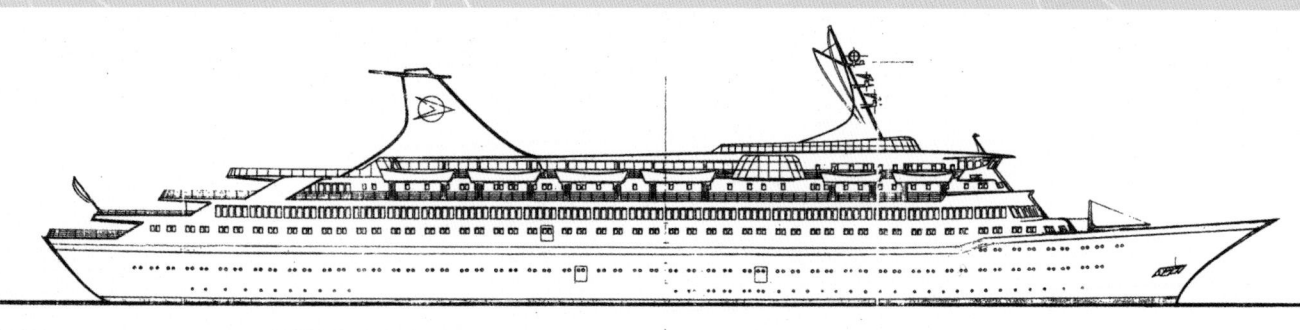

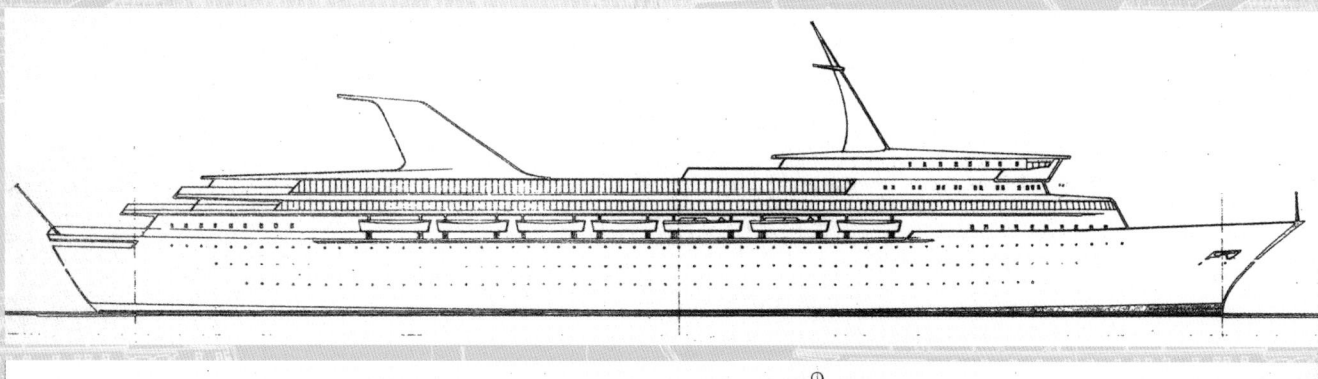

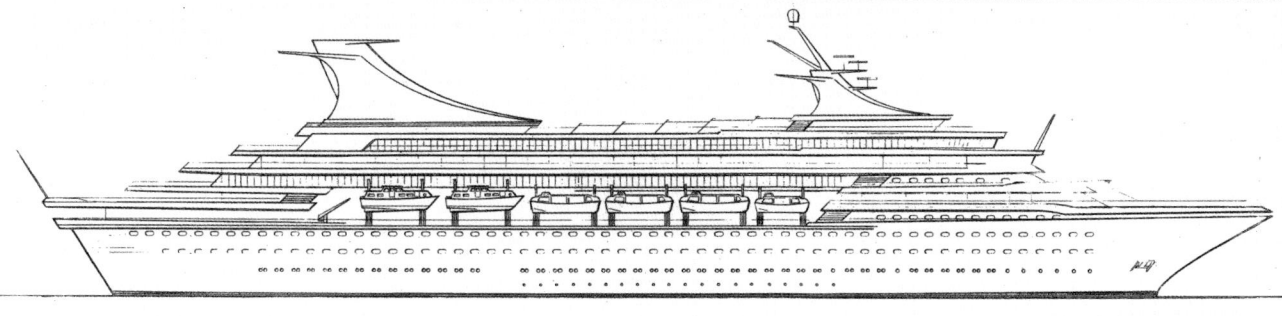

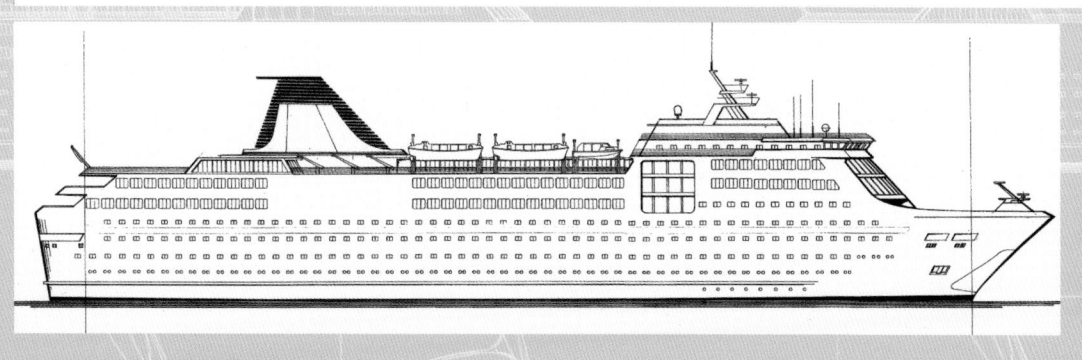

Above: A cruise ship design from 1983, showing elements of *Royal Princess* and *Crown Odyssey*.
(KNUD E. HANSEN Archive)

Left: A 1990 design for a cruise ferry for Rederi AB Gotland with a large forward-facing window, rather like the subsequent *Moby Freedom* and *Moby Wonder* for Moby Lines. (KNUD E. HANSEN Archive)

The jumbo ferry era

The *Norsea* on trials on the Measured Mile off Arran in the Firth of Clyde in April 1987. (ShipPax archive)

Top left: Two of the pioneering Stena jumbo ferries under construction at Rickmers Werft in Bremerhaven in the mid-1970s. Their double-deck freight capacity and superstructures extending fully aft brought a new approach to ferry design.
(Rickard Sahlsten collection)

Top right: The *Stena Nordica*, pictured shortly after entering service.
(Rickard Sahlsten collection)

When, in 1970, Boeing launched their 747 airliner, which was two-and-a-half times the size of their existing best-selling long-haul jet, the 707, and offered significant economies of scale, it was perhaps inevitable that the largest short-sea vessels of the era would become known as 'jumbo ferries.'

As demand for ferry capacity grew, particularly with regard to freight lane metres and expanded passenger facilities, and as sharply increasing crew and fuel costs demanded greater economies of scale, a problem for naval architects designing a new generation of large ferries was that most existing port infrastructure could not cope with vessels significantly longer than the 1960s generation, the majority of which measured between 90 and 140 metres. If the size of port installations could not be changed to accommodate bigger ferries, then the vessels themselves would need to become taller and wider, rather than longer. Thus, the new generation of 'jumbo' ferries less resembled small passenger liners, as had many of their 1960s predecessors, and instead were conceived as floating platforms to generate revenue, both through maximising the size of their payloads and by providing more inboard deck space for expanded retailing.

Four ferries designed by Dag Rogne for Stena and built by the Rickmers Werft in Bremerhaven, West Germany, represented a radical departure from existing design practice. Because Stena's owner, Sten A. Olsson, had come to believe that ships were primarily 'beautiful' on the balance sheet, Rogne was employed to work out how capacity could be greatly increased within similar hull dimensions to the earlier series designed by KEH and built in Yugoslavia. This work gave rise to the box-shaped 5,441 grt *Stena Nordica*, *Stena Normandica*, *Stena Nautica* and *Stena Atlantica*, ships that put the desire for a large freight capacity ahead of aesthetic concerns. This quartet was intended principally for the lucrative charter market and was delivered between October 1974 and November 1975. The origin of their design was explained by Stena's former technical director, Sven Erik Råwall, in the World Ship Society's history of Stena 1939–1989:

> 'Sten, whom we used to call "Olsson the Engineer", was always extremely interested in the project work. He followed each detail and very often pointed out that we had not utilised the ships' dimensions to a maximum. 100% was never enough and the worst of all was that he usually was right. When we were finished, a 10 litre bucket always contained 12 litres … As we planned these measures we noted that necessary stability improvement for a future enlargement of the vessel by taking bigger quantities of ballast water was uneconomical as the ship had to operate with a bigger draught than wanted and thus bigger bunker consumption as a consequence. Then the idea of side sponsons emerged, which we later complemented by a changed bulbous bow design and stern arrangement to compensate for the negative influence on speed.
>
> Sten had long reacted against the existing passenger vessels and their streamlined superstructures. He meant that if we could extend the accommodation to the stern this would add cream only to the profit. "Now we are running away from the result", he used to tell us. Our arguments that the stability did not allow bigger superstructures and that accommodation above the propellers was unsuitable due to vibrations did not impress Sten. At this time a ferry was built in Germany where a "ring" of steel cement was constructed against the outer hull right above the propellers to reduce the vibrations. Could this be the solution?
>
> In cooperation with our consultants in Copenhagen, Knud E Hansen, we attacked the vibration problem (the stability problem could always be solved, e.g. increased breadth) and found that we could change the stern frequency considerably by changing the form to a twin-skeg. We made a lot of model tests to see how speed was influenced and repeated tests confirmed what

Top left: The Langeland-Kiel ferry *Langeland To*.
(Ambrose Greenway)

Top right: The *Frigg Sydfyen*.
(Bruce Peter collection)

we never had thought possible. For the same speed, the effect was reduced by 5–6%.

In connection with the model test of a lengthened version of the ship we found that the speed increased further by about 0.5 knots at a certain trim. When the vessel was on trial, we noted reduced vibrations, better course stability and improved steering capability. When our results became known in the world, our stern was copied for practically every ro-ro and passenger ship built worldwide. We also looked for reduced vibration capabilities and we managed, but we also unexpectedly gained reduced bunker consumption. As the twin-skeg also improved stability there were no longer any obstacles to enlarging the superstructure. "Ugly ships" some said – "they look like shoe boxes." "Efficient –beautiful", others said.'

Tage Wandborg, who was not personally involved in their design, recalls that 'the naval architects designed the four ships exactly as Stena wanted and then went to the plan chest and got out my funnel drawings for the Yugoslavian-built sisters and plonked them on top, so at least they looked half decent from the boat deck upwards.' What these ships lacked in looks, fortunately, they made up for in capacity and, within hull dimensions not dissimilar to the recently delivered Yugoslavian-built series, they could accommodate 1,460 passengers and 500 cars, an impressive total.

Next, Stena and Knud E. Hansen A/S set about optimising the capacities of Stena's existing ferries. In 1976–77, the three-year-old Yugoslavian-built Gothenburg–Frederikshavn day ferries *Stena Danica* and *Stena Jutlandica* were subjected to radical rebuilding at the Wilton-Fijenoord shipyard at Schiedam in the Netherlands. Their superstructures were cut away and jacked up while steelwork for a new deck was inserted to make their upper car decks double-height so that commercial vehicles could be loaded on two levels. In order to mitigate the consequently raised centre of gravity, sponson tanks were welded onto each side of their hulls at the waterline. Dag Rogne, who took charge of this project, recalls:

'Stena correctly reasoned that ro-ro freight was becoming an increasingly important trade all year round, so our experimental lifting of the superstructure on these ferries might provide an excellent opportunity to increase Stena's profits by carrying trucks, especially during the winter when the existing upper car deck was otherwise empty. When the two ferries' captains first saw what we were proposing to do, they were unconvinced and argued that the ships might not be safe. In reality, however, they became significantly more stable than they had been before the rebuilding, thanks to the new sponson tanks. They certainly didn't look as attractive as when first delivered, but our client was happy.'

During the latter 1970s, Knud E. Hansen A/S carried out a significant amount of ferry rebuilding work to increase capacity. DFDS' Copenhagen–Oslo vessels *Kong Olav V* and *Prinsesse Margrethe* were fitted with superstructure extensions containing additional cabins. Other well-known ferries for which KEH produced jumboisation plans were Larvik-Frederikshavn Fergen's *Peter Wessel* and the DFDS-owned Mols Linien ferries *Mette Mols* and *Maren Mols*, operating between Sjællands Odde and Ebeltoft. The vessels' superstructures were to have been raised and sponsons added to their hulls, but neither scheme proceeded beyond the planning stage.

From the mid-1970s onwards, the European economy picked up and Knud E. Hansen A/S began once again to develop new projects. These included a new Bagenkop–Kiel ferry, the 1,500 grt *Langeland To*, which was built by the Scheepswerf Hoogezand in the Netherlands and delivered in 1977. For the Sydfynske Dampskibsselskab, which operated short Danish domestic routes from Spodsbjerg to Taars and from Bojden to Fynshav, Knud E. Hansen A/S designed the 1,479 grt *Thor Sydfyen*, built in 1978 by Dannebrog Værft in Århus, and the *Odin Sydfyen* and *Frigg Sydfyen*, both of which were constructed by Svendborg Skibsværft, entering service in 1982 and 1984 respectively.

A much larger ferry design commission came from the Dutch North sea ferry operator Stoomvaart

168 KNUD E. HANSEN • 80 YEARS

Above: The *Prinses Beatrix* crunches through the North Sea off the Hook of Holland. (Ferry Publications Library)

Below: The Bornholm ferry *Jens Kofoed*. (Bruce Peter collection)

Left: The Canadian National/Marine Atlantic ferry *Abegweit*.
(Bruce Peter collection)

Below: BC Ferries' *Queen of Saanich* is shown following lengthening and heightening through the insertion of an extra upper car deck.
(Bruce Peter collection)

Left: The DSB Great Belt train ferry *Prins Joachim*. (Bruce Peter collection)

Above: The 'ferry square' in the centre of the superstructure on the *Dronning Ingrid*. (Bruce Peter collection)

The *Jens Kofoed* is seen in Copenhagen in the late-1970s. (Bruce Peter collection)

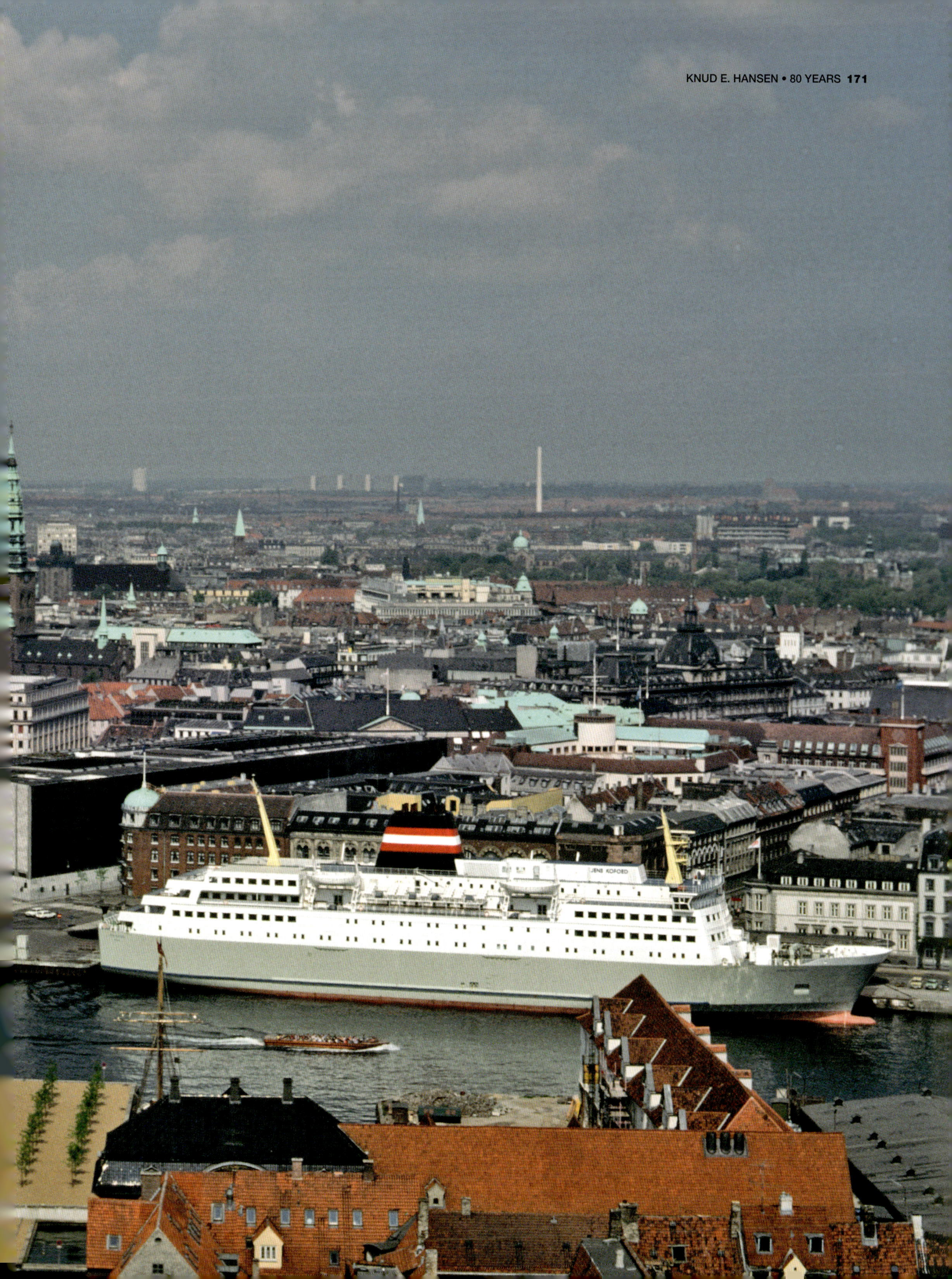

Maatschappij Zeeland (SMZ), operating on the Hook of Holland–Harwich route. The 9,356 grt *Prinses Beatrix*, was built by the Verolme Scheepswerf Heusden B.V at Heusden in the Netherlands and delivered in 1978. Her design emerged at a crucial stage of transition in ferry design thinking. Elements of the layout and appearance of Knud E. Hansen A/S ferries from the early to mid-1970s were combined with broader and more fulsome hull lines and a rather bluff bow with a slightly convex profile above the waterline, similar to that of the recent Stena Searunner freight ferries and DFDS' *Dana Maxima*. The rectilinear design of the *Prinses Beatrix*'s aft hull initially caused pronounced vibration at certain speeds, though this problem was later partially cured by welding in additional steelwork to stiffen the structure.

In 1978, upon his return from Iraq, Hans Kjærgaard produced designs for a new 13,482 grt double-ended ferry for Canadian National, the ferry fleet of which already included two second-hand Knud E. Hansen A/S-designed ferries from the 1960s, the *Leif Ericson* (ex-*Prins Bertil*) and the *Lucy Maud Montgomery* (ex-*Stena Danica*). The new vessel was for use on a short link between Cape Tormentine in New Brunswick and Borden on Cape Breton Island. Delivered as the *Abegweit* in 1982, she was propelled by six Ruston diesels, giving substantial redundancy, and she could transport 950 passengers and 200 cars each crossing with simultaneous loading on her main vehicle deck and upper car deck.

On Canada's Pacific Seaboard, meanwhile, Knud E. Hansen A/S planned conversions for four of BC Ferries' existing vessels, the *Queen of Esquimalt*, *Queen of Vancouver*, *Queen of Saanich* and *Queen of Westmins*ter, all of which had been built in the early-1960s and lengthened in 1969. Following the precedent of the *Stena Danica* and *Stena Jutlandica*, BC Ferries wanted an additional upper car deck to be inserted between the hull and superstructure to increase capacity on the busy routes to Vancouver Island.

Ferries for Danish state operators

In the early 1970s, the Danish Government began a major programme of modernisation of Denmark's transport infrastructure. As part of this strategy, a new state-owned company called Bornholmstrafikken was created, to serve the island of Bornholm. Knud E. Hansen A/S was asked to produce a design for its new ferries, the 8,203 grt *Povl Anker* and *Jens Kofoed*. Nearly twice as big as the largest of their predecessors on the routes to Bornholm, they accommodated 1,500 passengers and 270 cars. Their hull configuration was developed from that of the *Stena Danica* and *Stena Jutlandica*, which had recently entered service when planning commenced. The Bornholm ferries' hulls were shorter and beamier, however, better to fit the confines of Rønne harbour, and they had twin stern ramps.

In 1976, an order was placed with Aalborg Værft, with delivery scheduled for 1978 and 1979.

The *Povl Anker* and *Jens Kofoed* acted as reference ships for the quality of design expected of the Danish Government's next ferry projects, a trio of commodious 10,600 grt train ferries for DSB's route between Nyborg and Korsør. Once again, Knud E. Hansen A/S was consulted to produce a suitable general arrangement for these vessels, the task being directed by Gerhard Erichs. In the early 1980s, investments in new ferries were viewed politically as welcome means of staving off the closure of some of Denmark's struggling shipyards. Therefore, two of DSB's new train ferries, the *Kronprins Frederik* and *Prins Joachim*, were ordered from Nakskov Skibsværft, while the third, named the *Dronning Ingrid*, was built in Helsingør.

These ferries were unusually long and broad, measuring 152 x 23.7 metres. Their design was, however, atypical of the Knud E. Hansen A/S' usual ferry output, partly because of their highly specialised purpose and also because DSB's own architects and technical staff made significant contributions. Able to load and unload simultaneously on two tracks via their bows, each had train deck space for 18 26.4-metre-long Inter-city coaches on four tracks. As constant operation was necessary without interruption by breakdowns, six B&W-Alpha diesels were installed, only four of which were actually used at any one time, with one undergoing maintenance and another in reserve. So that replacement parts could be easily lowered to the engine room, electric cranes were installed atop the superstructure with hatches below accessing service shafts. The three ferries all entered service in 1981 and, thereafter, served DSB very reliably for 15 years.

Stena Line's third generation

By the latter 1970s, the existing fleet on Stena Line's cross-Kattegat routes, linking Sweden, Denmark and Germany, was reaching capacity, especially during the summer season. Stena's business philosophy was to provide relatively inexpensive mass transportation, subsidised by considerable onboard revenues generated by the bars, restaurants and slot machine gaming. Its existing vessels, dating from the early 1970s, were no longer sufficiently capacious to transport thousands of passengers and many hundreds of cars in up-to-date retail-orientated environments. In 1978, therefore, Knud E. Hansen began design work for a new generation of Stena Line jumbo ferries.

Two for the Gothenburg–Frederikshavn route were to be the world's largest for daytime operation.

Left: The launching of the *Stena Danica* at Chantiers du Nord et de la Méditerannée on 30 August 1980. (Bruce Peter collection)

Below: The *Stena Danica* is seen approaching Gothenburg. (Bruce Peter collection)

Bottom: Interiors of the *Stena Danica*, showing her restaurant, forward lounge and part of her hallway amidships. (Bruce Peter collection)

The *Stena Scandinavica* is seen at Frederikshavn.
(Bruce Peter collection)

Each was planned to carry 2,300 passengers and 630 cars, loaded through bow and stern doors at the lower level and through side doors to port into a full-height upper garage deck. This arrangement had first been tried out with the conversions to their 1970s predecessors and it was found to be successful. On the four larger overnight vessels, two of which were for the Gothenburg–Kiel route, the vehicle decks were similarly arranged, but with cabins on either beam; out of a total capacity of 2,500 passengers, 2,204 were berthed. In addition, there was space for 550 cars.

The lowest bids came from the Chantiers du Nord shipyard at Dunkirk in France to build the day ferries and from the state-owned yards of Communist Poland in Gdynia and Gdansk to construct four overnight vessels, each with delivery scheduled to commence in 1982. Unfortunately, there were delays at all three shipyards and so the French-built *Stena Danica*, was not ready until the summer of 1983.

Inboard were ranges of facilities not hitherto seen on a route of only 3½ hours' duration. They had two saloon decks, entirely given over to restaurants, bars, lounges, gaming arcades and a vast tax-free supermarket. This was located aft on the lower saloon deck, filling the entire width of the rather beamy hull.

Unfortunately for Stena, the four overnight ferries under construction in Poland were more heavily delayed. The country's disliked Communist regime was in decline and there was both a shortage of finance and a poorly motivated workforce. By the mid-1980s, talk of revolution was in the air and the

The *Stena Jutlandica* arrives at Gothenburg.
(Bruce Peter collection)

KNUD E. HANSEN • 80 YEARS **175**

Left: The launch of the *Visby* at Landskrona on 25 January 1980. (ShipPax archive)

Below: The *Visby* as she appeared upon entering service. (Bruce Peter collection)

Centre left, centre right and bottom left: Inboard, *Visby*'s public rooms were colour-coded. Here we see her brown reclining seat and observation saloon, Red Lounge and Blue Restaurant. (Bruce Peter collection)

Bottom right: The *Visby*'s sister, the *Wasa Star*, under charter to Vaasanlaivat for service across the Gulf of Bothnia in the Northern Baltic. (Klas Brogren)

Top left: The Viking Line ferry *Viking Saga*. (Viking Line)
Top right: The DFDS Scandinavian World Cruises cruise ferry *Scandinavia* is pictured off Grand Bahama Island. (Bruce Peter collection)
Centre left: The Broadway Lounge on the *Scandinavia*. (Bruce Peter collection)
Centre right: The *Scandinavia*'s Windows on the World Restaurant. (Bruce Peter collection)
Bottom: The 'Gulfspan' ferry *Caribou*. (ShipPax archive)

Solidarity movement gained momentum with the Gdynia and Gdansk shipyards as its centrepiece. For Poland, the bravery of the shipyards' workers led eventually to a new democratic system of government, but for Stena Line, there was only frustration as one proposed delivery date after another slipped past with little evidence of progress.

Eventually, in 1986, Stena enlisted the Swedish construction company Skanska to complete the outfitting of the first two ships, named the *Stena Germanica* and *Stena Scandinavica*, while the orders for the second pair were cancelled. The *Stena Germanica* finally entered service in the summer of 1987 with her sister following in the spring of 1988, after being completed in Gothenburg. The two remaining hulls were sold in incomplete states, one passing initially to Fred. Olsen Lines before being sold on to Anek Lines in Greece for completion in Perama as the *El. Venizelos*. The hull of the fourth vessel, meanwhile passed to other Greek owners for completion as a cruise ship, but was instead laid up near Perama as a derelict hulk and, later, sold for scrap.

While Stena Line was enthusiastic about the revenue-earning potential of jumbo ferries on international routes, Rederi AB Gotland, which provided subsidised domestic ferry services from the Swedish mainland to Gotland, found itself being pushed somewhat reluctantly into the jumbo ferry era. Largely to keep the ailing Öresundsvarvet Shipyard at Landskrona in business, the Swedish government provided substantial subsidies to entice the Gotland company to commission two new ferries, each measuring nearly 15,000 grt. They were designed in 1979 by a team lead by Holger Terpet, while Tage Wandborg worked on the interiors. As with the Stena ships, the superstructure was built right out to the stern, the problem of vibrations from the propellers disturbing sleeping passengers being mitigated by locating nearly all the cabins in a 'hotel block' filling the forward two-thirds of the superstructure with public rooms spread over two decks to the rear. In an attempt to break up the ferries' rather boxy silhouette, Terpet decided that the recessed superstructure from the boat deck upwards should be painted pale blue to distinguish it from the white-painted mass below and a rather elegant conical-shaped design for the both the funnel and foremast was devised.

The original contract price for the first of the new sisters, to be named the *Visby*, was 165 million Swedish Kroner, but this escalated first to Skr 210 million and then to Skr 237 million with government aid to the Landskrona yard probably pushing the final figure close to Skr 400 million. The *Visby* was finally delivered to Rederi AB Gotland five months behind schedule in October 1980, which cost the yard a further Skr 5 million in penalty charges. At this juncture, Rederi AB Gotland began having second thoughts about the need for two ships with well over 1,100 overnight berths, each on crossings of no more than four or five hours' duration. Consequently, after the *Visby* was completed late, her sister, due to have been named the *Gotland*, was chartered to Vaasanlaivat before completion and launched as the *Wasa Star* for service across the Gulf of Bothnia in the Northern Baltic from Vaasa to Sundsvall and briefly Umeå. Some time thereafter, she was bought by Larvik-Frederikshavn Fergen to become its fourth *Peter Wessel*.

In 1978, Rederi Ab Sally approached Knud. E Hansen A/S, to produce the preliminary drawings for new Helsinki–Stockholm ferries. As the route formed a 'sea bridge' on the E3 motorway, Sally specified a high vehicle capacity with two full-height vehicle decks, vertically stacked, the upper of which was accessed by long fixed internal ramps. Passenger accommodation was arranged in a similar manner to the *Visby* and *Wasa Star* with cabins mainly forward-located and public rooms aft. Because the ferries were intended for winter navigation, not only were their hulls ice-strengthened, but the crew needed accommodation above the waterline as, lower down, it would be too noisy for sleep. As was typical of other recent Baltic ferries, the crew cabins were placed in casings on either side of the lower vehicle deck. Above these were recesses containing the lifeboats – an unusually placement for ferries

A design drawing for the Gulfspan ferry type for Cape Breton-Newfoundland service; as built, the vessels lacked the applied styling shown here.
(Per Jensen collection)

of the era, but one that was subsequently to become standard. The steelwork forming the casings therefore continued vertically behind these and into the superstructure. As with other recent Knud E. Hansen A/S-designed ferries, a twin-skeg after hull was specified.

The order to build the ferries was won by the Wärtsilä Turku Shipyard, whose own drawing office substantially re-worked the design. In the end, the ferries, which delivered in 1980 as the *Viking Saga* and *Viking Song* measured 13,900 grt and had a capacity for 2,000 passengers plus an impressive 936 lane metres for freight. As built, they had more in common with Wärtsilä's design approach of the era than that of Knud E. Hansen A/S and, in service, they performed effectively.

In 1979, the expansionist DFDS decided to build two very large ferries for its Copenhagen–Olo route with Knud E. Hansen A/S providing a design featuring a similar layout to the *Visby* and *Wasa Star*. Before orders could be placed, DFDS had a change of plan, deciding instead to invest heavily in a new American subsidiary called Scandinavian World Cruises to operate cruise-ferry services from both New York and Florida ports to the Bahamas. The design for the Copenhagen–Oslo vessel was modified for the route from New York with a somewhat longer hull and a lido complex on the topmost deck and an order was placed with the Dubigeon-Normandie shipyard at Nantes, in France, for delivery in 1981.

The 26,748 grt *Scandinavia*'s route would take her round North Carolina's infamous Cape Hattaras, where the warm Gulf Stream meets the colder North Atlantic and where frequent storms can whip up the shallow waters into long swells, causing severe pitching motion. Where great Atlantic liners were once built with long hulls better suited to riding out sea conditions such as these, the *Scandinavia*'s dimensions were restricted by the tight confines of Freeport's relatively small harbour to 185 metres by 27 metres and a draught of not more than 6.58 metres. Unlike on European overnight ferries, it was necessary to provide full cruise service to all of the 1,606 passengers with a consequently larger crew and more extensive galley and laundry facilities. A stern-loading vehicle deck was arranged around a long, narrow, centreline casing. Unusually for a ferry of her era, DFDS reverted to twin Burmeister &Wain slow-speed diesels to power her as similar engines had proven their worth in the rigours of Atlantic service on DFDS' fleet of cargo liners.

For DFDS, the entire Scandinavian World Cruises concept was a big gamble. Their Annual Report to shareholders in 1980 ominously confessed to 'butterflies in the stomach' over the project. The *Scandinavia*, meanwhile, was delayed at the shipyard and did not enter service between New York and Freeport until the summer of 1982. The *Scandinavia* continued on the New York–Freeport/Nassau route only until November 1983, when she was ordered back to Copenhagen and, after brief modifications, introduced on DFDS's Copenhagen–Oslo route. The Scandinavian World Cruises venture had cost DFDS a great deal of money – indeed, it nearly bankrupted the company and so it was decided to sell

The Danish Royal Yacht *Dannebrog* for which Knud E. Hansen A/S designed a substantial refit. (Søren Lund Hviid)

the *Scandinavia* to recoup some of the losses. Under subsequent owners, however, she found success as a cruise ship.

Gulfspan ferries for Canada

Since the early 1970s, a number of Knud E. Hansen A/S-designed ferries had operated on Canada's Eastern Seaboard, initially for Canadian National and, later, for their successor, Marine Atlantic. By the 1980s, Marine Atlantic was using two of the Rickmers-built ex-Stena freight and passenger vessels on its principal route from North Sydney in Nova Scotia to Port Aux Basques in Newfoundland. These were replaced in the middle of the decade by the first of two substantial new buildings, the planning of which had commenced in 1980.

Known as 'Gulfspan' ferries, the *Caribou* and *Joseph and Clara Smallwood* were largely designed by Holger Terpet and Svend A. Bertelsen, although each had their own ideas as to how they might best be shaped. Bertelsen tended to favour the rectilinear jumbo ferry approach preferred by European owners, while Terpet insisted upon the curvilinear aesthetic ultimately chosen, arguing that their hulls would require relatively fine lines to slice through the big Atlantic swells. (The failure of the KEH-designed *Scandinavia* in this regard may have been a winning argument.) The owners' technical team was headed by CN Marine's Director of Vessel Development, Alex Lawrence, an experienced marine engineer with considerable expertise in ice-breaking technology from his research work with the governments of Canada, West Germany and the Soviet Union. The vessels were ordered from the Versatile Davie Shipyard at Lauzon in Quebec for delivery in 1986 and 1989.

The *Caribou* and *Joseph and Clara Smallwood* were utterly distinct from any of Knud E. Hansen A/S's previous output. Of impressive appearance with sweeping lines and tall funnels, located two-thirds of the way aft, they were planned to meet the needs of widely varying trading circumstances between the busy summer holiday season, with the four-hour round trip made twice daily at 22 knots, and only a single crossing each way in winter when the voyage time was potentially much longer due to storm conditions. Four MaK diesels gave a high level of redundancy, meaning that the ships could continue in service in the event of a single engine breakdown. The hulls were ice-strengthened to enable continued service throughout the winter and spring months.

As with Marine Atlantic's existing ferries on the route, they were able to carry freight units, loaded on two levels. While as many as 350 cars could be carried and simultaneously loaded or off-loaded from the main and platform decks, to meet summer-season demand, up to 196 twelve-metre trailers can alternatively be carried during the low season. On either side, broad casings contained passenger cabins. Unusually, even although many of these were directly behind the shell plating, perhaps either to save money or to afford better storm protection, few had windows of any kind. In the superstructure, a great deal of space was given over to reclining chairs and dormitories as the vessels were intended to provide high-density mass transportation, rather than luxury.

The *Caribou* and *Joseph and Clara Smallwood* served Marine Atlantic for around a quarter of a century before being sold for scrap. The harsh environment in which they operated meant that, in the end, they were so run down that no buyer could be found for further trading.

Rebuilding the *Dannebrog*

While the trio of Knud E. Hansen A/S designed ro-ro freighters for Iraq were being built at Helsingør Skibsværft in 1981, a concurrent project for KEH at the same yard was the rebuilding of the Danish

Top left: The *Vesterålen*, one of three new passenger and freight vessels for Norway's 'Hurtigruten' coastal service along the scenic West Coast from Bergen to Kirkenes. (Ian Boyle collection)

Top right: Completed in 1981, the *Sundbuss Pernille* was a new addition to the Moltzau-owned fleet linking Helsingør and Helsingborg, designed by the KEH naval architect Hans Stevelt. (Bruce Peter collection)

The diving support vessel *Stena Wellservicer* nears completion on the River Tyne in 1988. (Bruce Peter collection)

Royal Yacht *Dannebrog*. Originally constructed by the Orlogsværftet in Copenhagen in 1932, the yacht was a very modern vessel for her era but, after nearly 50 years' service, she required a substantial overhaul. In 1980, Knud E. Hansen A/S was awarded the prestigious contract to upgrade her without compromising her original appearance.

The renovation involved the complete renewal of her engines, propellers and electrical systems. Hitherto, the *Dannebrog* had used DC electricity, but she was converted to AC instead. Also, she was fitted with a bow thruster and controllable pitch propellers. Her new engines could be controlled directly from the bridge, rather than by using telegraphs to communicate with the engineers. The conversion project involved Hans Kjærgaard in upgrading the accommodation and Steen Nielsen, who dealt with electrical and mechanical aspects. Both worked in the shipyard's drawing office for the duration of the project. Kjærgaard recalls:

'Like all ships of her era, the *Dannebrog* was built of very combustible materials – wood, asphalt, cork – and so it would have been disastrous if a fire had started on board. As part of the rebuilding, her accommodation was very carefully dismantled and new steel divisions and draught stops were put in to enhance fire safety. The Queen and Prins Henrik were consulted quite regularly and they visited the ship several times while the project was progressing. Our

The Finnish-built river dredgers *Anabar* (left) and *Jamal* (right) were a-typical but very complex designs by Knud E. Hansen A/S, built to work in extreme conditions of cold. (STX Europe)

plans were sent to Amalienborg for approval and even the Queen occasionally commented on the proposed designs, which showed how well she knew the yacht's layout. For example, I made a sketch for upgraded accommodation for stewards aft on the port side and this was returned from Amalienborg with advice to make better use of space below an adjacent staircase, so an extra crew cabin was included there. Towards the end of the project, the Queen also chose the textiles to make the Dannebrog suitably homely.'

Back in Knud E. Hansen A/S' Copenhagen offices, a concurrent project was to design a new generation of passenger and cargo ships for the Hurtigruten in Norway, a lengthy coastal voyage from Bergen northward to Kirkenes, calling briefly at numerous intermediate ports. Before Western Norway's oil wealth enabled a vast expansion in road infrastructure from the 1970s onwards, the Hurtigruten really was the only practicable way of accessing some coastal towns and villages. With the ongoing construction of new roads, tunnels and landing strips for aircraft, the Hurtigruten's role gradually changed from mainly providing transport for locals into a tourism phenomenon (although tourists for long had been important customers for the service).

Knud E. Hansen A/S were asked to provide a design for a new type of coastal passenger and cargo ship, designed with tourists in mind but also able to side-load cargo into a freight and vehicle deck while using the existing pier infrastructure. The solution was a 4,072 grt twin-screw vessel with berths for 166 passengers. Cargo could either be loaded using an aft-located electric crane, or through a side-hatch in the hull. This was designed so that, when opened, it could be raised level with any pier and, inboard, there was an elevator to raise or lower vehicles and cargo palettes to vehicle deck height (a similar principal already was used on Norwegian coastal cargo vessels).

Three examples of the design were subsequently ordered from Trondheims Mekaniske Verksted – the *Narvik*, *Midnatsol* and *Vesteralen* – owned respectively by Ofotens Dampskipsselskap, Troms Fylkes Dampskipsselkap and Vesteralens Dampskipsselskap. Delivered in 1982–83, they proved practical and reliable, though they were overshadowed in the 1990s when the remainder of the Hurtigruten fleet was replaced by much larger and more glamorously designed cruise-style vessels.

At the smaller end of the scale, an additional 'Sundbuss' was designed in 1980 for Ragnar Moltzau's Helsingør–Helsingborg passenger service. The *Sundbuss Pernille*, was built Lindstøls Skibs og Båtbyggeri at Risør, entering service in 1981. Stylistically, she had a more angular silhouette than her older fleetmates with streamlined twin exhaust uptakes, somewhat similar to those on ferry the *Terje Vige*.

The *Seaboard Sun* (ex-*Mercandian Sun II*) was one of a series of eight freight ferries built in Frederikshavn in the 1980s for the charter market.
(Mick Lindsay collection)

Stena oil supply ships

In 1976, Stena negotiated a deal to take over contracts for two pipe carriers under construction in Norway for the North Sea oil industry. Stena wanted the hulls to be lengthened by 12 metres, giving them the maximum possible dimensions for supplying pipes to pipe-laying barges while at anchor. When the *Stena Piper* and *Stena Supplier* were delivered, however, Stena found that it was actually more lucrative to charter them to BP for use in the Forties oil field.

This success led Stena to commission Knud E. Hansen A/S to assist in designing further examples that were larger still. The 5,823 grt *Stena Constructor*, *Stena Seaspread*, *Stena Inspector* and *Stena Protector* had ice-strengthened hulls and diesel-electric propulsion, power being generated by five Nohab V-diesels much as on the ferries *Visby* and *Gotland*. Built by Öresundsvarvet in Landskrona, they were completed in 1980. Subsequently, Knud E. Hansen A/S collaborated with Stena in the design of the 8,158 grt *Stena Seawell* and *Stena Wellservicer*, which were sophisticated diving support, maintenance and fire-fighting vessels for the offshore oil industry built by North East Shipbuilders in Sunderland and delivered in 1987 and 1989 respectively. With triple-screw diesel-electric propulsion and three thrusters, they could hold position in all but the most extreme conditions.

Left and above: The launch of the *Norsea* at Govan on the Clyde on 9 September 1986. (Bruce Peter collection)

The *Norsea* on trials off Arran in the Firth of Clyde in April 1987. (ShipPax archive)

The 'mini jumbo' ferry *Langeland III*, operated between Bagenkop and Kiel. The lack of windows in her aft superstructure indicates the extent of her tax-free supermarket.
(Jan Vinther Christiansen)

Siberian river dredgers

The 450 dwt *Jamal*, *Javaj*, *Anabar* and *Indirka* were highly specialised dustpan/trailing suction dredgers designed by Knud E. Hansen A/S in 1983 and built in 1985–86 by Wärtsilä for use in summer on the Siberian rivers in the Soviet Union. In winter, temperatures dropped as low as -70 degrees and so they were laid up. Their dredging range was from 1.8 to 10 metres but their draft was only 1.9 metres, thus allowing for operations in very shallow waters. Jesper Kanstrup of KEH coordinated the design work. Unfortunately for him, no English or Danish translations could be found of the Soviet regulations for inland waterways but, after some searching, a Finnish translation was unearthed, from which an English version could be produced. Unfortunately, the translator engaged by KEH got drunk in Copenhagen and mislaid his nearly-complete English translation of the rules the day before the Danish naval architects were due to fly out to Finland for an important progress meeting; the only solution to this embarrassing problem was to suggest to the Finns that the document had been lost in an airline baggage mix-up.

Lengthy discussions took place with Wärtsilä engineers as to how the dredgers could be designed and all agreed that they would be nearly impossible to plan as they would need to be very narrow due to the restricted dimensions of the lock system on the River Ob, one of the waterways on which they were intended to operate. In the end, KEH and Wärtsilä succeeded and much was written about the dredgers in the shipping technical press.

The J. Lauritzen reefer ship *Knud Lauritzen*. (Bruce Peter collection)

Surveys, calculations and conversions

Designing new passenger ships was the most high-profile and glamorous aspect of Knud E. Hansen A/S' activities but for every new ship built, there were dozens of smaller but equally important tasks, such as conducting surveys for clients thinking of purchasing or converting a particular vessel, or carrying out calculations to ascertain the floodable length and damage stability of vessels on behalf of owners, national authorities, classification societies and international bodies such as SOLAS (the convention governing the Safety Of Life At Sea), or the International Maritime Organisation. Such work resulted in the preparation of reports and manuals for these different bodies, either relating to a particular ship or whole classes of vessels. Sometimes carrying out inclining experiments on particular ships, whereby weights would be loaded onto the superstructure and the heeling angle measured to pinpoint the centre of gravity and thereby assess the ship's stability. In addition, analyses of problems, such as vibration or cavitation and the recommendation of measures to correct these faults were carried out.

Niels Fisker-Andersen was one of Knud E. Hansen A/S' senior naval architects who dedicated his career to these very important aspects of naval architectural practice. Born in 1931, as with so many of his colleagues, Fisker-Andersen first studied naval architecture at the Helsingør Teknikum, graduating in 1956, then went to Britain to take a B.Sc. in Applied Science at the University of Durham and King's College, Newcastle, while working at J.L. Thompson's shipyard in Sunderland. Having graduated, he worked briefly for Burmeister & Wain in their steel department before joining Knud E. Hansen A/S in 1964. There, Fisker-Andersen was involved in providing calculations for numerous conversion projects – including the rebuilds of Port Line cargo vessels in Greece into the cruise ships *Danae* and *Daphne*, the transformation of the *France* into the *Norway*, the renovation of the *Dannebrog*, the upgrading in 1884-86 of Norwegian Caribbean Line's 'first generation' cruise ships *Starward*, *Skyward* and *Southward* in Jacksonville, Florida, plus the rebuilding of numerous ro-ro freighters.

Vessels undergoing conversion appear very different from when they are in service. Most of the fixtures and fittings seen by ferry and cruise passengers – the furniture, carpets, decorative wall and ceiling panels – are missing and, with the removal of this thin veneer of applied decoration, bare steel, exposed pipe work and vast numbers of dangling cables, fairly dim temporary lighting, piles of construction debris, men in hard hats and boiler suits and occasional showers of sparks from welding are the principal characteristics. Amid such scenes of organised chaos, naval architects quietly go about their problem-solving roles, liasing with shipyard workers and managers, surveyors, ship's officers and owner's representatives to ensure that the process is completed in as timely and orderly a manner as possible. After all, the vessel's first-post conversion voyage will already have been advertised and so the re-delivery deadline must be met.

Niels Fisker-Andersen is particularly proud of his work in Santander, Spain in connection with the lengthening in 1995-96 of DFDS' 1978-built North Sea ro-ro freighter *Dana Maxima*. The project was particularly challenging because, once the ship was cut in half, the existing forward section required to be floated out so that the new mid-body could be moved into place, then the forward part returned with all three sections in perfect alignment so that they could be welded together. Thanks to Fisker-Andersen's predictive calculations as to how the various sections would behave when the dock was flooded, the whole operation went very smoothly, but the margins for error were extremely tight. As a result of this work, the *Dana Maxima* continued in service until 2012, latterly as a member of P&O Ferries' North Sea fleet.

Left and right: The lengthening of the *Dana Maxima* at Santander in 1995-96. (Niels Fisker-Andersen collection)

Other diverse early 1980s projects included the design of a new ice-strengthened cargo ship, the 6,759 grt *Nuka Ittuk*, built by Ørskov in Frederikshavn for the Denmark–Greenland service and subsequently extensively rebuilt as the container ship *Arina Arctica*. Four approximately 22,800 grt semi-submersible heavy lift vessels were designed for the Norwegian specialist ship owner Jan-Erik Dyvi. The *Dyvi Swan* and *Dyvi Tern* were built in Kaldnes in Norway, while Samsung in South Korea constructed the *Dyvi Swift* and *Dyvi Teal*; delivery was between 1981 and 1984. Samsung also built the 38,465 dwt oil tanker *Osco Stream* for Ole Schrøder of Oslo. In Denmark, meanwhile, Knud E. Hansen A/S assisted in designing a new series of large ro-ro freight ferries for Mercandia, the 15,375 gt *Mercandian Globe*, *Mercandian Arrow*, *Mercandian Giant*, *Mercandian Continent*, *Mercandian Ocean*, *Mercandian Sea II*, *Mercandian Sun II* and *Mercandian Universe*. Built By Frederikshavn Værft in the 1984–86 period, these were single-screw vessels intended for charter to liner operators and each contained 2,191 lane metres spread over four decks. In 1986 Frederikshavn also completed a single smaller version of the type measuring 12,189 gt, specifically for Mercandia to charter to DFDS for North Sea service as the *Dana Cimbria*.

The era after Svend A. Bertelsen

Knud E. Hansen A/S' long-serving and hard-working managing director Svend Aage Bertelsen died in 1985. His untimely demise was followed by significant changes in the structure of the company during which other long-serving employees came to the forefront of project management. Bertelsen's replacement as managing director was Franklin Petersen, who created three teams of naval architects, working under the direction of senior naval architects to develop projects on a rolling basis. One of the teams was led by Holger Terpet, another by Hans Kjærgaard and the third by Steen Nielsen, who had been a Knud E. Hansen A/S employee since 1973, the year he graduated from Helsingør Teknikum. Terpet and Kjærgaard now took responsibility for the majority of passenger ship design work while Nielsen's team carried out a diversity of projects, ranging from conversions of existing tonnage on the one hand to designing luxury yachts on the other. Morten Skrydstrup, who had first been employed by Knud E. Hansen A/S in 1968, then worked at Helsingør Skibsværft between 1971 and 1973, before re-joining KEH, dealt with calculations and theory. Born in 1944 and another graduate of the Helsingør Teknikum, Skrydstrup had for many years managed KEH new building projects and conversions of ro-ro and passenger ferries with a special focus on matters relating to stability. Together, this group steered Knud E. Hansen A/S through leaner years in the latter 1980s and 1990s, dealing with a wide variety of design work in the process.

An early success for Hans Kjærgaard's team in this period was the design of the first of two large new ro-pax ferries for the Anglo-Dutch North Sea Ferries route from Hull to Rotterdam. The *Norsea* project was initiated by P&O, the British partner in the combine, and the vessel was ordered from Govan Shipbuilders on the River Clyde in Glasgow. In the Netherlands, it was hoped that her Nedlloyd-owned, Dutch-flagged sister ship would be built by the Van der Giessen shipyard at Krimpen, which was at that point constructing a large ferry for the rival SMZ/Sealink service from the Hook of Holland to Harwich. In the end, when the Dutch government refused to subsidise the yard and so the Nedlloyd ship, named the *Norsun*, was ordered instead from Nippon Kokan in Japan using the *Norsea*'s general arrangement but with detailed design being carried out at the shipyard there.

In dimensions and appearance, the 31,727 gt *Norsea* barely resembled any previous ferry designs from Knud E. Hansen A/S. As she was required to navigate through a tidal lock at the mouth of the King George V Dock in Hull, her width was severely restricted, meaning that, as with the *Tor Britannia* and *Tor Scandinavia* over 20 years previously, a long and narrow configuration was developed. Whereas the 'Tor' ships were sleek and fine-lined, the *Norsea* had an unusually fulsome and rectilinear hull form. An emphasis on freight traffic necessitated two main vehicle decks plus a ramp-accessed hold space forward of the machinery spaces. With sectioned hoistable car platforms fitted above the upper trailer deck, the total capacity was 850 cars, 191 twelve-metre trailers or various combinations of these. As the Hull–Rotterdam service was leisurely with only nightly sailings in each direction, the *Norsea* was not particularly fast. Four Sulzer diesels enabled the 197-nautical-mile passage between Hull and Rotterdam to be covered overnight in 14 hours at 18.5 knots eastbound and 16.5 knots westbound, compensating for the hour's difference between the UK and Continental time-zones. Above were three passenger decks, with cabins located forward and public rooms aft; 446 cabins occupied the forward part of the superstructure, accommodating 1,124 passengers.

The *Norsea* was delivered in 1987 and, ever since, she has operated from Hull. Following the introduction of larger ships to serve Rotterdam, she now sails to Zeebrugge as the *Pride of York*.

The *Langeland III*, designed in 1985 by Preben Agner, brought the 'jumbo ferry' form to a smaller ship of only 6,721 gt. To illustrate the point, this vessel, which was constructed by Svendborg Værft and delivered in 1989, measured only 91.8 metres in length, yet she could transport 1,080 passengers

Top left: Shin Nihonkai Ferry's *Ferry Hamanasu* during her career in coastal service on the Sea of Japan.
(Peter Therkildsen collection)

Top right: The *Lissos*, ex *Ferry Hamanasu* is shown undergoing conversion in Greece.
(Bruce Peter collection)

Above: The *Lissos* as she appeared in the wake of her radical reconstruction in Anek Lines' service from Piraeus to Crete. (Bruce Peter collection)

Left: The *Tropicana*, ex *Prinses Paola* is pictured in the process of being rebuilt in Greece from a Belgian cross-Channel passenger vessel into a casino ship for service in Florida.
(Niels Fisker-Andersen collection)

Above: The Indonesian-built Rederi AB Gotland ro-pax ferry *Gotland*, the building of which nearly ruined Knud E. Hansen A/S. (Bruce Peter collection)

Below: BC Ferries' high-density Tsawassen-Swartz Bay route demands efficient ferry tonnage. Here, the *Spirit of Vancouver Island* sails through the narrows, half way between the two ports. (Bruce Peter collection)

Above: The sister ship, *Spirit of British Columbia*, passing the same location. (Bruce Peter collection)

Below: The *Prins Filip*, Belgium's flagship cross-Channel ferry of the 1990s on the Dover-Oostende route. (Mike Louagie)

and 140 cars, almost twice the capacity of her 70-metre-long predecessor on the Bagenkop–Kiel route (see above). This great increase in capacity was, of course, achieved by making the ship broader and by extending the superstructure forward and aft, with a bluff and stubby blow profile to give a wide and completely regular vehicle deck. Much of the Langeland III's superstructure was given over to a large tax-free supermarket (hence the lack of windows) as this was perhaps the most important aspect of her profitability. As a result, her subsequent career was closely linked to the future of tax-free shopping which, within the European Union, began to look increasingly uncertain. When this was abolished, the vessel was sold in 1998.

Tankers, bulk carriers and reefers

In 1987, Knud E. Hansen A/S designed a variety of tankers all of which entered service in 1989. The 29,995 dwt Bunga Anggerik was built by Hanjin Heavy Industries' Mokopo shipyard in South Korea for Raffles Shipping in Singapore. Next, the Greek-flagged 46,538 dwt Samothraki was completed by Hanjin's Pusan shipyard, while the 39,977 dwt Torm Herdis and Torm Helene were delivered from Hyundai in Ulsan for Dampskibsselskabet Torm of Copenhagen. Meanwhile, the 14,300 dwt Thuntank 9 was constructed in Inchon for the Swedish owner Thuntank. In 1989, Hanjin's Pusan yard also built a single Kund E. Hansen A/S-designed bulk carrier, the 47,980 dwt Probo Bani.

In the latter 1980s, Knud E. Hansen A/S became involved in the Danish Ministry for Industry's 'Project Ship' venture, which involved various specialist consultancies and manufacturers in Denmark in the development of an advanced and highly competitive cargo ship type to boost the revival of the Danish merchant fleet. Not only would this have low fuel consumption thanks to ongoing developments in engine technology and hull hydrodynamics, but also the incorporation of an unprecedented amount of advanced automation would enable the crew to be reduced. The prototype vessels exemplifying these developments were four 14,406 gt refrigerated cargo ships for J. Lauritzen. These were known as the 'Family class' as they bore the names of leading Lauritzen family members – Ditlev Lauritzen, Ivar Lauritzen, Knud Lauritzen and Jørgen Lauritzen. Knud E. Hansen A/S devised the hull lines, but their builder, Danyard in Frederikshavn, carried out much of the remaining planning. Delivered in 1990–91, their sophisticated design and computerised control systems had a profound impact on Danish merchant ships constructed during ensuing years.

Greek ferry conversions

In the latter 1980s, Knud E. Hansen A/S developed a lucrative relationship with Anek Lines, a well-known Cretan ferry operator founded in Chania in 1967 by a consortium of local farmers, businessmen and Orthodox Church clerics. Since the early 1970s, Anek had been enthusiastic purchasers of recently built second-hand ferries from Japan. Evidently pleased with these, they made two more acquisitions in 1987. These were the Ferry Hamanasu, originally delivered in 1972 to Shin Nihonkai for their Sea of Japan coastal service from Otaru to Tsuruga and Maizuru, and the 1975-built Varuna, ex-Daisetsu, which originally sailed for Taiheyo Ferry on Japan's Pacific coast, linking Nagoya, Sendai and Tomakomai. As built, the Ferry Hamanasu was a rather eccentric-looking craft. Because her year-round coastwise routing involved sailing during the typhoon season in heavy seas, her forward mooring deck and superstructure up to wheelhouse height was entirely enclosed by a bulbous dome. Amidships, her cinema auditorium was in a large dummy funnel, while exhaust from her main and auxiliary engines was routed separate pairs of stacks on either beam. Thus, she possessed no fewer than five 'funnels' of various shapes, sizes and purposes. Otherwise, she was a fairly typical Japanese coastal ferry of her era, being long and broad relative to her height and having a spacious, unobstructed vehicle deck, significantly overhanging the hull on either beam. Passenger accommodation included a high proportion of open dormitories, in which it sleeping on the floor was expected.

In 1987, Anek commissioned Knud E. Hansen A/S to convert the ferry into one suitable for Piraeus

The Grand Manan V.
(Laurie Murison)

–Crete service with the new name *Lissos*. Ole Olesen, who designed and supervised the conversion, recalls:

'Knud E. Hansen A/S began to work with Anek purely by chance. There was a Greek lady, married to a Swede, who attempted to design ship interiors and needed our advice for an earlier project. She knew someone on Anek's Board of Directors and recommended us. When I was surveying a vessel in Finland, I was contacted and asked to go next to Perama in Greece to examine Anek's newly-acquired *Lissos*. She was berthed among many other ships of different types and, already, she was in the process of being stripped out. There was not much time to redesign her so that she would be complete in time for the summer season.'

Olesen observes that satisfactorily converting Japanese ferries for Greek service was no easy task. A fundamental problem was that their underwater hull lines were remarkably fine in contrast with their rather bluff profiles above the water. This meant that, even before their new owners' requirements for extra passenger decks were taken into account, they had a worrying lack of excess buoyancy and therefore also a limited deadweight capacity for cargo. The best solution was to add sponson tanks to either side of the hull below the waterline and this could be achieved quite neatly due to them almost invariably having large vehicle deck overhangs and rounded bottoms which sponsons could 'square off' with little discernable negative effect on speed, manoeuvrability or sea-keeping characteristics. According to Olesen, 'Anek's directors included clerics, a school teacher and a farmer and they were not very sure about why we were proposing such radical changes, After a detailed explanation was given, they understood and the conversion was a great success.'

The *Lissos* lost her domed bow but gained a great deal of additional top hamper – an entire deck, no less – stretching all the way aft and slightly overhanging her stern. Thereafter, Knud E. Hansen A/S were involved in rebuilding every subsequent Japanese-built ferry Anek Lines purchased.

In 1986, Anastasios Kyriakiades, a Greek business entrepreneur based in Miami, contacted Knud E. Hansen A/S with a view to converting the incomplete hulk of a Greek ferry called the *Taygetos*, the building of which had begun in Perama in 1979 but had never progressed to the fitting out stage, into a casino ship. Kyriakiades had first made his fortune in the electronics business as Chairman of Lexington Corporation, which successfully manufactured pocket language translators. Subsequently, in 1984, he founded Regency Cruises before establishing Sea Venture Cruises.

Hans Kjærgaard was sent to Perama to survey the shell of the laid-up former *Taygetos*, which already was renamed *Sea Venture*. Kjærgaard's verdict was that the vessel would never be able to put to sea due to her chronic lack of stability and so he suggested that Kyriakiades find a different ship. As a result, in 1987 he bought the 1966-vintage Dover–Oostende passenger vessel *Prinses Paola* and Kjærgaard was sent to Piraeus to oversee her conversion in Perama to the casino ship *Tropicana*. While the rebuilding was successful, unfortunately, Knud E. Hansen A/S were never paid for their work and a loss of four million Danish kroner was recorded on the project.

While the *Lissos* and *Tropicana* conversions were underway in Greece, in Knud E. Hansen A/S' Copenhagen offices, a substantial 25,996 gt ro-pax (combined passenger and freight) ferry was being designed for Rederi AB Gotland. The idea was that she should be the first of a series of new and highly adaptable ferries for chartering out or for subsequent use on services between Gotland and the Swedish mainland with a larger superstructure retro-fitted over the weather deck. (As RAB Gotland had lost the right to operate these state-subsidised routes in 1987, for the next decade, it concentrated on chartereting out tonnage.)

As in the past, Rederi AB Gotland was keen to control costs and so an order was placed with a newly-established shipbuilder called Dok Kodja Bahri at Jakarta in Indonesia. When the contract was signed, the yard itself had not been built beyond the launchway and so a great deal of construction work remained to be carried out before the ferry's keel could be laid. Eventually, this took place in 1990 but thereafter the construction process fell seriously behind schedule. For Knud E. Hansen A/S, the design and project supervision contract was worth 12 million Danish kroner, of which they were paid 10% upon commencement, 15% at launching and the remainder upon the vessel's delivery. Evidently unperturbed by the shipyard's lack of completion, Knud E. Hansen A/S accepted a second similar contract worth Dkr 9 million to design and supervise the building there of the 16,839 dwt tanker *United Axel* for United Tankers of Gothenburg and, inevitably, she too was severely delayed until 1995. As the bulk of the payments owed to Knud E. Hansen A/S for these projects were due to be made after wage and travel costs had been incurred, the severe delays caused KEH to accumulate considerable debt.

Worse was to follow. At the launching of the ferry in 1992, which was named the *Gotland*, the incomplete hull got stuck on the slipway, meaning that there were still more delays in paying Knud E. Hansen A/S for their accumulated work. The shipyard allegedly diagnosed the problem as having been caused by attempting to launch the hull without there being a full moon and its management insisted that matters would only be resolved by waiting for the next lunar cycle. Not surprisingly, Knud E. Hansen A/S's directors found it difficult to persuade their bank in Copenhagen that this was a valid reason for extending emergency loans to the company to tide it over its short-term difficulties. Taken together, the lack of payment for the *Tropicana* conversion and the débacle in Indonesia threatened to cause ruination. The offices in Bredegade, valued at 16 million Danish kroner, were used as collateral but the property market for such premises collapsed and so bankruptcy became a very real possibility.

In Jakarta, meanwhile, the *Gotland* was eventually launched properly but, as the outfitting process was protracted, fixtures and fittings delivered from suppliers in Europe were left to rust in the tropical humidity, meaning that nearly three times more inventory had to be purchased than expected to replace damaged items. In the end, the outfitting work was actually completed at Dunkerque during a break in the delivery voyage. The *Gotland* finally entered service in 1997 a decade after the project to design and build her had first commenced.

The cumulative effect of these unfortunate circumstances persuaded Knud E. Hansen A/S' directors that there could be no other option than to put the wounded business up for sale. While they awaited a buyer, however, a slimmed down drawing office continued as best possible with ongoing project work.

While the *Gotland* project was making painfully slow progress in Indonesia, a small passenger and car ferry, the 3,833 gt *Grand Manan V*, was designed for the Ministry of Transport of New Brunswick in Canada. Completed to schedule in 1990 by the Bodewes Scheepswerf Volharding at Foxhol in the Netherlands, she was capable of carrying 312 passengers and 64 cars between Grand Manan and Blacks Harbour.

A more complex concurrent ferry project was for a large new Belgian cross-Channel ferry for operation between by Regie voor Maritiem Transport (RMT) between Oostende and Dover. Frustratingly, the 28,883 gt *Prins Filip*, completed in 1991 by the Boelwerf at Temse, presented problems of her own. Back in the early 1980s, RMT had chartered KEH-designed and converted tonnage from Stena Line, which introduced the concept of full-height car decks on two levels on the route.

In the wake of the sudden capsize of the *Herald of Free Enterprise* off Zeebrugge in 1987, the Belgian authorities and trade unions were most anxious that their new ship should be designed with a safety margin well in excess of existing regulations. This meant that extra buoyancy was built into her hull and there was a lot of duplication in the engine room to ensure that she would always have sufficient power in the event of a mechanical breakdown. In that sense, the design was ahead of its time. The unions also insisted that there should be individual accommodation for all crew so that those working onboard would feel both familiar with, and responsible for, the vessel's safe operation, right from the outset.

These factors complicated the design and construction of the *Prins Filip* and, when sea trials took place, there were troublesome vibrations to be eradicated. The Boelwerf shipyard was crippled financially by the project, though when the vessel finally entered service in May 1992, she impressed all who experienced her and set a new standard for Dover Strait ferry design.

In 1989, Knud E. Hansen A/S began work with Canada's BC Ferries, an old customer from the early 1960s, and with the Yarrows Shipyard, located on Vancouver Island, on the design of two large new ferries, the 18,747 gt, 2,100-passenger *Spirit of British Columbia* and *Spirit of Vancouver Island*, for the busy Tsawwassen–Swartz Bay route (between Vancouver and Vancouver Island in British Columbia). There, they would supplement vessels jumboised by KEH in 1981–82. Like these existing ferries, the new 'Spirit' class, as they were known, were to have an additional upper car deck, giving a total capacity of 470 cars.

For political reasons, the *Spirit of British Columbia* and *Spirit of Vancouver Island* were built in local shipyards, none of which alone had the capacity to assemble such large 167.5 metre long hulls. Consequently, an ingenious (but complicated) solution was reached whereby the bow sections were built by Allied Shipbuilders in Vancouver, with the mid-body and stern sections being constructed at the Esquimalt dry dock, near Victoria. Each hull was then welded together at Esquimalt, before being towed to the Yarrows Shipyard for the installation of machinery, consisting of two MAN diesels. After that, the ferries were towed again, this time to the Pacific Rim shipyard, south of Vancouver, where a prefabricated superstructure was fitted as a series of modules, which were welded together.

Such a complex construction process might have been expected to produce an unattractive result, but it was to the great credit of the designers and builders that the *Spirit of British Columbia* and *Spirit of Vancouver Island*, delivered in March and December 1993 respectively, were of notably orderly appearance. In each ship, the greater part of two entire decks were given over to passenger usage with a series of recliner saloons and catering facilities, all surrounded by large picture windows through which to enjoy the passing scenery.

The turbulent nineties

KNUD E. HANSEN
SHIP DESIGN SINCE 1937

The *Superfast X* leaves Rosyth at the start of a North Sea crossing to Zeebrugge. (Bruce Peter)

Right: The Greenland coastal passenger ferry *Sarpik Ittuk*. (Bent Mikkelsen, Søfart archive)

Below: The Norasia container ship *Norasia Sharjah*, one of a series of vessels designed without hatch covers to save weight and speed loading. (Bruce Peter collection)

Knud E. Hansen A/S struggled to recover from the losses incurred on the *Gotland* project and, besides, most of Hansen's colleagues who had inherited the company in 1960 had either retired, or were reaching retirement age. In 1991, Morten Skrydstrup reluctantly replaced Franklin Petersen as managing director but his tenure lasted only four years because early in 1995, the remaining original trustees sold the company to the Swedish Pelmatic Group, which otherwise consisted of a variety of specialist engineering consultancies.

As Pelmatic wanted a fresh start, it employed a Swede, Bengt Olof Jansson, in place of Skrydstrup, who was relieved to be reverting to project management work in the new role of technical director. Jansson did not find favour with his colleagues, who grew increasingly frustrated by what they saw as his autocratic approach. After only two years, he was dismissed by Pelmatic to be replaced by Niels Prip, a Danish naval architect who had previously been a director of a rival firm, Dwinger Marine Consult A/S. He proved very effective in developing new projects, which generated welcome cash flow. To cut overheads, the old offices in Bredegade were vacated in favour of cheaper, but more modern space at Islands Brygge with ducting for computer work stations.

While these managerial changes were underway, Knud E. Hansen A/S' day-to-day business of designing ships continued. In the early 1990s, the decision was taken to modernise the coastal passenger service around Greenland. Thus, Knud E. Hansen A/S designed three small but very robust vessels, 1,211 gt *Saqqit Ittuk*, *Sarfaq Ittuk* and *Sarpik Ittuk*, which were built by the Ørskov shipyard in Frederiskhavn and delivered in 1992.

At around the same time, Knud E. Hansen A/S designed a series of six large 42,323 gt, 2,780 TEU, 22-knot container ships for Norasia, a Swiss operator known for its forward-thinking approach. These were, in fact, the first big container vessels Knud E. Hansen A/S had designed in their entirety and the solution arrived at was unusual in that they were designed without hatch covers to save weight and expense. Instead, the containers on deck were protected by an enclosed forward mooring deck and by corrugated steel panels which unfolded on top of the container stacks. The class – consisting of the *Norasia Fribourg*, *Norasia Kiel*, *Norasia Singa*, *Norasia Shanghai* and *Norasia Hong Kong* – was built by the Howaldtswerke Deutsche Werft in Kiel in the 1992–94 period.

Thereafter, considerable success was had designing various sizes of broadly similar feeder container ships for the Ørskov shipyard in Frederikshavn. First to be completed in 1994 was the 6,297 gt, 703 TEU *Gertie* for Bidsted & Co, followed by the similar *Mærsk Euro Quinto* for A.P. Møller, who additionally bought three 724 TEU versions, the *Mærsk Euro Primo*, *Mærsk Euro Tertio* and *Mærsk Euro Quarto*. Next came the 960 TEU *Norasia Melita*, *Norasia Adria* and *Mærsk Lima*. The *Katherine Sif*, *Flemming Sif* and *Colleen Sif* were bigger again, with space for 982 TEU. Subsequently Ørskov built further expanded versions able to accommodate 1,128 TEU (the *Ratona Sopa*, *TSL Valiant* and *Inger C.*) and 1,467 TEU (the *Kirsten Sif* and *Helen Sif*). These designs were then licensed to the Yardimci shipyard in Tuzla and the Kalkavan shipyard in Istanbul where yet more were built. Thus, the type became a standard feeder container ship, found in many ports around the world.

In addition, during early-1990s, a couple of small chemical tankers were designed Danish owners; these were the 8,603 dwt *Anne Sif*, built in 1993 by the Hyundai Ulsan shipyard in South Korea and the 2,400 dwt *Kilgas Champion*, built in 1995 by Ørskov. The former's bridge was designed for navigation with only one officer on duty when operating in coastal waters.

The early 1990s was, however, a torrid period for ferry operators. Not only was there a deep recession in Europe but also two serious tragedies undermined confidence in the industry. In April 1990, the Bahamian-flagged *Scandinavian Star* (ex *Massalia*) was destroyed by fires set by an arsonist while on passage across the Kattegat from Oslo to Frederikshavn, killing 159 of her passengers, most of whom suffocated due to smoke inhalation. Once the flames were extinguished, the wreck was towed to Copenhagen where the Danish authorities engaged Knud E. Hansen A/S as part of their criminal investigation. Hans Kjærgaard carried out this work with the assistance of British experts in the behaviour and spread of fires. He recalls that:

> 'It was easily the most unpleasant task of my entire career and but working with my British colleagues was strangely fascinating. On board the wrecked ship, they could map out where the fires had begun and how they had then spread. The *Scandinavian Star* had been put in service too quickly and her crew were not trained. Her operator only wanted to make money and took no thought about safety. The disaster was a wake-up call for the entire passenger shipping industry.'

Only four years later, in September 1994, the Baltic ferry *Estonia* (ex *Viking Sally*) foundered in a storm while en route through the Gulf of Finland from Tallinn to Stockholm. The locking pins securing her bow visor suffered metal fatigue and failed sequentially. Consequently, the visor came loose and began to move from side to side. As the fold-down ramp forming a watertight seal behind extended into a housing at the top if the visor, this movement caused the ramp to open and so the vehicle deck flooded. The *Estonia* lost stability and sank, killing 851 passengers and crew.

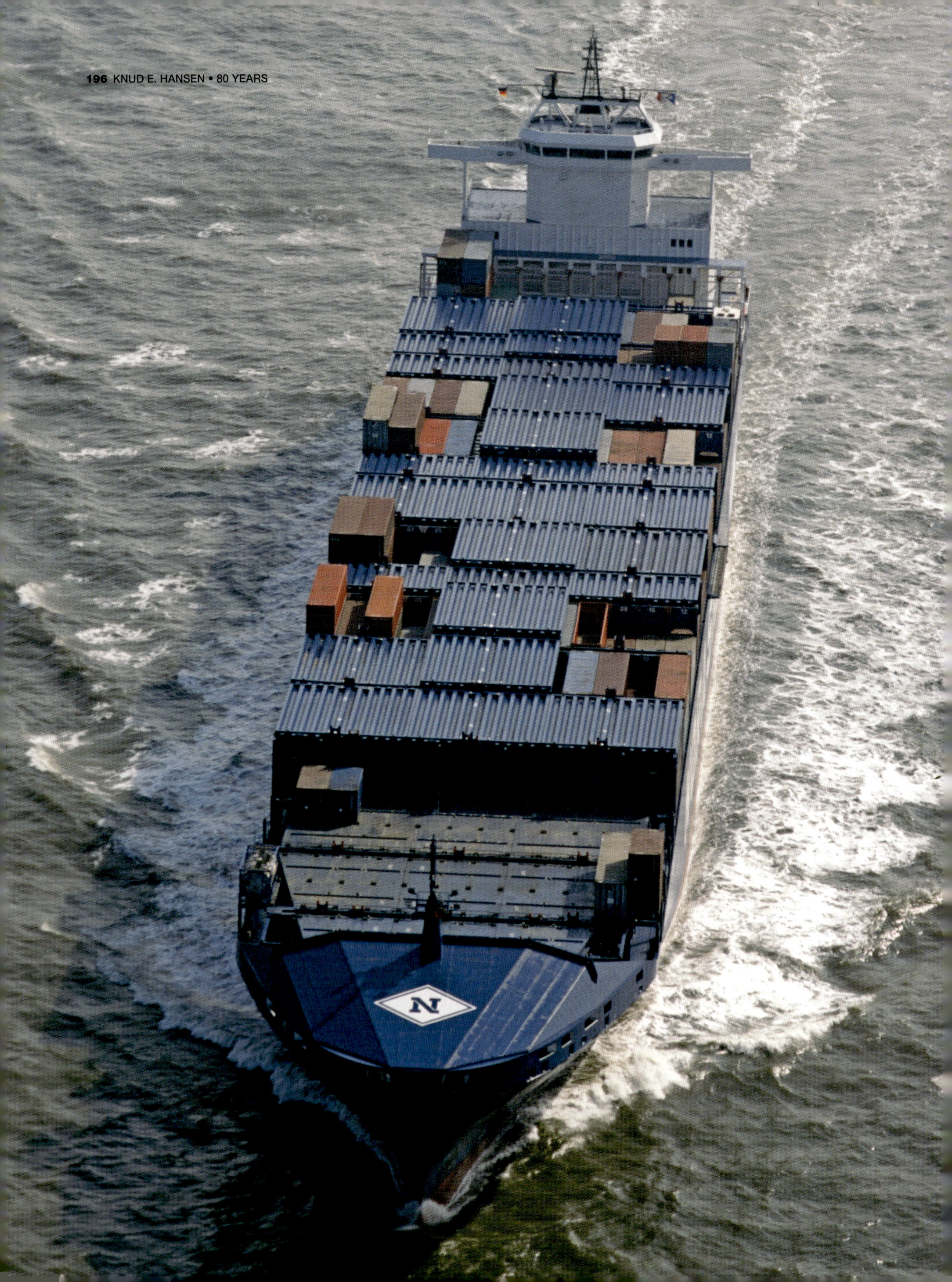

This tragic event caused national and international maritime authorities and classification societies to re-appraise the damage stability criteria for ferries and, while this process continued, there was a temporary moratorium on new orders being placed. Seven Northern European countries with ferry fleets signed the Stockholm Agreement of 1996 and this specified that all ferries should have far superior damage stability and also better protection for their vehicle decks. The Stockholm Agreement created a vast amount of welcome additional work for Knud E. Hansen A/S, as nearly all of the leading ferry operators sought their advice on how best to upgrade existing vessels. Typical solutions were to fit an additional watertight bow door behind the existing ramp, to install retractable flood control barriers across the vehicle deck to contain flood water while reducing free surface effect, or to add sponsons to the hull sides or stern to improve the damage stability margin. As most ferry designs are unique, each vessel affected required analysis on an individual basis and a bespoke solution applied.

Opposite: A dramatic aerial view of the *Norasia Kiel*. (Bruce Peter collection)

Some vessels examined by Knud E. Hansen A/S were found to need radical alteration. For example, the 1975–76-built former *Tor Britannia* and *Tor Scandinavia* which in the 1990s traded for DFDS as the *Prince of Scandinavia* and *Princess of Scandinavia*, were fitted in 1998 with very large side and stern sponsons, plus modified bulbous bows to bring them within the new damage stability criteria.

Three new ferry projects which did come to fruition during this period were for Scandlines, an operator created in 1997 through the amalgamation the Danish, German and Swedish State Railways' shipping interests. Firstly, Knud E. Hansen A/S was commissioned to design the hull lines for two new Danish-flagged double-ended ferries for the hour-long Rødby–Puttgarten route across the Southern Baltic between Denmark and Germany. The 14,822 gt *Prins Richard* and *Prinsesse Benedikte* were otherwise designed in-house by Scandlines and built by Ørskov in Frederikshavn.

For the Swedish part of Scandlines, owned by SweFerry, Knud E. Hansen A/S designed the 42,705 gt train ferry *Skåne*, built in Spain by the Astilleros Españoles shipyard in Puerta Real and delivered in 1998 for service between Trelleborg and Rostock. She could carry 600 passengers, all berthed, and 55 railway wagons, some of which were lowered by elevator to twin tracks installed on her tank top deck, ahead of the engine room. Otherwise, her 3,295 lane metres for trucks made her an important part of the 'sea bridge' between Southern Sweden and Germany.

As the European economy picked up, there was an unprecedented growth in freight traffic while, concurrently, the appearance of so-called 'low-cost' airlines and the expected ending of tax-free shopping between EU member states meant that ferries changed from a passenger-focus to a freight focus (tax-free shopping finally came to an end in 1999). In response to these trends, during the latter 1990s, the ferry industry in Europe generally switched to ro-pax ferries, typically with two or three freight decks and proportionally smaller passenger accommodation than the 1980s generation of jumbo ferries.

In this period, Ireland experienced unprecedented growth, particularly in banking and other service industries, and so there was a parallel expansion of traffic across the Irish Sea. To handle this increase, Irish Ferries asked Knud E. Hansen A/S to design a new passenger and freight ferry for the Dublin–Holyhead route. At the same time, they were also contacted by the Van der Giessen shipyard in the Netherlands, which offered to build a ro-pax ferry of their own design. As this was evidently a cheaper option than Knud E. Hansen A/S' proposal, the new 22,365 gt *Isle of Innisfree* was indeed built largely according to Van der Giessen's specifications, although Irish Ferries retained Knud E. Hansen A/S to evaluate and modify the Dutch shipyard's design. Completed in 1995, the ferry was followed by two others, the 34,031 gt *Isle of Innismore*, delivered by Van der Giessen in 1997, and the 50,938 gt *Ulysses*, largely designed and built by Aker Finnyards in Rauma, Finland. Irish Ferries once again consulted Knud E. Hansen A/S to evaluate the plans and additionally to design a striking silhouette for the vessel. Indeed, with 4,101 lane metres for freight, she was the highest capacity ro-pax ferry in the world when delivered in 2001. Klaus Horn, an interior architect working together with KEH on the project, styled her exterior, adding a wedge-shaped funnel and a sweeping profile to her aft superstructure.

In 1999, Knud E. Hansen A/S worked with Irish Ferries' rivals, P&O, on three new 20,800 gt ro-pax ferries ordered from the Mitsubishi Shimonoseki shipyard in Japan for their own Irish Sea routes. The *European Causeway* and *European Highlander* were built for the Cairnryan–Larne service while the third vessel, named the *European Ambassador*, was for use on a new route from a purpose-built ferry port at Mostyn in North Wales to Dublin; all were delivered in 2000–2001 and have proven very economical and effective.

During the 1990s, the collapse of Communist regimes in the former Warsaw Pact countries, many of which aspired to join the European Union, boosted ferry services across the Adriatic. Secondly, the outbreak of Serbian nationalism which followed the disintegration of Yugoslavia led to a civil war from 1991 until 1995, meaning that traditional overland routes through the Balkans were closed. Hence,

The *Mærsk Primo* (delivered as *Mærsk Euro Primo*) fitting out at the Ørskov shipyard in Frederikshavn. (Bruce Peter collection)

The feeder container ship *Mærsk Euro Tertio*. (Bent Mikkelsen, Søfart archive)

lorries heading East would instead have to cross by ferry from Italian ports to Igoumenitsa and Patras in Greece. To provide extra capacity, existing ferry companies acquired as much used tonnage as possible, while numerous upstart operators appeared.

One such ambitious newcomer was Superfast, owned by Knud E. Hansen A/S' long-standing client Pericles Panagopoulos. When the cruise industry had consolidated from the latter 1980s onwards, Pericles Panagopoulos decided to sell his Royal Cruise Line, retaining only a few senior employees, including Costis Stamboulelis, to assist in establishing Magna Marine, a company owning and operating dry bulk carriers. Even although the sale of Royal Cruise Line to Kloster contained a clause forbidding Panagopoulos from re-entering the cruise industry for five years, Stamboulelis began working with Steen Nielsen of Knud E. Hansen A/S to develop a new 2,500-passenger cruise ship, the idea being that an order would be placed as soon as the five-year term had elapsed. The project was code-named 'Pan Max' and was analysed with both diesel and gas turbine propulsion. When quotations came in from shipyards, however, it became clear that it would cost nearly as much to build as Panagopoulos had earned by selling Royal Cruise Line and so the scheme was abandoned. This notwithstanding, the idea of using gas turbine propulsion was prescient and subsequently it became briefly fashionable on cruise ships, with vessels for Celebrity Cruises, Royal Caribbean and Cunard all being gas-propelled.

Instead, Costis Stamboulelis observed that, with Greece's increasing participation in trade with its fellow European Union members, it would be sensible to develop a high-speed ro-pax ferry service on the 504-nautical-mile route between Ancona, on northern Italy's Adriatic coast, and the Greek mainland port of Patras. The idea came to him during a two-night Adriatic crossing on an old Japanese ferry belonging to Minoan Lines, which he thought was frustratingly slow. Alexander Panagopoulos, the son of Pericles, was quickly persuaded about the merits of the idea and became the driving force behind the project's development. Meanwhile, in 1993 Panagopoulos Senior purchased Attica Enterprises, a Greek business conglomerate which he renamed Attica Group. Within this, Superfast was developed as a new ferry brand to operate fast 20-hour Ancona–Patras crossings.

In November 1993, an order was placed with Schichau Seebeckwerft in Bremerhaven for two ships for this service, the 23,663 gt *Superfast I* and *Superfast II* which were the first ferries to be purpose-built for Adriatic service since the early 1960s. Their overall structural resolution was derived from the shipyard's earlier ro-ro freighters *Nils Dacke* and *Robin Hood*, built for TT-Line in 1988–89 and P&O's Dover Strait vessels *European Seaway*, *European Highway*, *European Pathway* and *Pride of Burgundy*, introduced in 1991–93. To provide the required 25.5-knot service speed, four powerful Wärtsilä-Sulzer 12-cylinder diesels were specified and the hull had a particularly fine-lined bow configuration while the underwater form further aft was derived from that of the of the 1986–87-built *Peter Pan* and *Nils Holgersson*. All of these vessels had hull lines supplied to Schichau Seebeckwerft by Knud E. Hansen A/S.

The majority of the hull and superstructure volume on the Superfast vessels was given over to two commodious freight decks arranged around centre casings with additional space ahead of the engine room, giving a total of 1,850 lane metres. Above, there were three passenger decks, designed to accommodate a very wide diversity of travellers ranging from budget-conscious backpackers to tourists and truck drivers. All cabins were forward-located and outfitted to a very high standard. Public rooms were towards the stern and arranged around a U-shaped circulation plan.

During the development of the Superfast ferry project, Costis Stamboulelis recommended to Schichau Seebeckwerft that they should consult Holger Terpet of Knud E. Hansen A/S to evaluate and modify the general arrangement drawings and to participate in the ferries' detailed design. Terpet also designed the distinctive Superfast funnel with upturned winglets on either side, much like those of

An unbuilt design by Knud E. Hansen A/S for a large ro-pax vessel for Irish Ferries. (KNUD E. HANSEN Archive)

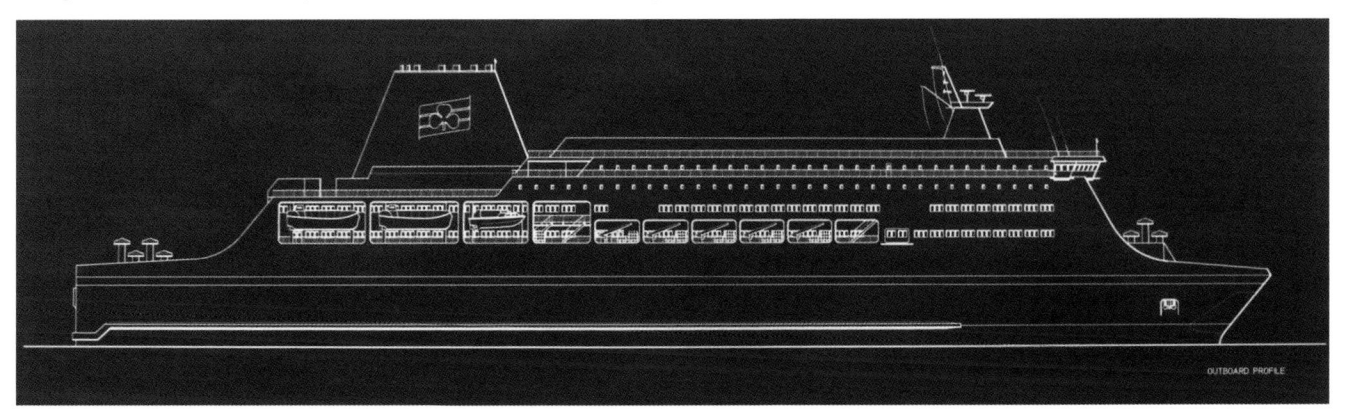

Above: Irish Ferries' flagship, the *Ulysses*, with external styling by Klaus Horn. (Bruce Peter collection)

Below: The Rødby-Puttgarten Scandlines ferry *Prins Richard*. (Bruce Peter collection)

Top: The Trelleborg-Rostock train and road freight ferry *Skåne* – a complex vessel in terms of her vehicle deck ramp and lift arrangements.
(Bruce Peter collection)

Left: P&O Irish Sea's Japanese-built ro-pax ferry *European Causeway* is seen here leaving the mouth of Loch Ryan.
(Bruce Peter collection)

Right: A stern-quarter view of the *Superfast I*, berthed at Patras. (Bruce Peter collection)

Below: The *Superfast III* at Patras. (Bruce Peter collection)

The *Superfast V* at speed on the Adriatic Sea. (Bruce Peter collection)

The *Superfast VI* arrives at Patras. (Bruce Peter collection)

A lounge on the *Superfast III*, illustrating the high standard of interior design on these vessels. (Bruce Peter collection)

recent airliners, based on a sketch given to him by Alexander Panagopoulos, who also devised the new ferries' striking Ferrari red and white livery.

Shortly, Attica acquired 16% of the shares in another leading Greek ferry operator, Strintzis Lines. Then, in August 1999, 38.8% of the shares of Strintzis Lines were acquired and, later still, this figure was increased to 48.8% and Alexander Panagopoulos decided to re-brand the company as Blue Star Ferries, taking the colours of the European Union flag for inspiration. This meant that Attica very quickly became the dominant player not only on international ferry routes from Greece, but, through Blue Star Ferries, on domestic services as well.

From the outset, Attica's Superfast operation was a great success, so much so that a further 10 examples of the type were ordered for delivery between 1998 and 2003, not only to expand Adriatic operations, but also to introduce three North European routes – a remarkable initiative for a Greek ship owner. In 1998, the 29,067 gt *Superfast III* and *IV* were delivered by Kvaerner Masa Yards (the former Wärtsilä Marine shipyard) in Turku to an improved design though, once again, Holger Terpet was employed to evaluate and adjust the plans. Next, Terpet drew up the basic design for no fewer than six further vessels for Superfast, the *Superfast V* to *X*, all of which were built by Howaldtswerke Deutsche Werft in Kiel in the 2001–2003 period.

The 32,728 gt *Superfast V* and *VI* had a slightly higher service speed of 29 knots to enable time for a call at Igoumenitsa, a Greek port near the border with Albania popular with truck drivers, while en route between Patras and Ancona. The subsequent 30,285 gt *Superfast VII* to *Superfast X* were also built in Kiel as operations expanded into the Baltic with new services to the former East German port of Rostock from Södertälje in Sweden and Hanko, Finland's nearest port to Continental Europe. On these examples, the internal layout of the passenger decks was changed from a vertical subdivision of cabins and public rooms to a horizontal arrangement with the main lounge facing forward, rather than aft as before, and the decks narrowing towards the stern. Furthermore, they were built to the highest ice class notation for ferries. While the Finland–Germany route performed satisfactorily, the one from Sweden was a flop and so the ferries were quickly redeployed to open a new service from Rosyth in Scotland to Zeebrugge in Belgium. Two final vessels, the 30,902 gt *Superfast XI* and *XII*, were delivered in 2002 by Flender Werft's yard in Lübeck, again for the Ancona–Patras service, replacing the original *Superfast I* and *II*. They also adopted the horizontal layout of public rooms and forward outlook of the Baltic ships.

All Superfasts, with the exception of *Superfast XI* and *XII*, were designed for a very efficient double-deck simultaneous loading of trailers, and Holger Terpet designed the interfaces between the linkspans in the ports of Patras, Södertälje, Hanko, Rostock, Rosyth and Zeebrugge and the ferries. While not all of Superfast's routes lived up to expectations, the Superfast concept was widely emulated and revolutionised ferry travel all over the world.

The *Superfast XII* is seen off the Greek coast on her way to Italy. (Bruce Peter collection)

The *Superfast VII* approaches Travemünde. (Bruce Peter collection)

Superfast were the first of several Greek ferry companies to invest heavily in new tonnage during the boom years of the 1990s, aided by Greek and German banks suddenly being very willing to extend loans to finance the purchase of vessels on an unprecedented scale. In 1996, Anek Lines bought from Shin Nihonkai Ferry in Japan two very large freight-orientated ferries to strengthen its Ancona–Igoumenitsa–Patras route, the 27,239 gt *New Suzuran* and *New Yukari*, both of which dated from 1979. Ole Olesen produced a conversion plan for these, the most significant aspect of which was the fitment of sponsons below the waterline to enhance their deadweight capacities. Upon the completion of this work in Perama, they entered Adriatic service as the *Kriti I* and *Kriti II*. Once the Balkans War ended, however, they were switched to provide extra freight capacity between Piraeus and Heraklion as the farmers of Crete, who had helped found Anek, continued keenly to support the company's provision of ships with plenty of space for large trucks to bring their wares to the mainland.

Shortly thereafter, in 1998 Anek added the first of two further Japanese ferries to its Adriatic fleet, purchasing the *Hermes* of Nighashi Nihon Ferry for a lengthy coastal route between Patras and Trieste, skirting past the war-torn Balkans. Again, Knud E. Hansen A/S planned the vessel's conversion from which she emerged as the *Sophocles V*. Two years later, Anek also bought one of her sisters, the *Hercules*, for the same service and she was renamed *Lefka Ori*. Both were large ro-pax ferries of rather eccentric design, but high build quality, dating from 1990 and 1992 respectively.

To compete with Superfast on equal terms on the Patras–Igoumenitsa–Ancona route, Anek next ordered their first ever new buildings, the 32,694 gt *Olympic Champion* and *Hellenic Spirit*, from Fosen Mekaniske Verksted, near Trondheim in Norway. The construction of their hulls and superstructures was subcontracted to Bruce's Shipyard in Landskrona, Sweden, from which they were towed to Fosen to be fitted out. Although designed largely by their builder, Anek Lines retained Knud E. Hansen A/S to evaluate and approve plans and to supervise their construction until up to the point of delivery in 2000 and 2001 respectively.

A third leading Greek operator of ferries across the Adriatic, Minoan Lines, bought no fewer than 10 new fast ro-pax ferries. Three of these were ordered from Fosen Mekaniske Verksted, four from Finncantieri in Italy and a further three from Samsung in South Korea. Knud E. Hansen A/S provided the design for this latter trio, using a basic formula similar to that developed for the Superfast fleet, albeit with a longer 221-metre hull and a less extensive superstructure. The *Oceanus*, *Prometheus* and *Ariadne Palace* were delivered in 2001–2002.

In 2001, Moby Lines, operating ferries on Italy's West Coast to Corsica and Sardinia, also received Knud E. Hansen A/S-designed ferries from South Korea. The 36,093 gt *Moby Wonder* and *Moby Freedom*, built by Daewoo Shipbuilding & Heavy Machinery Ltd, were high-capacity vessels, their most outstanding feature being a large forward-facing tiered lounge with a three-deck-high panoramic window overlooking the bow. During the summer and at weekends they operated in 'cruise ferry' mode with live entertainment and a variety of eating options. On weekdays out of season, they sailed in 'ro-pax' mode with fewer passenger facilities in use and a predominance of freight carried on the vehicle decks.

New Gotland ferries

Having worked with Rederi AB Gotland to design and deliver successive generations of innovative ferries, Knud E. Hansen A/S was employed once again to develop a further pair of vessels for the company's principal routes from Nynäshamn and Oskarshamn to Visby. The new *Visby* and *Gotland*, however, marked significant departures for both their designers and owners in several respects. Firstly, they were very fast vessels, powered by four mighty Wärtsilä diesels capable of speeds of up to 28.5 knots and so they were able to do the work of dedicated fast ferry tonnage as well as carrying out more conventional passenger, car and freight-carrying roles. By using fewer engines, slower passages could be made in the winter, meaning that the two ships could cope well with seasonal fluctuations in demand. Each could carry 1,500 passengers (mainly in reclining seats) and 500 cars, making for a very efficient high-capacity transportation system to the island. For longer overnight sailings, 300 cabin berths were included.

Secondly, they were the first large ferries to be built in China for a European passenger ship operator. Each cost a mere 550 million Swedish Kronor, or well below half of the price of similar vessels built in Northern Europe. For Knud E. Hansen A/S, working with China's Guangzhou Shipyard was both a challenge and a new opportunity. The *Visby*'s keel was laid in November 2000, with the *Gotland* following in July 2001. For both the designer and the builder, the construction process in China presented a steep learning curve, but vessels were built efficiently with completion in January and October 2003.

The ro-pax ferry *Kriti I* was converted in Greece from the Japanese *New Suzuran*. (Bruce Peter collection)

Above: Anek Lines' *Olympic Champion* arrives at Ancona. (Bruce Peter)

Seen at Igoumenitsa, Anek Lines' *Lefka Ori* was rebuilt from the Japanese ro-pax *Hercules*. (Bruce Peter)

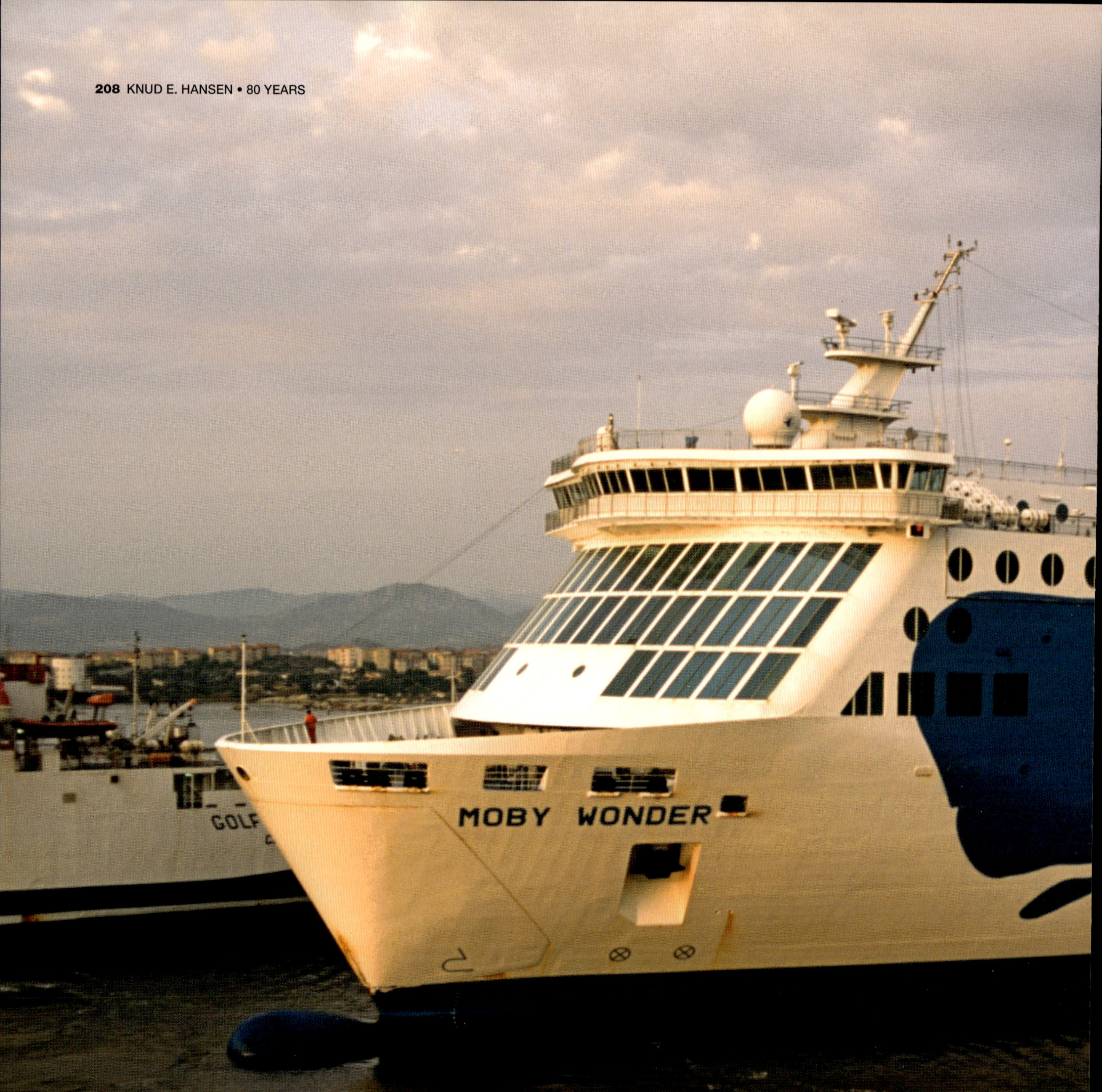
MOBY WONDER

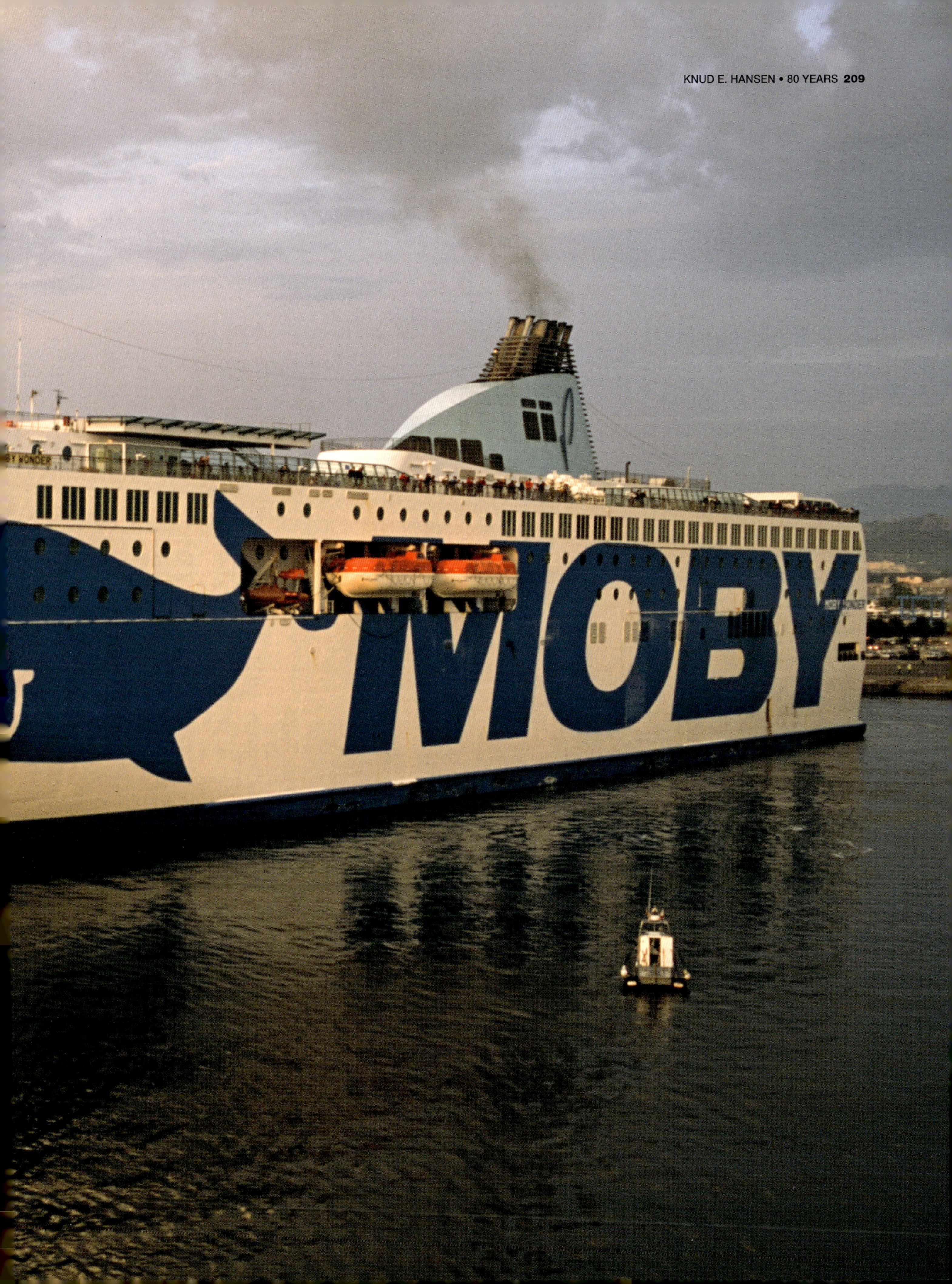
MOBY
MOBY WONDER

Above: The South Korean-built *Ariadne Palace*, one of three KEH-designed fast ro-pax ferries delivered to Minoan Lines in 2001-2002, is seen off Igoumenitsa. (Bruce Peter collection)

Right: The *Visby* arrives at her namesake port on the island of Gotland in the summer of 2011. (Bruce Peter collection)

The Chinese-built Rederi AB Gotland ro-pax ferry *Gotland* off Visby. (Bruce Peter collection)

New ferries for the Atlantic Isles

Since 1983, the stormy Atlantic route from Norway to the Shetland Isles, Tórshavn in the Faroes and Seydisfjördur in Iceland had been in the hands of the Knud E. Hansen A/S-designed *Norröna* (ex *Gustav Vasa*) of 1973, a ship never intended to sail out of the sheltered confines of the Southern Baltic (as described above). As by the late 1990s, her freight capacity was found insufficient, Smyril Line decided to build anew and appointed Knud E. Hansen A/S to produce a suitable design.

As DFDS' *Scandinavia* had shown in attempting to sail from New York to the Bahamas in the early 1980s, a standard jumbo ferry was quite unsuitable for Atlantic service and so, for Smyril Line's new *Norröna*, an approach more akin to Marine Atlantic's *Caribou* and *Joseph and Clara Smallwood* would be necessary. However, as the ferry would also need to manoeuvre in fairly confined harbours on her weekly routing from Denmark via Norway, the Shetland Isles and the Faroes to Iceland, her hull would need to be short. Thus, Knud E. Hansen A/S proposed a rather unusual looking 35,966 gt vessel with a length of only 164.56 metres, but a 30-metre breadth.

Late in 2001, the new *Norröna* was ordered from the Neue Flensburger Schiffbau in Flensburg but for political reasons, construction actually took place at the Flender Werft in Lübeck which was lacking orders to keep its workforce employed. The keel was laid in January 2002 and the ship was ready for delivery only 13 months later. In appearance, she was quite different from any other larger ferry of her generation with a distinctive chiselled bow form. This design appears to have been arrived at jointly with the Flensburger shipyard's naval architects, who went on to use a similar approach for numerous ro-ro freight ferries subsequently built at the yard. The *Norröna*'s bow was substantial with a breakwater to deflect large waves away from the bridge windows. The fenestration in her forward superstructure was small and sparse, again quite unlike other recent ferries, but a wise precaution given the sometimes ferocious nature of her operating environment. Power was provided by four Caterpillar MaK diesels, giving a 21-knot service speed.

Within, the *Norröna* accommodated 1,482 passengers, all but 159 of whom were berthed (another unusual feature of the ship was that the cabins were handmade in Poland, rather than being modular constructions, as this was found to be slightly cheaper). From an economic perspective, the vessel's generous freight capacity of 1,870 lane metres was essential to her success, carrying lorry loads of Icelandic and Faroese fish and seafood exports to Scandinavia all year round, while significant numbers of passengers were an added bonus during the brief summer season.

The *Norröna* project was followed in quick succession by a commission from the Faroese transport company Strandfaraskip Landsins to design a new ferry for operation within the Faroe Islands between Tórshavn and Suderø. After two years of planning to develop a suitable design, the 12,320 gt *Smyril* was ordered in 2002 from the IZAR shipyard in San Fernando, Southern Spain. There followed a lengthy construction process, the vessel finally being delivered in 2005. In comparison with the rather fore-square *Norröna*, the *Smyril* is externally sleek, having a slight resemblance to the *Visby* and *Gotland*, while inboard she is spacious and comfortable and has proved highly popular with islanders.

High-speed cruise ships

In the cruise ship field, Holger Terpet designed the silhouette and arranged the passenger accommodation for two innovative fast vessels for the Greek Royal Olympic Cruises – the 24,391 gt *Olympic Voyager* (soon renamed *Olympia Voyager* following an infringement claim by the American Olympic Committee) and the *Olympia Explorer* – delivered in 2000–2001. These were, in fact, Royal Olympic's first ever new buildings and the idea behind their design, developed in great secrecy by the builder, Blohm & Voss of Hamburg, was to be able to call in ports in Europe, Asia Minor and Africa all in a week-long cruise. This required a speed of as much as 33 knots and it was from German warship design research that a suitable hull form was chosen. This had an aft-body configuration in which the twin propeller shafts were unusually deeply submerged and located very close together with the blade tips nearly touching. The hull steelwork above formed a semi-tunnel, thereby intensifying the thrust while minimising vibration. The wave-making resistance of this design was significantly lower than for conventional hull forms intended for high-speed operation and allowed for an undisturbed flow of water to the propellers. Propulsion was from four 9-cylinder Wärtsilä engines, any two of which could together maintain a 22-knot speed.

Although Blohm & Voss was responsible for the hull form, the superstructure and interior layout was devised by Holger Terpet of Knud E. Hansen A/S, whose detailing had a strong horizontal emphasis, capped by a large streamlined funnel, emphasising the vessels' great speed. Unfortunately, the vessels were not economically successful and were quickly sold for use elsewhere.

The sturdy Faroese ferry *Norröna* approaches Hirtshals in August 2012. (Bruce Peter collection)

Above: The *Norröna* is seen entering Hirtshals harbour. (Bruce Peter collection)

Below: The Faroese inter-island ferry *Smyril* is a very sleek vessel with a long bow and a breakwater to protect her superstructure from mountainous head-seas. (Søren Lund Hviid)

A stern-quarter view of the *Smyril* at Tórshavn. (Søren Lund Hviid)

Freighters for Stena Ro-Ro

In the mid-1990s, Knud E. Hansen A/S produced concepts for three similar classes of ro-ro freighter with various capacities for Stena Ro-Ro to build in Guanzhou in China. Unlike the enduringly successful mid-1970s 'Searunner' class, the three new types had forward-located superstructures but, as before, the possibility of subsequent lengthening was considered from the outset and the weather deck could be enclosed, if need arose. As with the *Visby*, *Gotland* and *Smyril*, and the earlier Norasia container ships, the three Stena Ro-Ro designs were distinguished by the sculptural appearance of the forward superstructure, the mooring deck being enclosed and with a steep downward rake.

Instead of Guanzhou building the smaller 21,104 gt, 2,715 freight lane metre examples as first intended, Stena instead ordered four of them from the Società Esercizio Cantieri in Viareggio, Italy. After only two were delivered in 1998 (the *Sea Centurion* and *Stena Forwarder*), the yard went bankrupt and it was five years before Stena could extricate the remaining incomplete examples. In 2003, however, one was completed in Marina di Carrara as the *Stena Carrier*, while the other was towed to Kraljevica in Croatia and finished as the *Stena Freighter*. Meanwhile, Stena Ro-Ro ordered three of the medium-sized 24,688 gt, 3,000-lane metre type from a Chinese shipyard in Dalian – the *Stena Forerunner*, *Stena Forecaster* and *Stena Foreteller*, all of which delivered in 2002–2003. No orders were placed for the biggest of the three types, which would have had 3,540 lane metres.

At the same time as the small and medium-sized Stena Ro-Ro classes were being built, three new Knud E. Hansen A/S-designed freighters for DFDS' North Sea routes were also being built by Fincantieri in Ancona, Italy; these were the 24,196 gt, 2,800 lane metre *Tor Selandia*, *Tor Suecia* and *Tor Britannia*, completed in the 1998–2000 period. To ensure the comfort of their crew and 12 passengers, the superstructure was placed two-thirds aft, where pitching motion would be felt less severely than were it forward-located, as on the Stena vessels.

At the beginning of the year 2000, Knud E. Hansen A/S was sold by Pelmatic to the Swedish industrial technology and design company Semcon AB. The opportunity was then taken to streamline and reorganise KEH in line with Semcon's approach.

In 2003, Finn Wollesen Petersen was appointed as Knud E. Hansen A/S' new managing director and he immediately instituted a policy of diversification into a number of lucrative niche markets and also set about developing additional subsidiary offices around the world to bring Knud E. Hansen A/S' expertise closer to its clients. Beforehand, Wollesen had a diverse career, encompassing many aspects of shipping, engineering and business. Initially, he followed his father by becoming a seaman on J. Lauritzen's well-known polar and reefer ships (there are even Wollesen Islands in the Antarctic, resulting from his father's visits there). Thereafter, during the latter 1980s, he trained as a mechanical engineer at Århus Teknikum. Later, he specialised in designing and commissioning ship's heating,

Royal Olympic Cruises' *Olympic Voyager* at Piraeus at the commencement of her short career with the company. (Andrew Kilk)

ventilation and air conditioning (HVAC) systems – a hidden, but vital element in modern passenger ship design.

When Wollesen joined Knud E. Hansen A/S, he brought with him a small but highly experienced team of HVAC engineers, who subsequently carried out major design, consultancy and supervision in HVAC and electrical automation on numerous large cruise ships, including members of the MSC, Carnival Corportation and Royal Caribbean fleets. The success of these schemes was a significant factor in landing Knud E. Hansen A/S a large and lengthy contract to supply HVAC design and coordination for the British Royal Navy's new aircraft carriers (HMS *Queen Elizabeth* and HMS *Prince of Wales*, completed in 2017 and 2019). The scope of this project urgently required an expanded project team with new employees recruited from Spain, Lithuania, Italy and Australia, headed by a French Project Manager, Stéphane Geslin. In terms of hours, it turned out to be the biggest task ever handled by Knud E. Hansen A/S in their entire history and, throughout, Geslin remained in charge.

Early ship design projects of the Wollesen era included two 6,300 dwt chemical tankers, the *Inge Wonsild* and *Marianne Wonsild*, which was designed for the Danish ship owner, Wonsild & Søn, and built by Sekwang Heavy Industries Co Ltd of Mokpo in South Korea. For the shipyard, which lacked sufficient experience with chemical tankers, the Inge Wonsild proved unexpectedly complicated to construct and so the process lagged behind schedule. Only ten days into his new job as Managing Director, Finn Wollesen flew to South Korea to try to solve the difficulties. As he recalls,

'I was immediately in at the deep end but, with the help of my new colleagues and the ship owner, we managed to assist the shipyard with advice on how to overcome the difficulties. In the end, the tankers performed very well and are still in service under the Danish flag. As a result, I developed a very good relationship with one of Wonsild's managers, Henning Loesch, and subsequently he was made a director of Knud E. Hansen A/S.'

The *Inge Wonsild* and *Marianne Wonsild* were delivered in 2005 and 2006 respectively.

Another contract was to design a pair of new 873 gt 'Sundbuss' passenger ferries for Moltzau's Helsingør–Helsingborg link. These had distinctive streamlined external profiles which were devised in collaboration with the Norwegian cruise ship and yacht designer, Petter Yran. Not surprisingly, they somewhat resembled the 'Sea Goddess' cruise ships styled by him in the early 1980s. Eventually, an order was placed with the Remontova shipyard at Gdansk in Poland but during the construction process, Moltzau sold the Sundbuss operation to another Norwegian ship owner, Eitzen Group, which re-branded it as ACE-Link. The two ferries were

HMS *Queen Elizabeth* at Portsmouth. (Wikimedia Commons)

Knud E. Hansen A/S' current Managing Director Finn Wollesen Petersen has overseen the expansion of the company with a new headquarters in Helsingør and additional local offices around the world, making use of modern communications to bring the company closer to its customers.
(KNUD E. HANSEN Archive)

The *Stena Freighter* in Kiel with the *Stena Scandinavica* astern in October 2010.
(Bruce Peter collection)

intended to move the route upmarket and the emphasis was to be on dining and relaxation, as well as the more traditional attraction for Swedes of shopping for cheap alcoholic drinks and tobacco products. After a lengthy building process, they entered service as the *Simara Ace* and the *Siluna Ace* during the winter of 2007–2008. Unfortunately, there was insufficient traffic for such capacious 400-passenger vessels and so they were quickly sold to a Dutch company for use as service ships in relation to the offshore energy business.

In 2005–2006, a series of four ro-ro freighters were built to a Knud E. Hansen A/S design by Astilleros de Huelva shipyard in Spain for Seatruck Ferries, a subsidiary of the successful Danish bulk shipping specialist, Clipper Group. The hull form of the *Clipper Point*, *Clipper Pace*, *Clipper Pennant* and *Clipper Panorama* was optimised to maximise the payload within the constraints of the Port of Heysham, the ferries' UK port on their regular Irish Sea service.

The Seatruck ro-ro projects were followed by a contract for Ven Trafiken to provide the basic design of a double-ended ferry for the operator's route to the island of Ven, located between Denmark and Sweden. The vessel was to have been built by Asterillos MCIES Shipyard in Vigo, Spain, which was also building a Knud E. Hansen A/S-designed fishery protection and rescue vessel for operation in the North Sea for the Danish Directorate of Fisheries. Unfortunately, along with a number of other Spanish shipyards, MCIES ran into financial difficulties. The fishery inspection vessel was eventually launched in January 2009 but the Ven ferry project was abandoned and a new contract was signed with the Hvide Sande shipyard in Denmark. The 1,151 gt vessel's steelwork was constructed in Poland and outfitted in Denmark; she entered service in 2012 as the *Uraniborg*.

While carrying out these varied ferry design projects, Knud E. Hansen A/S also provided design assistance to Danish Yacht, a specialist builder of luxury motor yachts, based at Skagen in the North of Jutland, with plans for large and fast yachts, as well as the development of future concept vessels. The yachts are technologically sophisticated, making use of advanced composite materials for their hull constructions.

In December 2006, Knud E. Hansen A/S was sold by Semcon to the Danish private owner Mogens Larsen, whose ML Group specialised in a range of marine-related technologies, including offshore design. A new Knud E. Hansen A/S subsidiary office was opened in London, the first of a number of branch offices to be created over the next five years. By then, Knud E. Hansen A/S had a number of employees with links to Britain and so it was logical to establish a permanent London base, led by the naval architect Christian Bursche, to serve the UK shipping and marine industries.

Immediately prior to this, Stena Line had approached KEH for assistance in lengthening its 2003 South Korean-built ro-pax ferry *Stena Britannica*, at that time operating on the Harwich–Hook of Holland route. The project was ambitious and would for a short time turn the vessel into the largest lane metre capacity ro-pax in the world, with four trailer decks and 4,220 lane metres. Lloyd Werft in Bremerhaven carried out the lengthening and, while it was in progress, Knud E. Hansen A/S' London office team moved there to support the shipyard and coordinate the flow of information. Short lines of communication and fast reaction times were key factors in the project's successful outcome. The *Stena Britannica* was delivered back to Stena after just 49 days' intensive work.

Two years thereafter, Stena again approached KEH to add even more accommodation to the vessel and, at the same time, her interiors were partially refurbished by Stena's regular architects, Figura. During this conversion, new cabin suites with outdoor Jacuzzis and garden lawns were added on the topmost deck and the vessel was renamed *Stena Scandinavica* for operation between Gothenburg and Kiel.

In 2007, A.P. Møller-Mærsk approached Knud E. Hansen A/S to investigate the possibility of lengthening of their year-old South Korean-built Dover–Dunkerque ro-pax ferries *Maersk Dunkerque*, *Maersk Delft* and *Maersk Dover*. They also requested designs for lengthening a series of car carriers (PCTCs). While the ferries remained unaltered, in 2011, however, Höegh Autoliners purchased the car carriers and went ahead with their lengthening, engaging KEH to develop and finalise the design work before the project was executed in China.

Another long-standing customer of Knud E. Hansen A/S to return was Anek Lines, who wanted to convert the 1998-built Japanese Blue Highway Line ro-pax ferry *Sunflower Tsukuba* as a flagship vessel for its principal route to Crete from Piraeus to Chania to offer a similar standard of accommodation to the purpose-built *Olympic Champion* and *Hellenic Spirit*. At Perama, an extensive new superstructure was added and even a new parabola-shaped funnel was fitted. Renamed the *Elyros*, she entered service in August 2008. So thorough was the rebuilding work that, unless one knew of her Japanese origins, it would be difficult to imagine that she was anything other than a brand new ship.

The area around Piraeus is one of the world's ship-owning hubs with numerous shipping-related offices overlooking the Great Harbour and repair yards stretching far to the west. To be at the heart of the action in the Mediterranean's shipping scene, in 2009 Knud E. Hansen A/S opened a Piraeus office.

The move to Helsingør

With so many projects in progress, one problem faced by Knud E. Hansen A/S was a lack of space in its Copenhagen head office at Islands Brygge. The solution to this was a radical one – to move out of the city centre for the first time since the company was established. Having examined a

The *Stena Freighter* is seen approaching Kiel. (Bruce Peter collection)

A stern-quarter view of the *Stena Freighter* manoeuvring off her berth in Gothenburg. (Bruce Peter collection)

Above: The launching of the tanker *Inge Wonsild* at the Sekawan Heavy industries shipyard. (Henning Loesch collection)

Right: A stern-quarter view of the *Marianne Wonsild*. (Henning Loesch collection)

variety of possible solutions, Finn Wollesen and his colleagues decided that the best option was to move north to new premises in Helsingør, the town in which Knud E. Hansen himself had worked at the local shipyard nearly 80 years previously. For customers visiting from overseas, Helsingør is only a short direct train journey away from Copenhagen Airport.

In late-2008, Knud E. Hansen A/S acquired an elegant neo-classically-styled former naval hospital, known as Lundegården, which is located close to Kronborg Castle. The building has been carefully renovated to reflect the maritime traditions it shares with its new owners. As well as providing a spacious new headquarters for Knud E. Hansen A/S, it also includes office space for other tenants who appreciate the building's history and unique location. A vast removal operation from Islands Brygge to Helsingør then took place in June 2009, during which the company's 72-year archive of plans and correspondence was shifted north and carefully re-shelved in the basement at Lundegården. On the floors above, however, nearly everything was new with spacious, comfortable offices to engender the best possible working environment and with sufficient room for future expansion. Certainly, the clean computer-based working environment is very different from the original offices in Bredegade, which were filled with drawing boards and piles of paperwork and in which nearly everyone smoked at their desks. It is also far superior to the slightly cramped conditions at the subsequent Islands Brygge office, modern and well equipped though it was.

Among the final projects undertaken at Islands Brygge prior to the move north was a major upgrading for Stena Line's 1983-built Kattegat ferry *Stena Danica*, including the building of a new aft body featuring a larger ducktail sponson and a new keel tank to increase its buoyancy in line with the forthcoming SOLAS (Safety of Life At Sea) 2010 convention. Lloyd Werft also carried out this rebuilding.

Subsequent conversions for Stena included the *Superfast VII* and *Superfast VIII*, which were chartered by Stena Line for use on a new Cairnryan–Belfast service across the Northern Irish Sea. To enable the carriage of taller lorry trailers (known as 'hi cubes'), the free height in the main vehicle deck was increased by cutting into the structural framing above. Extra vertical stiffening was then inserted between the vehicle lanes to compensate for this. On the passenger decks, meanwhile, partitions and casings were removed to open up the public rooms across the full width of the each vessel's superstructure. Cabin blocks were dismantled and Figura designed new interiors, suitable for short-haul daytime service. The alterations were carried out in Poland, after which the ferries entered Irish Sea service in late-2011 as the *Stena Superfast VII* and *Stena Superfast VIII*.

The lower hull of the *Tor Selandia* takes shape in Fincantieri's shipyard at Ancona.
(Bruce Peter collection)

Above: The *Tor Selandia* executes a tight turn during trials prior to entry into service. (Bruce Peter collection)

Below: The *Tor Selandia* is seen leaving Gothenburg. (Bruce Peter collection)

Above: The ACE-Link passenger ferry *Siluna Ace* at Helsingør. (Bruce Peter collection)

Left: The *Siluna Ace* and the *Simara Ace* at Helsingborg. (Bruce Peter collection)

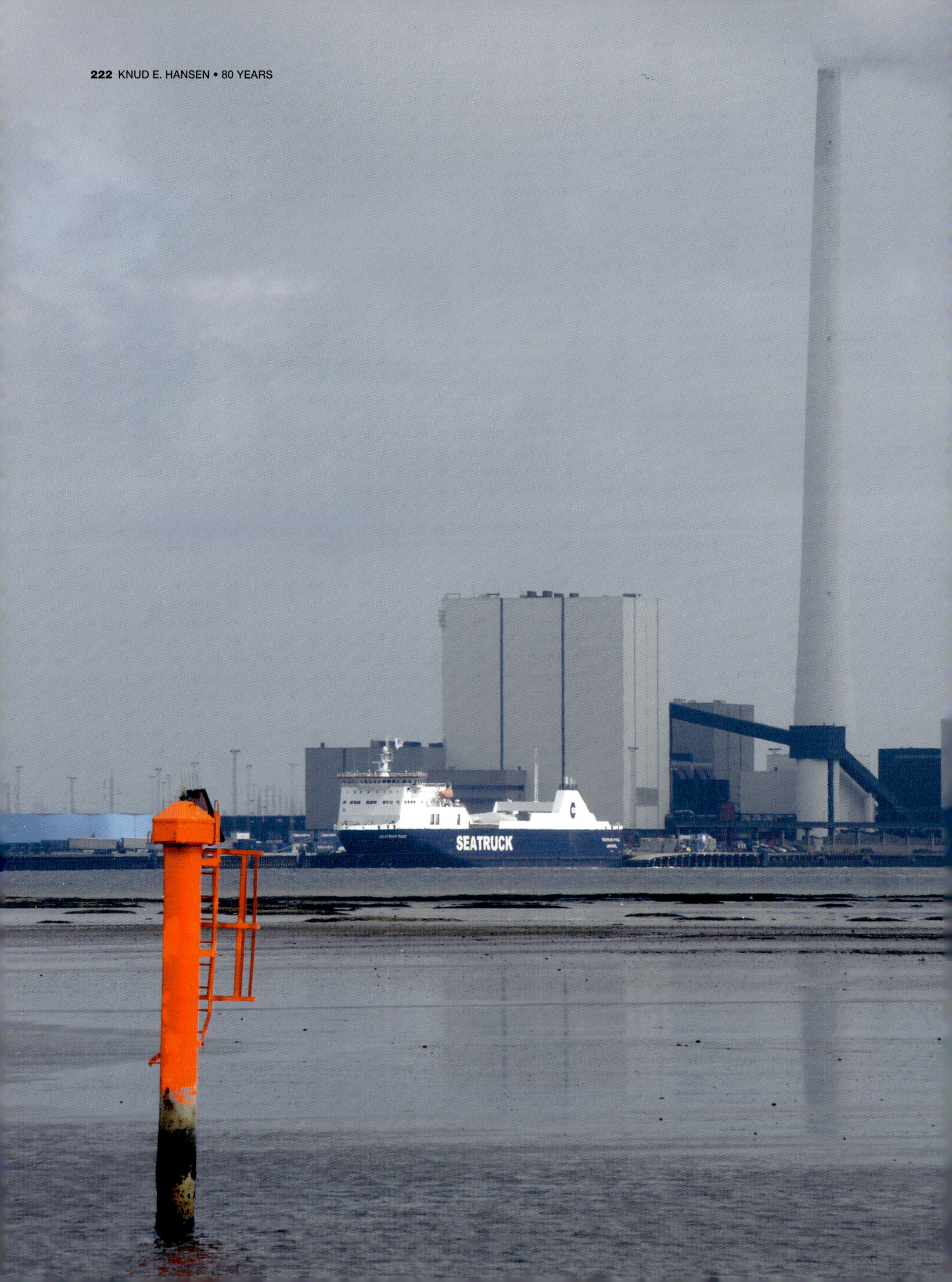
SEATRUCK

The new Blue Stars

In early 2002, Blue Star Ferries had pioneered a new generation of Greek domestic ferry, designed by Deltamarin in Finland and built by Daewoo Shipbuilding and Engineering in South Korea. The *Blue Star Ithaki*, *Blue Star Paros* and *Blue Star Naxos* were to have been followed by a further pair constructed by Hellenic Shipyards in Greece, but severe delays eventually led to Blue Star Ferries abandoning these vessels, the hulls of which were completed for Hellenic Seaways. Once Blue Star Ferries was taken over by the Attica Group, in 2003 Holger Terpet and Costis Stamboulelis began work to design the vessels which eventually materialised in 2011–2012 as the 18,498 gt *Blue Star Delos* and *Blue Star Patmos* – each nearly twice the size of the earlier series. The contract for their construction was delayed because of state legislation regarding domestic ferry services and by the sale of Attica Group by Pericles Panagopoulos in 2007. By the time the project was revived, Holger Terpet unfortunately had died. Stamboulelis observes that his passing 'was a great loss for Knud E. Hansen and most certainly for me.' Thereafter, Stamboulelis worked with Christian Bursche, who progressed the scheme into the basic design phase and assisted with the shipyard evaluations.

Eventually, two vessels were ordered from Daewoo Shipbuilding and Engineering. Measuring 18,498 gt, the new *Blue Star Delos* and *Blue Star Patmos* are notably capacious, even in comparison with the earlier Deltamarin-designed trio for the same operator. In a hull measuring only 145.9 by 23.2 metres, they can carry 427 cars, or a combination of cars and trucks. This is achieved by there being no fewer than five car decks, the lowest two of which are ahead of the engine room, with a main vehicle deck above in which additional platform decks can be lowered with further car capacity in the aft two-thirds on Deck 5 above. Higher still, two entire decks are given over to very comfortable passenger facilities accommodating up to 2,400 in summer, designed by Molindris & Associates. There are also extensive sheltered outdoor deck spaces, features sadly lacking on the fast catamarans with which they compete.

Four MAN B&W diesels generate 32,000 kW of power, enabling 26 knots to be maintained and so the *Blue Star Delos* is able to reach Santorini from Piraeus in just over eight hours, with three stops en route, meaning that a daily return circuit can be scheduled. So far as passengers are concerned, the speed advantage of a fast catamaran is marginal, but the operational cost is far higher and so Blue Star Ferries should be well positioned to gain additional market share.

The *Blue Star Patmos* operates from Piraeus to Chios and Mythilene on Lesvos, a longer route requiring more cabins and dining facilities for overnight voyages, but less lounge space. Thus, although externally she is nearly identical to the *Blue Star Delos*, her interior layout is slightly different. Externally and within, the two ferries are of outstanding quality and represent the best of modern ferry design.

The offshore energy sector

Knud E. Hansen A/S sought to increase its presence as a designer of specialist vessels for the offshore energy market. This has involved recruitment, training and the purchase of specialist software. As new wind farms were planned around Northern Europe's exposed coastal fringes, a variety of unprecedented ship types came to be required, some capable of transporting wind turbine components to installation sites, others able to install the turbines and, additionally, accommodation ships to house workers involved in installation projects.

Kicking off this new area of development, in 2001, Knud E. Hansen A/S produced a highly innovative design for the world's first ever self-elevating offshore wind turbine installation vessel, the *MPI Resolution*. Built for Mayflower Energy by the Shanhaiguan Shipyard at Chenwei in China and delivered in 2004, the vessel carries the parts of turbines to the installation site, where it transforms into an elevated construction platform with six legs lowered to the seabed and the hull jacked up on these.

Three years thereafter, a Danish company, Blue Ocean A/S, approached Knud E. Hansen A/S, seeking a design for a much larger turbine installation vessel as, in the interim, turbines had increased in size. Shortly, Blue Ocean A/S was taken over by the Hong Kong-based Swire Group and they placed an order for Knud E. Hansen A/S' design with Samsung Heavy Industries' Geoje shipyard in South Korea, who completed the vessel in 2012 as the *Pacific Orca*. Her 1,200 ton capacity stern-mounted crane can lift turbines and blades to the top of 120 metre-high towers and, operating in 'ship' mode, her four bow thrusters and dynamic positioning system enable very precise manoeuvrability. Using a high-speed jacking system, the vessel's hull can be lifted 22 metres above the water, meaning that it is above even the highest waves, and can work at depths of up to 75 metres. This exceeds current and planned wind farm water depths, anticipating the needs of future installations and opening up countless possibilities for wind farm locations. A space saving innovation has been achieved by integrating the craft's main crane into the housing for one of her jack-up legs.

Opposite: The freight ferry *Clipper Pace* is seen berthed in Esbjerg. (Bruce Peter collection)

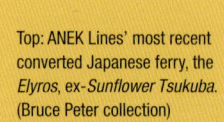

Top: ANEK Lines' most recent converted Japanese ferry, the *Elyros*, ex-*Sunflower Tsukuba*. (Bruce Peter collection)

Above: The *Uraniaborg* crosses passes pleasure craft while crossing from Landskrona to Ven. (Bruce Peter collection)

Right: The little ferry *Uraniaborg* serves the island of Ven. (Bruce Peter collection)

Meanwhile, the Danish bunkering company Mojasa set up a new subsidiary called C-Bed to purchase, convert and operate old ferries as floating accommodation ships for workers engaged in the offshore wind energy industry. Between 2008 and 2012, Knud E. Hansen A/S were called upon to advise on how best to convert the former *Prinsessan Christina*, *Prinsessan Birgitta* and *Olau Britannia* into the *Wind Solution*, *Wind Ambition* and *Wind Perfection* (none of these ferries was originally designed by KEH, however.)

Knud E. Hansen A/S also secured an ongoing contract, involving it in the Anholt Offshore Wind Farm project off the Danish coast in the Kattegat, the principal contractor for which is the leading Danish construction company MT Højgaard A/S. KEH participation covered a wide spectrum of projects, such as converting cargo vessels to carry wind turbine components and to interface with the floating crane *Svanen*. A novel device was designed to support a monopole (wind turbine tower) in the horizontal position but which can swivel to vertical as the crane lifts the monopole, while still providing it with adequate support. Other Green design projects included work with Floating Power Plant A/S to design a wave energy platform which also supports wind turbines and a project with DK Group to help develop their patented air bubble system which uses a cushion of air bubbles to reduce the resistance of ships' hulls in water.

In the oil energy sector, Knud E. Hansen A/S designed the *Technip*, a pipe installation vessel for the offshore oil industry, built by STX in South Korea and capable both of laying rigid steel pipes and flexible pipes on 2,800-ton reels. A design was also produced for a Shallow Water Oil Recovery Vessel (Sworc) with a catamaran hull which could be packed into a standard shipping container for fast dispatch by air, road and sea to oil spill locations.

In 2010, Knud E. Hansen A/S added two further branch offices, one at Fort Lauderdale in Florida and the other in Perth, Australia. The opening of the Perth office coincided with a contract to provide on-site supervision at the fast ferry builder Austal for the Clipper Group's new Bornholm catamaran, *Leonora Christina*. A further office was then added in Tórshavn in the Faroe Islands.

The Shallow Water Oil Recovery Vessel (Sworc) vessel. (KNUD E. HANSEN Archive)

Knud E. Hansen A/S' Head Office at Lundegaarden in Helsingør. (Bruce Peter collection)

226 KNUD E. HANSEN • 80 YEARS

The *Blue Star Patmos* is pictured at her berth in Piraeus. (Bruce Peter collection)

The *Blue Star Delos* off the island of Syros. (Bruce Peter collection)

Left: The hallway on the *Blue Star Patmos*; the exceptionally well-detailed interiors are by the Greek firm of Molindris & Associates. (Bruce Peter collection)

Below: The *Blue Star Patmos*' restaurant. (Bruce Peter collection)

228 KNUD E. HANSEN • 80 YEARS

Left: The cafeteria on the *Blue Star Patmos*. (Bruce Peter collection)

Above: The Goody's fast food outlet on the *Blue Star Delos*. (Bruce Peter collection)

Below: A stern-quarter view of the *Blue Star Delos* off Piraeus. (Bruce Peter collection)

KNUD E. HANSEN • 80 YEARS **229**

Left and below: The *MPI Resolution* sailing and with her hull jacked up to install wind turbines. (VROON)

The remarkable offshore wind turbine installation vessel *Pacific Orca*. (KNUD E. HANSEN Archive)

The Wollesen era

The Atlantic Container Line G4-type con-ro vessel *Atlantic Sail*. (Philippe Holthof)

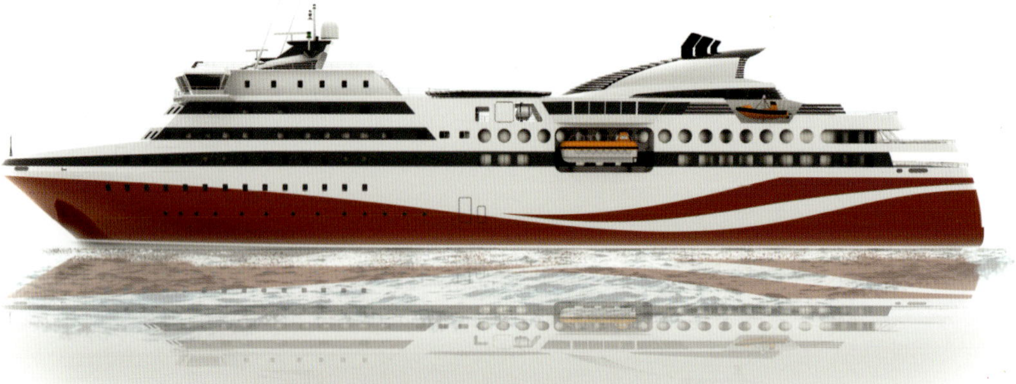

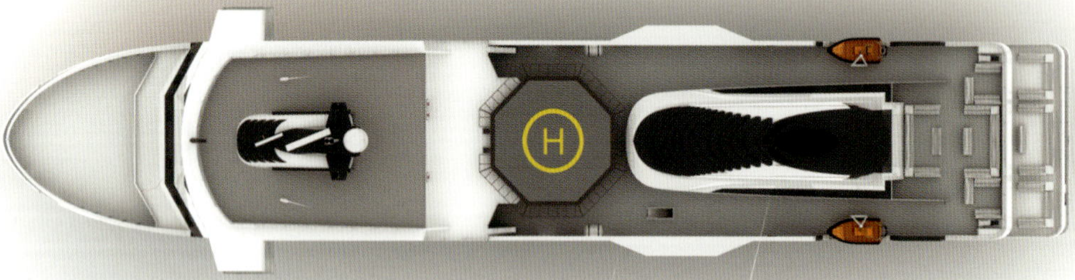

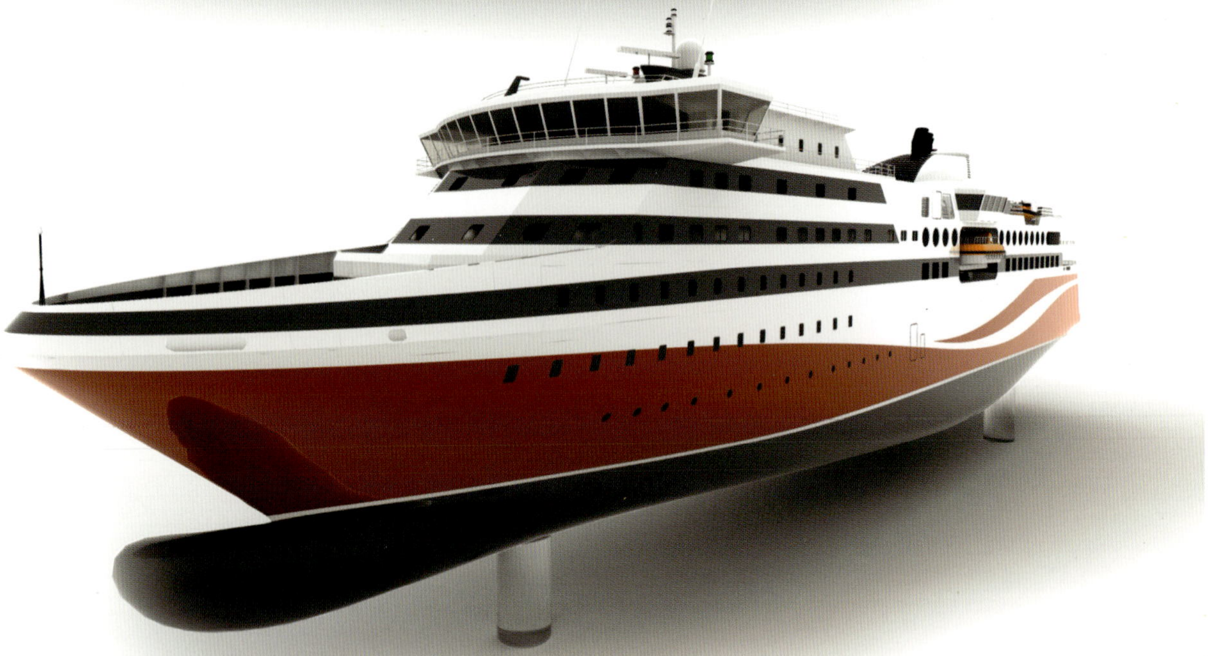

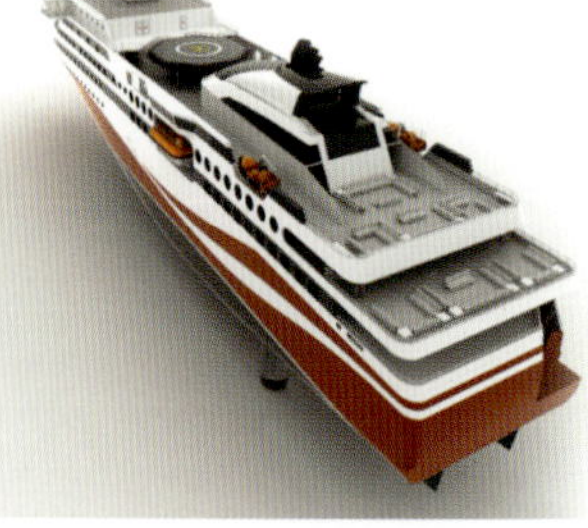

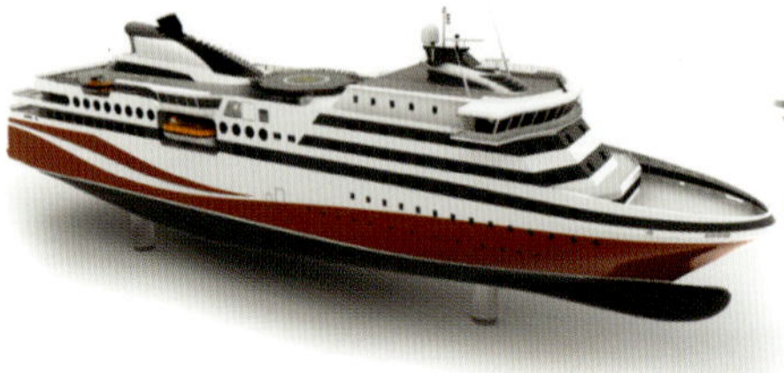

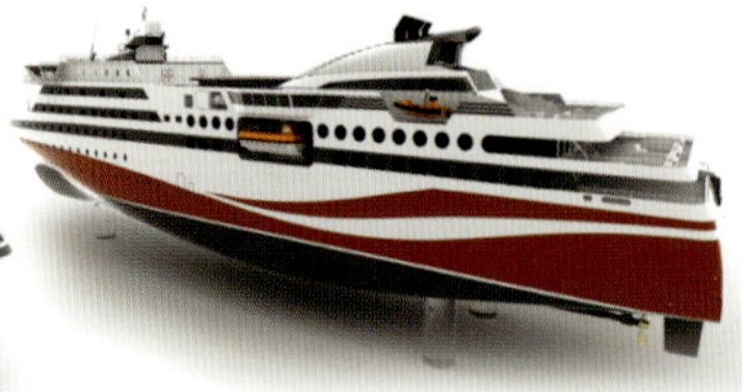

In the autumn of 2012, KNUD E. HANSEN's ownership status changed once again. When KNUD E. HANSEN's management realised that its owner, ML Group, was experiencing financial difficulties, they began searching for a new owner with whom to build a strong mutually beneficial relationship to enable a secure long-term future. An ideal partner emerged in the Dutch-headquartered global shipbuilding and engineering group, Damen. A family-owned company, established in 1927, Damen has over 40 shipbuilding and ship repair facilities around the world, building specialist commercial and military vessels of many kinds. To bring KNUD E. HANSEN – with its diverse naval architecture, HVAC and design expertise – into the Damen group would clearly be highly advantageous. Yet, a high degree of autonomy was also to be maintained so that KNUD E: HANSEN could continue as a unique brand serving its usual broad portfolio of clients, acting almost entirely independently of the new parent owner. As Managing Director, Finn Wollesen, put it, the take-over was a happy instance of 'Dutch and Danes united.'

In the past five years, KNUD E. HANSEN has designed a wide variety of outstanding merchant ships of many types and has also supplied designs of HVAC systems for numerous assorted vessels with an emphasis on cruise ships. Reflecting international trends for global companies to consider the perceptions of potential clients around the world, in 2015, KNUD E. HANSEN updated its image with a subtly modernised logo and the loss of the suffix 'A/S' (the Danish shortened form of 'aktie-selskabet', or 'shareholder company') – a term not widely understood by non-Danes.

The company has continued to design new examples of the ship type for which it was most famous – ferries. In 2010–2011, the firm designed two 80-metre-long ice-strengthened ferries for year-round operation to Fogo Island off the coast of Newfoundland and Change Island in Labrador. Named the *Veteran* and *Legionnaire*, they were built in Romania by the Dutch-owned Damen shipyard at Galati. Each can carry 200 passengers and 64 cars entered service in 2015 and 2016 respectively.

While that project was underway, in June 2011, a further contract was won from the Government of Newfoundland and Labrador to provide a basic design of a series of six ferries for operation on the south coast routes off Newfoundland. The south coast ferries were developed in close collaboration with the Canadian engineering and logistics company, Fleetway Inc., and the Government of Newfoundland and Labrador to ensure that the vessels could cope with the harsh Canadian climate to provide reliable lifeline services throughout the year.

Measuring 41 metres in length, each has a 36-passenger capacity with a multi-use cargo deck and a service speed of 12 knots. The south shore vessels are expected to be built locally in Newfoundland and Labrador, benefiting the communities that will also use them. The vessels utilise green technology and carry a number of additional class notations reflecting this.

KNUD E. HANSEN also designed a new a hybrid diesel-electric/battery-powered small ferry measuring 675 gt and capable of transporting 170 passengers plus 12 cars for the Faroese ferry operator Strandfaraskip Landsins' service between Nólsoy and Tórshavn. Designed to withstand treacherous conditions, she will have a double hull and be able to withstand water on deck with a significant wave height of three metres. Battery power and a waste-heat recovery system will spare enough energy to enable return trips to be made using electricity alone.

Building on its good relationships with Chinese shipbuilders, in 2013 KNUD E. HANSEN was commissioned by the Bo-Hai shipyard – the parent company of which also owns a ferry-operating company – to design a new ferry for its route from Qinglan Port near Wenchang City to Sansha on Yongxing Island. The 7,800 gt, 456-passenger *San Sha 1 Hao* was designed and built in just 24 months and is arguably the first purpose-built 'cruise ferry' to be constructed and operated in China. 350 lane metres of cars and freight can be loaded via a quarter ramp on the starboard side. Passenger facilities include an Internet café, a cigar bar, library and conference rooms, cinema, VIP dining area and a 200-seat cafeteria. The ship is also equipped with a helicopter landing platform, which makes it convenient for maritime rescue and island patrolling. Powered by a single diesel engine, her service speed is 19 knots. The vessel's silhouette and interiors were designed by Francesca Arini, KNUD E. HANSEN's in-house interior and exterior designer, who joined the company in 2012 having previously worked in the shipping industry in Italy.

Cruise ship conversions

Between November 2011 and March 2012, KNUD E. HANSEN oversaw the refitting of Saga Cruises' newly-acquired *Saga Sapphire*, a vessel originally built in West Germany in 1982 for Hapag-Lloyd as the *Europa*. Saga is a British company, specialising in traditional and comparatively expensive cruises for older people. Before she was purchased by Saga, KNUD E. HANSEN evaluated the vessel for structural integrity, stability, safety and fire protection. Thereafter, her upper decks were substantially altered with the installation of new cabins with balconies, new restaurant layouts and installation of elevators to allow disabled people to access all areas of the vessel. The refit was carried out by the Fincantieri shipyard at Palermo in Italy.

In 2015, KNUD E. HANSEN designed a radical conversion for the Norwegian coastal cruise operator Hurtigruten of a Portuguese ferry, the *Atlantida*, which had been built by the Estaleiros Navais de Viano do

Opposite: 3D renderings for the Chinese ferry *San Sha 1 Hao*. (KNUD E. HANSEN Archive)

234 KNUD E. HANSEN • 80 YEARS

Right: The launching of the Canadian coastal ferry *Veteran* at the Damen shipyard at Galati in Romania. (KNUD E. HANSEN Archive)

Below: An aerial view showing the *Veteran* as she appeared upon delivery. (KNUD E. HANSEN Archive)

Bottom: The completed *San Sha 1 Hao*. (KNUD E. HANSEN Archive)

The Hurtigruten coastal passenger ship *Spitzbergen*. (KNUD E. HANSEN Archive)

Costelo shipyard in 2009 for operation in the Azores but had been rejected due to being overweight, meaning that her intended payload could not have been carried. Having languished for seven years, Hurtigruten realised her potential for conversion as an exploration cruise ship and the complex project was carried out by the Fosen Shipyard in Norway. The two car decks were converted as cabins and a storage area for zodiacs. Cabins with balconies are were added to the aft superstructure and the public rooms were redesigned with the addition of a sauna and gym complex. The vessel entered service in 2016 as the *Spitzbergen*.

The need to save fuel has become a vital issue for the cruise industry for reasons of economy and environmental sustainability. For this reason, KNUD E. HANSEN has developed special skills to evaluate possible energy saving measures for operators to implement in their newbuilding or to retrofit them on their existing vessels. A major energy optimisation project has recently been carried out on behalf of Carnival Cruise Line.

Con-ro vessels

Deep sea con-ro (combined container and ro-ro) vessels were built in large numbers in the 1970s and 80s, but in the period since, fewer were constructed and it was more typical that pure container vessels were built for 'long-haul' international liner operations. Due to their inherent flexibility, con-ro ships remained useful, but most were ageing and badly needed replacement with more modern, reliable and efficient examples.

In 2010, KNUD E. HANSEN's naval architect Christian Damsgaard led a team to design a new con-ro vessel type for the National Shipping Company of Saudi Arabia (BAHRI)'s service from Arabian Gulf ports to the East Coast of North America. KEH also assisted BAHRI in the contract phase by providing technical expertise and advice. In March 2011, six such vessels were ordered from the Hyundai Mipo shipyard in South Korea.

Measuring 50,714 gt, they had dedicated space for 364 containers plus 24,800 square metres of vehicle deck space for ro-ro freight on three main levels with additional hoistable decks, dimensioned for the transport of American-manufactured trucks and sports utility vehicles. (Alternatively containers can be stowed double-stacked on the main internal decks, giving a total capacity of 2,025 TEU). The vessels are also designed to operate as military transports in time of war and therefore are fitted with two 120-tonne capacity cranes. Main vehicle deck access is via a stern-quarter ramp while, towards the bow, a well-deck enables special project cargoes, mainly for the oil industry, to be stowed. The design also can accommodate aluminium, which is transported from Qatar to Houston and Savannah for industrial use.

The advanced single-skeg hull form has relatively fine lines while still giving sufficient deadweight capacity and, unusually, is double-skinned up to Deck 4, enhancing survivability in the event of collision and avoiding a need for transverse bulkheads across the vehicle decks. A single 6-cylinder Wärtsilä main engine provides a 17-knot service speed. The first vessel, named the *Bahri Abha*, entered service in 2013.

Subsequently, the French operator Compagnie Maritime Nantaise (CMN) ordered two KEH-designed con-ro vessels of their own from Hyundai with an option for a third unit. Their design – which was co-ordinated by KEH's London-based naval architect, Christian Bursche – is different from the Saudi Arabian examples and resulted from close work over the past year with CMN. A number of options were studied taking into consideration constraints of the operating areas, including the size limitations of port facilities. The main deck is loaded via a stern and a quarter ramp and so the layout has been

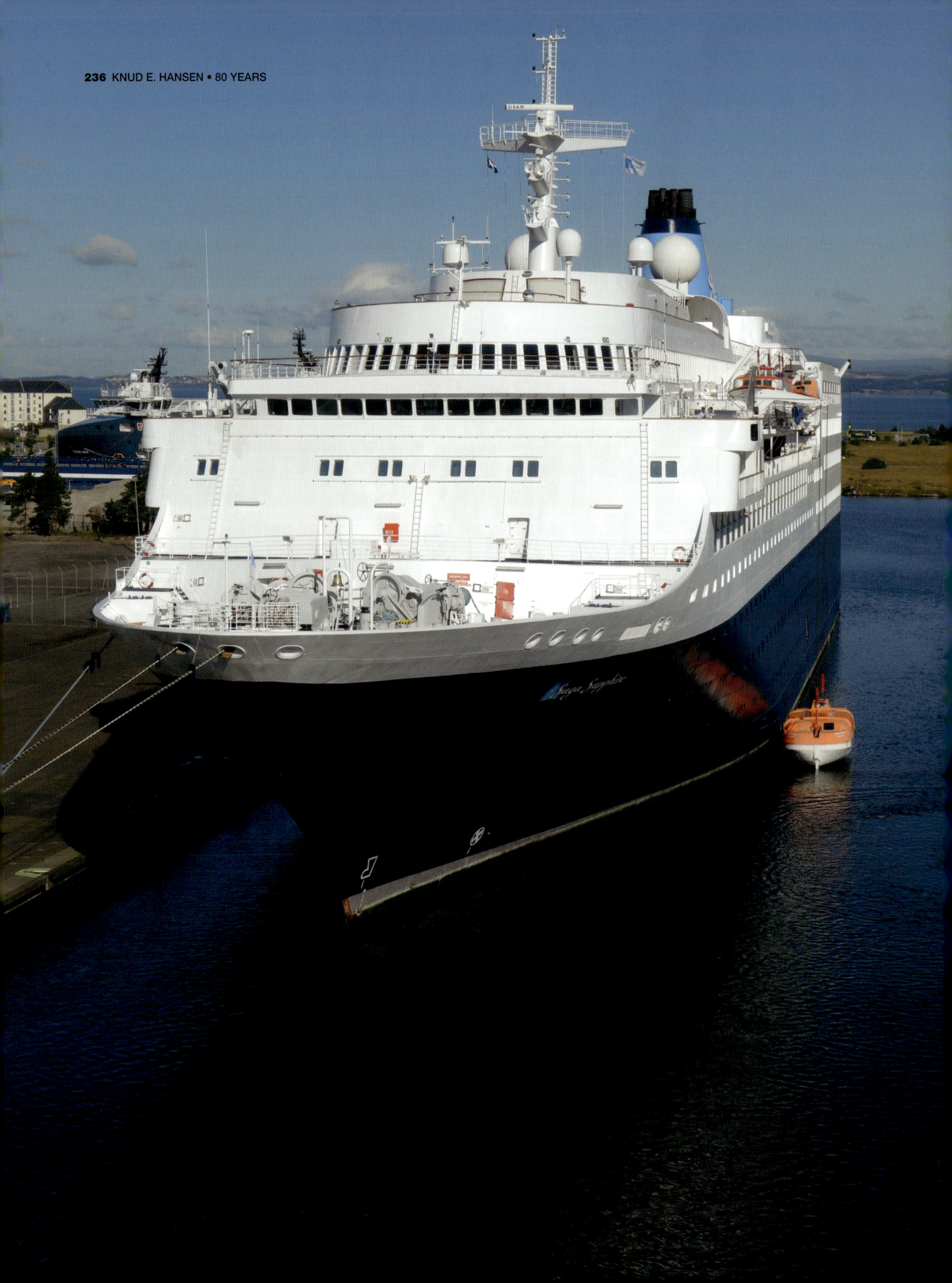
Saga Sapphire

optimised to ensure a steady cargo flow to and from all decks even when using this, as well as enabling controlled shifting of cargo between the decks while at sea. In addition, the internal ramps to the upper deck have been carefully designed and located to make the most effective use of such space as is available. This has been essential in order to achieve the specified cargo uptake within the specified main dimensions. A unique feature is the flush deck hatches on the weather deck, enabling loading and unloading of containers directly onto the main deck, independent of the ramps.

A major project for KNUD E. HANSEN from 2011 onwards was to design and oversee the construction of a new generation of con-ro vessel for trans-Atlantic service, based upon a concept devised in 2008 by one of its retired naval architects. In the past, a major drawback of con-ro tonnage had been the low cargo density and consequently lighter weight of their ro-ro freight decks versus the heavy and dense top-weight of stacked containers carried as deck cargo. This necessitated considerable ballasting but nonetheless the number of layers of containers was limited. The entire forward half of the hull was configured like a conventional large container ship with cells reaching all the way down to the bottom. The ro-ro space occupied the hull aft of amidships and the superstructure above, with more container accommodation above and adjacent towards the stern. Without large ballast water tanks, the space utilisation was much enhanced.

The design proposal intrigued Atlantic Container Line and its parent company, Grimaldi – a major Italian owned international liner and ferry company, which needed to replace ACL's ageing existing tonnage, dating as it did from the mid-1980s. The only problem was finding a shipyard capable of translating the outline plan into a buildable vessel and then constructing it for an acceptable price. Having spent three years investigating potential options, in 2011 ACL and Grimaldi held discussions with the Hudong Zhonghua Shipyard in China at Changxing Island near Shanghai. In common with most Chinese shipyards, it had no in-house design department and so it commissioned KNUD E. HANSEN to produce a contract design with the intention of winning orders to build the new class of vessels. When the yard succeeded, it again employed KNUD E. HANSEN to develop a basic design. Among other content, this consisted of general arrangement and class drawings, hull structural design and lines plan, engine room arrangement, HVAC, electrical and automation design, CFD and model test assistance, intact and damaged stability and noise and vibration analysis; the steel construction drawings were, however, the shipyard's responsibility. Engineers from Hudong Zhonghua worked in KNUD E. HANSEN's office in Helsingør, where the naval architects Niels Georg Larsen, Christian Damsgaard and Brian Madsen managed the project, which involved between 15 and 30 other employees. The development process also involved ACL's technical staff, based in Gothenburg. ACL and Grimaldi found the KEH/ Hudong Zhonghua offer acceptable and a contract was signed in 2012 for five vessels to replace entirely the existing ACL fleet.

The design, known as 'G4' (i.e. the fourth generation of vessel for ACL) was intended to cope with extreme weather conditions, having a large breakwater at the bow to protect the forward container stacks, massive cell guides to provide structural rigidity. As the containers are not lashed, these guides needed to withstand horizontal forces exerted by the containers and so large triangular stiffeners were added on either side along the length of the upper hull. These structures were partly responsible for the vessels being measured at a mighty 100,430 gt (without them, they would otherwise have been only around 79,000 gt). Containers are stowed 13 across and 14 deep, giving a total capacity of 2,230 TEU. Ro-ro cargo can be stowed on six fixed decks with one fixed car deck and four levels of hoistable decks, accessed via a massive stern-quarter ramp; the upper levels are accessed via dog-leg ramps. Designing the junction between the container-carrying fore-body – effectively an 'open shoe box' tending to experience torsional flexing – and the ro-ro aft body, with its rigid horizontal elements, proved a major challenge. Two decks of crew accommodation are atop the superstructure; although 47 cabins are provided, under normal circumstances, a crew of below 20 is required. They height of the superstructure was circumscribed by a need to fit beneath the 43-metre-high Bayonne Bridge in New York.

During the design process, KNUD E. HANSEN's naval architects made several improvements to the complex layout of the aft body and ro-ro decks, removing unnecessary pillars and freeing up space for smoother cargo circulation. Extensive model tests were carried out jointly with the builder to confirm performance predictions. To maintain the best possible service speed in North Atlantic conditions, a vertical-stemmed bow without a bulb was chosen as this allowed for optimal performance at a wider range of load and weather conditions and drafts than a bow with a bulb would have done and, having less flare, also reduced slamming in head-seas. The stern has a trim wedge, extending beyond the transom. For optimal fuel economy, a remarkably compact single Wärtsilä 8RTflex 68-D main engine, generating 22,000 kW and driving a fixed-blade propeller was installed, as was a shaft generator to power onboard services (avoiding any need for auxiliary diesels). The exhaust is fitted with an Alfa Laval scrubber to remove sulphur dioxide emissions.

The *Atlantic Star*, *Atlantic Sail* and *Atlantic Sea* entered service in 2015, followed by the *Atlantic Sky* and *Atlantic Sun* in 2016. These vessels have been widely admired in the naval architecture and liner

Opposite: The cruise ship Saga Sapphire. (Bruce Peter collection)

238 KNUD E. HANSEN • 80 YEARS

Right: A 3D rendering of the Saudi Arabian con-ro vessels built in South Korea. (KNUD E. HANSEN Archive)

Below: An aerial view showing the first completed example of the type, the *Bahri Abha*, at sea. (KNUD E. HANSEN Archive)

shipping communities, their sophisticated yet highly flexible and efficient design representing a great advance over any existing con-ro tonnage.

Yet another contract from China was received in 2016 when the long-established Danish ferry operator DFDS announced plans to build a pair of unprecedently large 6,700 lane metre North Sea freight ferries at the Jingling Shipyard at Yizheng, near Nanjing on the Yangtse River. As with the ACL G4 series, the initial design for these vessels, supplied to DFDS for contract negotiation purposes, was by a different Danish firm of naval architects and KNUD E. HANSEN was employed by the shipyard to refine and optimise this, translating it into a basic design that could actually be built. Nowadays, designs for vessels of this type for operation in European waters must reflect so-called 'Energy Efficiency Design Index' (or 'EEDI') standards, meaning a strong focus on structural solutions and hydrodynamic capabilities. Thanks to their economy-of-scale capacity and optimised design, they will reduce energy consumption by 25% in comparison with DFDS' existing vessels. In June 2017, DFDS announced orders for a further pair of the type, taking the total contracted so far to four. The first pair are scheduled to enter service in 2019 with the second following in 2020.

Other specialised vessels

Apart from the traditional specialisms of ferries, cruise ships, con-ro and ro-ro vessels, in recent time, KNUD E. HANSEN have designed a very broad variety of diverse vessel types. In 2014, a conversion plan was produced to transform a feeder container ship, the 24,344 gt *Guanabara*, built in 1990 at Ulsan in South Korea, into a livestock carrier with space for either 75,000 sheep or 22,000 cattle. The rebuilding work was carried out in Batam in Indonesia and the vessel, renamed the *Awassi Express*, entered service for Corral Line between Australia and Indonesia. The vessel is fitted with sophisticated feeding and ventilation and also systems for processing animal waste. In 2017, another similar project was carried out for the same owner, this time to transform a 2,997 gt feeder container ship, the *TransNjord*, which had been built in 1995 by J.J. Sietas of Hamburg, into the livestock carrier *Alondra*. The steelwork was built by Nauta Ship Repair of Gdynia in Poland, after which the vessel was towed to Skagen in Denmark where Karstensens Skibsværft outfitted the accommodation. Finn Wollesen observes that the two Corral Line vessels carry more 'passenger' legs than the largest cruise ships and that great care was taken to ensure the wellbeing of their four-legged 'passengers' while in transit.

3D renderings of the new DFDS freight ferries, the detailed design and construction of which KNUD E. HANSEN is supervising in China. (KNUD E. HANSEN Archive)

In 2015, two 24-metre-long private yachts were designed; these share the same hull form, fabricated from steel, but with aluminium superstructures designed by Francesca Arini and customised according to each owner's preferences. Capable of being operated by only two persons, each can accommodate up to 12 persons in luxuriously-appointed surroundings. Most significantly, they are fitted with hybrid propulsion systems, consisting of diesel generators with batteries as an auxiliary power source, meaning that harmful emissions and engine noise can be avoided. When cruising at lower speeds, the hybrid system supports operating with one main engine only while running both propellers. They were built by Holland Jachtbouw in the Netherlands and delivered in 2017.

The first steel is cut in China for DFDS' large ro-ro ferries. (DFDS)

Above: An aerial view of the ACL con-ro vessel *Atlantic Star*. (Atlantic Container Line)

Below: The *Atlantic Star* at Gothenburg; note her vertical bow profile. (Philippe Holthof)

242 KNUD E. HANSEN • 80 YEARS

Right: The massive stern-quarter vehicle access ramp on the *Atlantic Star*. (Philippe Holthof)

Bottom: The massively-constructed container cells on the *Atlantic Star*. (Philippe Holthof)

The vehicle decks inside the *Atlantic Star*'s superstructure with inter-connecting ramps, enabling the stowage of cars and smaller industrial machines or agricultural and commercial vehicles. (Philippe Holthof)

A yacht design KNUD E. HANSEN, combining a 'traditional' exterior with state-of-the-art propulsive technology. (KNUD E. HANSEN Archive)

One of the new yachts is shown upon the completion of structural fabrication and upon completion, immediately prior to launching. (KNUD E. HANSEN Archive)

In 2016, KNUD E. HANSEN designed the 14,950 dwt bitumen tanker *Dania Désgagnes* – the first example of her type to use dual-fuel (either diesel or liquidised natural gas) propulsion, her engine being a Wärtsilä 5RT-flex 50DF type developing 5,450 kW. Built in turkey by the Besiktas Shipyard for use on the St. Lawrence Seaway and Great Lakes in Canada, she is ice-strengthened and to ensure optimal manoeuvrability, she is equipped with a variable pitch propeller, a 750 kW bow thruster, a 550 kW stern thruster and a dynamic positioning system.

Shortly after, a design was produced for a new Antarctic supply research vessel to be operated on behalf of the Australian government by the international public service contract provider, Serco. As with the recent KEH-designed Canadian ferries, the highly complex vessel is being built by the at Damen's Galati shipyard in Romania with project supervision by Damen Schelde Naval Shipbuilding, based at Vlissingen in the Netherlands. The vessel will be 156 metres in length, with a beam of 25.6 metres. She will be able to break ice up 1.65 metres at speeds of 3 knots and will supply Australia's permanent research stations in Antarctica and Macquarie Island with cargo, equipment and personnel. Designed with 500 square metres of on board laboratory and office facilities, she will have a crew of 32 plus up to 116 scientific personnel. The vessel will enter service in 2020 and will be named the *Nuyina*, a name meaning Southern Lights in the Tasmanian Aborigine language. The project has been particularly close to the heart of Finn Wollesen, who as a young man voyaged to the Antarctic on the Danish ice-strengthened cargo vessel *Nella Dan*.

Another recent project has been to assist in developing designs for two types of passenger-cargo ship for Indian domestic service. One pair of these are intended for operation from the Subcontinent to the Andaman and Nicobar Islands, carrying 1,200 passengers plus general cargo. The other pair, with space for 500 passengers are to serve as inter-island ferries. The two projects were developed jointly with an Indian partner, Smart Engineering & Design Solutions (SEDS). KNUD E. HANSEN devised the initial concepts for both vessels and also the basic design for the larger one, while SEDS developed equivalent plans for the smaller. All four will be built at Cochin Shipyard in India and will fly the Indian Flag.

Concept ships

As well as being responsible for designing and co-designing numerous complex ships of many diverse types, recently, KNUD E. HANSEN has also devised several innovative concept ships. These all take into account the need to minimise energy consumption while maximising safety – two of the key criteria for ship designers today.

With the international engineering conglomerate ABB, a project was initiated to develop a highly fuel-efficient 2,000 TEU feeder container vessel. The main dimensions were optimised for calling at Bangkok, reflecting its growing importance as a hub for feeder container ships in the Far East. The design's special characteristics include optimisation for variable service speeds, improved loading flexibility and increased container capacity including a higher than usual reefer capacity (and a commensurately reduced requirement for ballasting). Its greater capacity in combination with the fine hull lines and very efficient propulsion system gives the vessel a fuel economy 15–25% better per TEU than typical existing feeder vessels of similar size.

More recently, KNUD E. HANSEN has produced a design for an expedition cruise vessel for transporting passengers into polar regions; this project comes half a century since the firm designed the world's first polar cruise ship, the *Linblad Explorer*. The design measures 139.4 m by 120.2 m, conforms to Ice Class 1A standards and is suitable for itineraries of up to 21 days with 300 passengers on board. All passenger cabins have outside views, and those on the bridge deck have balconies. Public facilities are concentrated on two decks. Green technology is used to the greatest possible extent. The ship is specifically suited to operate in heavy winds, heavy seas and to ports with narrow entrances. A helicopter deck and aircraft hangar are located on top of the observation lounge and a 'sea garage' is installed within the transom stern section for easy launching and retrieval of watercraft.

Elevation drawings of the two passenger ship types developed for services in Indian territorial waters. (KNUD E. HANSEN Archive)

246 KNUD E. HANSEN • 80 YEARS

This page and opposite: Renderings of the new Australian research ship designed by KNUD E. HANSEN and presently under construction in Romania. (KNUD E. HANSEN Archive)

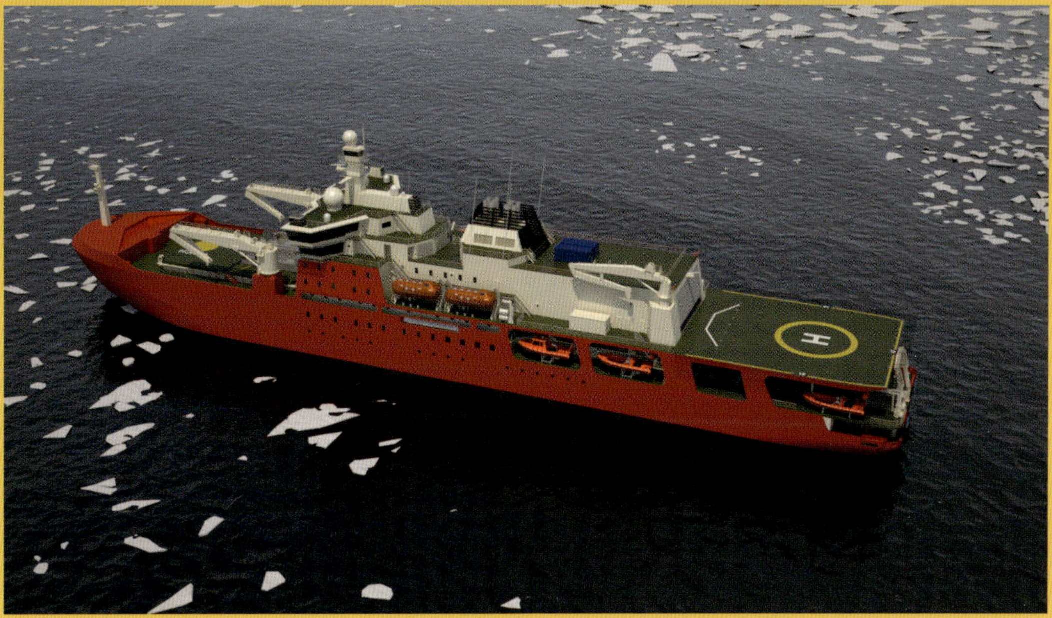

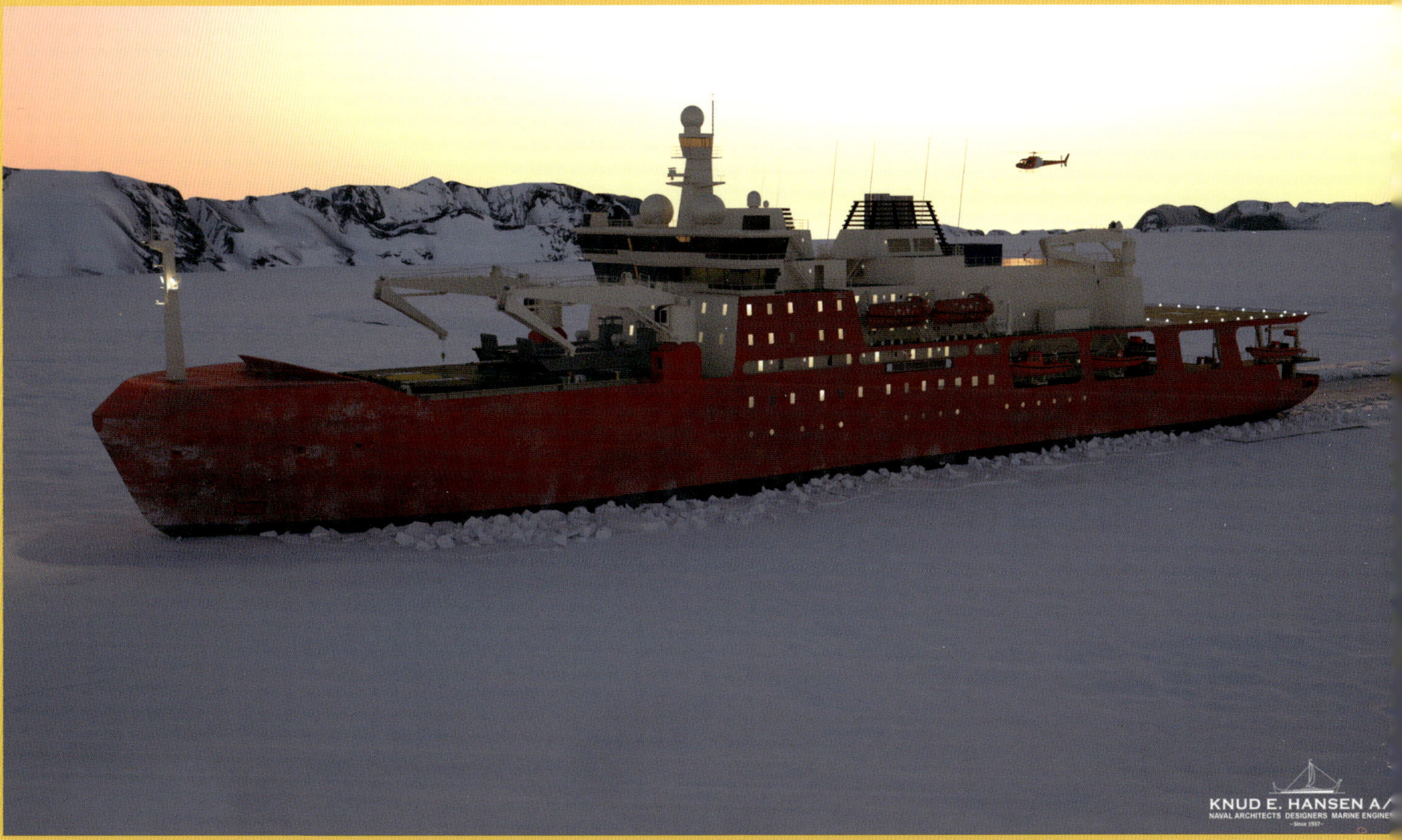
KNUD E. HANSEN A/

Recently, KNUD E. HANSEN have introduced an immersive virtual reality tool, enabling clients to visualise and experience design proposals. (KNUD E. HANSEN Archive)

Another recent speculative project has been the design of a new type of roll-on, roll-off reefer/trailer vessel, which has been developed in close cooperation with Stena Ro-Ro and Reefer Intel for worldwide operation in the banana trade. Able to carry 12,020 HC pallets, just over half on cassettes inside the ship with the remainder in refrigerated containers on the weather deck, special emphasis has been placed on fast and efficient cargo-handling in port. The vessel can operate as an ordinary ro-ro, including for the transportation of specialised project cargo.

For customers of naval architects – just as for those of architects and designers commissioning work on *terra firma*, a challenge is to visualise designs in a convincing way so that clients can see – or even 'experience' what is being proposed. Traditionally, graphic artists were hired to produce renderings and, in more recent time, computer-generated renderings have been employed. Recently, KNUD E. HANSEN has introduced a 3D visualisation tool, whereby employees and clients wear a headset over their eyes, enabling them to immerse themselves in – and explore – virtual shipboard environments. This tool reflects the company's determination to remain at the leading edge of design practices.

With a project portfolio spanning merchant ships of nearly every kind, KNUD E. HANSEN remains a leading global ship design consultancy. Presently, its staff numbers more than 80 with more than 20 nationalities represented, so although the management style may be Danish, many languages are spoken in the office and regular visits by clients from around the world add to the cosmopolitan mix.

Nowadays, KNUD E. HANSEN is structured into five divisions. These are Naval Architecture, employing 11 senior naval architects and four naval architects, Steel and Structure, employing 13 staff, Machinery and Systems with eight staff, Heating, Ventilation and Air Conditioning with 13 staff, Interior/Exterior Design with four staff and a separate USA Division with eight employees. The Interior/Exterior Design department is linked to the Sales and Marketing activities, which includes a Senior Naval Architect who makes concept proposals and a specialist in Virtual Reality who visualises these and other projects. The technology used in this rapidly growing area may be the most up-to-date, but the tradition of paying careful attention to styling dates back to the company's early years when Knud E. Hansen himself and subsequently Tage Wandborg took great care to design ships of harmonious appearance. Nowadays, all activities are overseen by a Director of Operations, who also has overall responsibility for the IT staff and other support services. As Managing Director, Finn Wollesen also takes charge of Sales and Marketing activities. Two employees, the naval architects Ole Olesen and Jesper Kanstrup, have recently celebrated their 40th anniversaries of working for KNUD E. HANSEN. Only nine staff are involved in senior management and support activities, while over 70 are employed to deliver the company's outputs. As with many successful Scandinavian companies, KNUD E. HANSEN exemplifies best practice with regard to so-called 'lean management' approaches. Efficiency not only means value for money for clients but also an attractive work-life balance for employees.

KNUD E. HANSEN's output to date has been a remarkable achievement by any standard of measurement and when one considers the extent to which ship design and construction have been transformed since the 1930s, one cannot begin to imagine how ships will look and be propelled another 80 years from now. During its long history, KNUD E. HANSEN has developed a global client base and its diverse expertise mean that it looks set to prosper for years to come.

A display of recent design awards in the corridor of KNUD E. HANSEN's office in Helsingør. These include ShipPax awards for *Smyril, Atlantic Star, Bahri Abha* and *Spitzbergen*. (KNUD E. HANSEN Archive)

Styling drawings for parts of the superstructure for a super-yacht and for an expedition cruise ship. (KNUD E. HANSEN Archive)

A design for a cruise ship for Celestyal Cruises, intended primarily for Greek island cruising. This and other recent KEH concept ships reflect the design input of Francesca Arini. (KNUD E. HANSEN Archive)

250 KNUD E. HANSEN • 80 YEARS

A design proposal for an expedition cruise ship.
(KNUD E. HANSEN Archive)

A design for a futuristic cruise ferry for Algerie Ferries, demonstrating how KNUD E. HANSEN can provide complete design 'packages', including the interiors. (KNUD E. HANSEN Archive)

Bibliography

Interview with Jens J. Kappel, former Head of Newbuilding, Maersk Line, by Bruce Peter on 28 April 2008.
Interview with Hans Kjærgaard, formerly of Knud E. Hansen A/S, by Bruce Peter in Copenhagen on 5th November 2005.
Interview with Niels Otto Knudsen, former Chief Naval Architect, Nakskov Skibsværft, by Bruce Peter by telephone on 29 January 2011.
Interview with John Kristiansen, formerly Technical Director of DFDS, by Bruce Peter at his home in Værløse, Denmark on 14 August 2012.
Interview with Kai Levander, formerly Project Manager of Wärtsilä Shipbuilders, by Bruce Peter in London on 25th January 2010.
Interview with Eric D. Nilsson, formerly Managing Director and presently Honorary Chairman of Rederi AB Gotland, by Bruce Peter at the ShipPax Conference on 17th May 2008.
Interview with Ole Olesen of Knud E. Hansen A/S at their offices in Helsingør on 13 August 2012.
Interview with Hens Henrik Petersen, formerly of Helsingør Skibsværft, by Bruce Peter by telephone on 15 January 2011.
Interview with Don Ripley, formerly Chief Draughtsman of British Railways' Naval Architecture Department, by Bruce Peter at the home of Ron Cox on 12th May 2002.
Interview with Dag Rogne, formerly of Knud E. Hansen A/S, by Bruce Peter at his home in Hummlebæk, Denmark on 11th October 2005.
Interview with Morten Skrydstrup, Technical Director of Knud E. Hansen A/S, at their offices in Helsingør on 13 August 2012.
Interview with Holger Terpet, formerly of Knud E. Hansen A/S, by Bruce Peter in Copenhagen on 6th November 2005.
Interviews with Tage Wandborg, formerly of Knud E. Hansen A/S, by Bruce Peter at his home in Snekkersten, Denmark on several occasions between 20th February 2000 and 14 August 2012.
Interview with Thomas Wigforss, formerly Tor Line's Project Manager, by Bruce Peter by telephone on 2nd June 1999.
Interview with Finn Wollesen Pedersen, Managing Director of Knud E. Hansen A/S by Bruce Peter at the Shippax Conference in Bastia on 17 May 2008.

Books
Axdal, Mike, Scandinavian Star: Mordbrand med statestøtte, Forlaget Nautilus, Frederiksværk, 2006.
Bakka Jr, Dag, Linjer Rundt Jorden, Seagull, Bergen, 2008.
Bannerman, Gary and Patricia, The Ships of British Columbia, Hancock House Publishers, Surrey BC, 1985.
Bergenek, Anders and Brogren, Klas, Passagerare till Sjöss: Den svenska färjesjöfartens historia, ShipPax, Halmstad, 2006.
Blomgren, Riitta, Malmberg, Thure and Raudsepp, Paul, Ett Skepp Anlöpte Helsingfors, Oy Raud Publishing, Helsinki, 1996.
Bornholmstrafikken 1866–1991, Bornholmstrafikken, Rønne, 1991.
Christensen, Jan Vinther, Den lige linie, Forlaget Nautilus, Frederiksværk, 2001.
Christensen, Jan Vinther, Med færgen fra Grenaa til Hundested, Forlaget Nautilus, Frederiksværk, 2008.
Cooke, Anthony, Liners & Cruise Ships 2: Some more notable smaller vessels, Carmania Press, Greenwich, 2000.
Cooke, Anthony, The Fred. Olsen Line and its Passenger Ships, Carmania Press, Greenwich, 2007.
Corlett, Ewan, The Ship: The Revolution in Merchant Shipping, National Maritime Museum, London, 1981
Cowsill, Miles, By Road Across the Sea: The history of the Atlantic Steam Navigation Company Ltd, Ferry Publications, Kilgetty, 1990.
Dawson, Philip, Cruise Ships: An Evolution in Design, Conway Maritime Press, London, 2000.
Denmark, Royal Danish Ministry of Foreign Affairs, Copenhagen, 1961.
Dumell, Matts, Sjövägen till Sverige, Schildts Forlag, Helsinki, 2007.
Eriksen, Erik, Værftet bag de 1000 skibe: Burmeister & Wain Skibsværft 1843–1993, Burmeister & Wain, Copenhagen, 1993.
Fantasia, Ferry Publications, Staplehurst, 1990.
Greenway, Ambrose, Cargo Liners: An Illustrated History, Seaforth Publishing, Barnsley, 2009.
Haresnape, Brian, Sealink, Ian Allan, London, 1982.
Harvey, W.J. et al, Stena 1939–1989, World Ship Society, London, 1989.
Holck, Jørgen and Simonsen, Jørgen D., Frit hav: Dansk skibsfart i 100 år, Danmarks Rederiforening, Copenhagen, 1984.

Jeppesen, Hans, Andersen, Svend Aage and Johansen, Hans Christian, Dansk Søfarts Historie 7 1960–2000: Containere & koncentration, Gyldendal, Copenhagen, 2000.
Johannesen, Ole Stig, Dansk-Fransk – skibene fra A/S Det Dansk-Franks Dampskibselskab, Editions Maritimes, Roskilde, 2005.
Johannesen, Ole Stig, Mærskbådene II: Skibene i årene 1955–1975, Editions Maritimes, Roskilde, 2007.
Johannesen, Ole Stig, The Torm Ships: The Torm Fleet Through 120 Years, Editions Maritimes, Roskilde, 2009.
Jørgensen, Bent, Helsingør byggede skibe i 100 år: Nybygninger fra værftet i Helsingør 1883–1983 og træk af skibenes og værftets historie, Nofoto Press, Helsingør, 2003.
Koch, Per, Nakskov Skibsværfts Historie: Episoder under teater, Per Kochs Forlag, Nakskov, 2005.
Lange, Ole, Logbog for Lauritzen 1884–1995: Historien om Konsulen, hans sønner og Lauritzen Gruppen, Handelshøjskolens Forlag, Copenhagen, 1995.
MacArthur, Ian C., The Caledonian Steam Packet Co Ltd: An Illustrated History, T. Stephenson & Sons, Prescot, 1971, pp157–158.
Malmberg, Thure and Stampehl, Marko, Femtio år med Silja, Tallink Silja OY, Helsinki, 2007.
Mikkelsen, Bent, Danske Rederier Volume 4: Mercandia, Forlaget Betty Nordgas, Ringkøbing, 2007.
Mikkelsen, Bent, Danske Rederier Volumes 7-8: The Lauritzen Fleet 1884–1945, Forlaget Betty Nordgas, Ringkøbing, 2009.
Olesen, Mogens Nørgaard, Over Storebælt i 1000 år, Lamberth, Copenhagen, 2000.
Olesen, Mogens Nørgaard, Østersøruterne og vejen gennem Danmark, Forlaget Nautilus, Frederiksværk, 2003.
Peter, Bruce, Knud E. Hansen A/S: Ship Design through Seven Decades, Forlaget Nautilus, Copenhagen, 2007.
Plummer, Russell, Superferries of Britain, Europe and Scandinavia, Patrick Stephens Ltd, Wellingborough, 1988.
Rasmussen, Frank A., Vedsted Rønne, Bendt, and Johansen, Hans Christian, Dansk Søfarts Historie, Volume 6: 1920–1960: Damp og Diesel, Gyldendal, 2000.
Ripley, Don and Rogan, Tony, Designing Ships for Sealink, Ferry Publications, Kilgetty, 1995.

Robins, Nick, Ferry Powerful: A History of the Modern British Diesel Ferry, Bernard McCall, Bristol, 2003.
Sjöström, Pär-Henrik, Vägen Över Havet: från pionjärer till marknadsledare, Viking Line and Breakwater Publishing, Gothenburg, 2009.
Taraldsen, Jan Erik, A/S Kristiansands Dampskipsselskap 1899–1999, Jan Erik Taraldsen, Kristiansand, 1999.
Thorsøe, Søren, Simonsen, Peter, Krogh-Andersen, Søren, Frederichsen, Frederik and Vaupel, Henrik, DFDS 1866–1991: Ship Development through 125 Years – from Paddle Steamer to Ro/Ro Ship, World Ship Society and DFDS, Copenhagen, 1991.
Witthöft, Hans Jürgen, Meyer Werft: Innivativer Schiffbau aus Papenburg, Koehlers Verlagsgesellschaft, Hamburg, 2005.

Journals

Architectura
Kjærgaard, Poul, 'Kay Fisker Til Søs, No 15, Copenhagen, 1993.

Arkitektur DK
'Nye DSB færger på Storebælt', April 1981, pp52–61.

Byggekunst
'Seks Skipsarkitekter: Arkitektfirma H.G. Finne & Co A/S', No 4, 1991, pp182–185.

Designs
Clegg, Paul, North Sea Ro-Ro: How It All Began, Designs 87, Marine Trading, Halmstad, 1987, pp28–29.
Dawson, Philip, 'In conversation with Director of Vessel Development, CN Marine, Alex Lawrence,' Designs 87, Marine Trading, Halmstad, 1987, p35–6.
Schilling, D., North Sea Ferries Ltd/Noordzee Veerdiensten BV: From Pioneer to Ferry Tycoon, Designs 87, Marine Trading, Halmstad, 1987, pp35–38.
Dawson, Philip, Robert Tillberg: Reflections on a remarkable career, Designs 04, ShipPax, Halmstad, 2004, pp90–95.
Boonzaier, Jonathan, Becoming BC Ferries, Designs 08, ShipPax, Halmstad, 2008, pp80–84.

DSB Bladet
'En markant færgeprofil', July 1980, pp12–14.

Ferry & Ro-Ro Designs
Onboard Scandinavia, Maritime Trading, Halmstad,1983, p32.

Guide
Reinikainen, Kari, 'Getting There: The ro-pax concept' Guide 96, ShipPax, Halmstad, 1996, pp pp84–88.

Hansa
Thode, H. and Lorenz, O., Passagier- und Trailerschiff 'Freeport' erbaut von der Orenstein-Koppel und Lübecker Maschinenbau AG für die Freeport Cruise Lines Ltd, Schiffbau: Schiffsmachinenbau – Schiffahrtstechnik, Hansa, 1969, Nr 3, pp211–230.

Jernbanen
Andersen, Ib V., Danake Statsbaners færger gennem 100 år, No.3, April 1972, p5–9.

The Motor Ship
The Motor Ship 'Venus': a 19½-knot passenger Sship for the Bergen S.S. Co's Bergen-Newcastle service. Pressure-charged airless-injection machinery of 10,000 shp, January 1931, pp430–437.
The Motor Ferry Ship 'Freia': built for the Korsör–Nyborg service, also for the open sea route from Kalundborg to Aarhus, December 1936, pp328–331.
A Large Ferry Motor Ship: 15 ½-knot vessel for the Danish–Norwegian route between Frederikshavn and Larvik, August 1937, pp168–171.
The Fastest Copenhagen–Oslo Passenger Ship, February 1938, p427.
Largest Danish Diesel Ferry Ship: fifth oil-engined vessel for the Great Belt service, April 1938, pp22–24.
An Anglo-German-built Passenger-car Ferry: the 'Jens Kofoed' with hull and superstructure constructed by Bartram and Sons, and engine installation and fitting-out by Bremer Vulkan. Twin C.P. propellers each driven by two 1,300 hp engines. To carry 1,200 passengers and 60–100 road vehicles, October 1963, pp280–283.
A 19-knot Passenger/Car Ferry for Gedser-Travemünde Service: four M.W.M. 2,000 bhp propulsion engines driving twin screws in the Moltzau Line's 'Travemünde', August 1964, pp210–212.
'Munster': first of a series of Irish roll-on, roll-off ferries, June 1968, pp141–144.
'Koningin Juliana', a Dutch-owned, British-built ferry, November 1968, pp360–362.
'Starward': a 13,100 gross ton cruise liner enters service in the Caribbean', March 1969, pp613–616.

Sea Lines
Harvey, Clive (ed) Dear Bliss: Freeport and Starward, No 22, Spring 2001, pp19–21.

The Shipping World
Car and Passenger Ferry 'Skandia': new vessel from Finnish shipyard, June 1961, p577.

Shipbuilding and Shipping Record
'Viking 1': New Channel roll-on/roll-off ferry for Otto Thoresen, May 1964, pp716–718.

Shipping World & Shipbuilder
Barclay, C., 'Sunward': Design Considerations, January 1967, pp247–253.
'Visby': ro/ro ferry for Baltic service: Yugoslavian-built car and passenger ferry incorporating Nohab-Polar uniform machinery, April 1973, pp439–441.
'Tor Britannia': first of two new ro/ro ferries for Tor Line' (Tor Britannia Feature), June 1975, pp2–15.

Vingehjulet
Nellemann, T., De ældeste Jærnbanefærger, No. 22, 25 August 1958, pp253–258.

Welt der Fährschiffahrt
Bergenek, Anders, Die vier 'Sherries' Teil 1: Ein neuartiger Dienst entsteht, April 1996, pp30–38.

Other documents
Biographical notes from Niels Fisker-Andersen, formerly of Knud E. Hansen A/S, supplied to the author.

Index

14 July, 54
14 Ramadan, 54
A.P. Møller A/S, 43, 87, 89, 145, 195, 217
A/S Bornholm-Færgen, 61
A/S Dalen Portland Cement Fabrik, 44
A/S Europafergen, 67
A/S Ramses, 85
Aalborg Maskin- og Skibsbyggeri, 17, 18, 22
Aalborg Værft, 25, 35, 46, 58, 61, 75, 77, 84, 155, 159, 172
Aalsgaard, Finn, 55
Abegweit, 172
ACE-Link, 215
Adda, 85
Adler Werft, 59
Admiral Atlantic, 142
Admiral Caribe, 142
Admiral Pacific, 142
Adrian Mærsk, 145
Ærøboen, 82
Ærø-pilen, 115
Ærøsund, 47, 59
Afrodite, 72
AG Weser, 87, 97, 103, 110
Agner, Preben, 28, 33, 40, 55, 85, 87, 89, 185
Ailsa, 44
Aker Finnyards, 197
Al Merbid, 91
Al Miqdad, 58
Al Omarah, 54
Al Waldid Al Saadi, 90
Al Zahraa, 145
Albert Mærsk, 145
Al-Khalij Al-Arabi, 91
Alli, 85
Al-Mansur, 160
Alondra, 243
Al-Rasheed, 54
Alssunds Skibsværft, 37, 40
Al-Waleed, 54
Amal, 44
Amely, 85
American Reefer, 25
AMK Design, 131
Amlie, Richard, 55, 87, 89
Anabar, 183
Anders Mærsk, 145
Andrew Salman, 85
Andwi, 55
Anek Lines, 177, 189, 190, 206, 217
Anette Mærsk, 43
Angamos, 25
Ångfartygs AB Bore, 51
Anna Mærsk, 145
Anne Bøgelund, 87
Anne Reed, 44
Anne Sif, 195
Antarctic, 32
Arcadia, 126
Arctic Gull, 35
Arctic Propane, 85
Argentinean Reefer, 25
Århus Flydedok og Maskinkompagni, 58, 85, 89
Ariadne, 145
Arina Arctica, 185
Arini, Francesca, 249
Arison, Ted, 82, 97, 155
Armement Deppe SA, 55
Arnatindur, 89
Arthur Mærsk, 145
Asterillos MCIES, 216
Asterillos Matagorda, 90
Astilleros de Huelva, 216
Astilleros Españoles, 197
Astrid Rarberg, 85

Ateliers et Chantiers de la Seine-Maritime, 67, 72
Atid, 44
Atid Mediterranean Lines, 44
Atlantic Container Line, 7, 79, 144, 237
Atlantic Project, 144
Atlantic Prosper, 144
Atlantic Sail, 237
Atlantic Sea, 237
Atlantic Sky, 237
Atlantic Star, 237
Atlantic Sun, 237
Atlantida, 233
Attica Group, 199, 204, 223
Aukra Bruk A/S, 85
Aurella, 114, 138
Australian Reefer, 25
Avon Forest, 135, 137
Awassi Express, 243
Axel Mærsk, 145
Babylon, 89
Baghdad, 89
BAHRI, 7, 235
Bahri Abha, 235
Balgees, 145
Bambi, 44
Banana, 87
Baron Ardrossan, 89
Baron Dunmore, 55
Baron Forbes, 55
Baron Inchcape, 89
Baron Wemyss, 89
Bartram and Sons Ltd, 61
Bastant, 85
Bastø I, 33, 35
Bastø V, 110
Bastø VI, 44
BC Ferries, 67, 172, 191
Beauval, 44
Bech, Søren, 37
Bel Geddes, Norman, 25
Bellatrix, 85
Bergens Mekaniske Verksteder, 55, 81
Bertelsen, Svend Aage, 28, 33, 36, 54, 55, 58, 84, 87, 91, 110, 122, 131, 144, 153, 179, 185
Besseggen, 44
Beta, 87
Betula, 84
Bewa Discoverer, 131
Bewa Line A/S, 131
Bidsted & Co, 195
Bijkers Aannemingsbedrijf, 43
Bijkers Scheepswerf, 87
Biologen, 89
Birger Jarl, 36, 51
Birka Line, 156
Birka Princess, 156
Bison, 138
Bjørn Bjiornstad & Co., 44
Black Sea Steamship Company, 99
Blohm & Voss, 145, 211
Blue Highway Line, 217
Blue Ocean A/S, 223
Blue Star Delos, 223
Blue Star Ferries, 204, 219, 223
Blue Star Ithaki, 223
Blue Star Naxos, 223
Blue Star Paros, 223
Blue Star Patmos, 223
Bodewes Scheepswerf Volharding, 191
Boelwerf, 191
Bo-Hai Shipyard, 233
Bolero, 98
Bornholms-trafikken, 172
Botnia, 111
Brandur Sigmundarson, 44
Bratt-Götha AB, 80
Bremer-Vulkan GmbH, 61
Bris, 55
Brisk, 85
Britannia, 79

British & Irish Line, 72
Brodogradiliste Jozo Lozovina Mosor, 110
Brodogradiliste Kraljevica, 110, 214
Brødrene Olsen, 44
Broen, 32
Bruusgaard, Karl, 35
Bruusgaard, Sigurd, 44
Buen Provecho, 44
Buffalo, 138
Bunga Anggerik, 189
Burmeister & Wain, 7, 13, 21, 25, 28, 32, 43, 54, 84, 131, 142
C. Clausen Dampskibsrederi, 25, 126
Cabo Frio, 44
Caledonian MacBrayne, 110
Cammell Laird & Co., 84
Canadian National, 172, 179
Canberra, 126
Canopus, 89
Cantieri Navali del Tirreno e Riuniti, 126
Cap Lambert, 137
Cap Lobos, 137
Cape Clear, 55
Cape Grafton, 89
Cape Grenville, 89
Cape Hawke, 89
Cape Horn, 89
Capella, 89
Cargospeed, 135, 137
Caribou, 179, 211
Carlsson, Rolf, 75, 79
Carnival Corportation, 215
Carnival Cruise Line, 155, 233
Carola, 66
Celebrity Cruises, 199
Cementine, 44
Centrumlinjen, 84
Chantiers de l'Atlantique, 77, 149, 156
Chantiers du Havre, 110
Chantiers du Nord, 174
Chesapeake Shipbuilding Corporation, 153, 155
Christensen, Hanne, 55
Christian Holm, 89
Christian IV, 77, 84
Christofer Polhem, 66
Christoffersen, Torgeir, 77
Circle Line, 155
Clipper Group, 216, 225
Clipper Pace, 216
Clipper Panorama, 216
Clipper Pennant, 216
Clipper Point, 216
Clipperen, 40, 43
Colleen Sif, 195
Colon Brown, 145
Compagnie Maritime Nantaise (CMN), 235
Copemar 1, 44
Copenhagen, 98, 99
Cort Adeler (I), 47, 61, 75
Cort Adeler (II), 138, 140
Costa Riviera, 153
Costanzi, Nicolò, 126
Costas, 85
Crown Odyssey, 159
Crystal Cruises, 156, 159
Crystal Harmony, 156, 159
Cunard, 123, 125, 131, 199
Cunard Adventurer, 125, 126, 127, 131
Cunard Ambassador, 125, 127, 131
Cunard Countess, 131
Cunard Princess, 131
Cynthia Bres, 85
Daewoo Shipbuilding and Engineering, 219
Dafra Line, 87
Daisetsu, 189
Dalian Shipyard, 214
Damen, 233, 245

Damen Schelde Naval Shipbuilding, 245
Dampskibsselskab paa Bornholm af 1866, 28, 61
Dampskibsselskabet Ærø, 47, 82
Dampskibsselskabet Jutlandia, 43
Dampskibsselskabet Øresund, 17
Dampskibs-Selskabet paa Bornholm af 1866, 21
Dampskibsselskabet Torm, 189
Dampskipsselskapet Ibis, 44
Damsgaard, Christian, 249
Dana Atlas, 142
Dana Cimbria, 185
Dana Futura, 142
Dana Gloria, 142
Dana Maxima, 142, 172, 184
Dana Scarlett, 66
Danae, 149, 184
Dania Désgagnes, 243
Danielsen, Otto, 44, 85
Danish Arrow, 145
Danish Dart, 145
Danish National Maritime Museum, Kronborg, 22
Danmark, 110
Dannebrog, 167, 179, 180, 181
Dannebrog Værft, 167
Da-No Linjen, 110
Danske Statsbaner (DSB), 17, 22, 25, 28, 32, 45, 46, 110, 172
Dansk-Fransk Dampskibs-selskab, 85, 87
Danyard, 189
Daphne, 149, 184
De Danske Sukkerfabrikker, 87
De Mervede Van Vliet & Co., 66
Det Bergenske Dampskipsselskap, 13, 28, 127
Det Forenede Dampskibs-Selskab (DFDS), 21, 49, 61, 92, 142, 145, 167, 172, 178, 185, 197, 211, 214, 237, 239
Deutsche Reichsbahn, 25
Dilling, Troels, 145
Disko, 99
Ditlev Lauritzen, 189
Ditlev-Simonsen, Sverre, 81
Ditte Holmo, 85
Djursland, 35, 36
Djursland II, 109
Dok Kodja Bahri, 190
Donghia, Angelo, 149
Dorthe Danielsen, 87
Dronning Ingrid, 172
Dubigeon-Normandie, 77, 98, 178
Duchess, 155
Duke of Yorkshire, 138, 140
Dyvi Swan, 185
Dyvi Swift, 185
Dyvi Teal, 185
Dyvi Tern, 185
Dyvi, Jan-Erik, 185
E. J. Smit & Zonen, 85, 87
Eagle, 98
East Asiatic Company, 7
Ebba Victor, 85
Edith Borthen, 44
Eitzen Group, 215
Eklund, Gunnar, 114
El. Venizelos, 177
Elizabeth Hentzer, 89
Elk, 144
Ellen Helleskov, 87
Ellerman Wilson Line, 77, 79
Elly, 89
Elly Jensen, 40
Else Danielsen, 85
Elyros, 217
England, 49
England–Sweden Line, 77, 80, 81
Eny Højsgaard, 87
Erichs, Gerhard, 28, 33, 35, 40, 43, 54, 55, 85, 87, 89, 172
Eriksbergs Varv, 32

Esbjerg, 58
Esbjerg Jernstøberi & Maskinfabrik A/S, 53
Estaleiros Navais de Viano do Costelo, 233
Estelle Mærsk, 43
Estonia, 195
Etly Danielsen, 85
Europa, 233
European Ambassador, 197
European Causeway, 197
European Highlander, 197
European Highway, 199
European Pathway, 199
European Seaway, 199
Falster, 142
Farcus, Joe, 155
Farsea, 54, 55
Farstad, Sverre, 54
Fearnley & Eger, 28, 44, 119, 122, 123
Federal Commerce & Navigation Ltd, 135
Federal Rhine, 145
Federal Schelde, 145
Federal St Lawrence, 145
Felania, 145
Felipes, 145
Fernfjord, 28
Fernwood, 44
Ferry Hamanasu, 189
Ficus, 145
Fincantieri, 214, 233
Finnboda Varv, 36, 45, 51, 85, 135, 145
Finnlines, 113
Finska Ångfartygs Aktiebolaget, 51, 85
Fisker, Kay, 13, 21, 28
Fisker-Andersen, Niels, 184
Fjordshell, 145
Flagship Cruises, 122, 123, 127
Flammulina, 145
Flemming Sif, 195
Flensburger Schiffbau-Gesellschaft, 82
Floria, 85
Fossarina, 145
Fossarius, 145
Fr. Lürssen Werft, 84
France, 85, 92, 149, 184
Fred. Olsen & Co., 13, 85, 177
Frederikshavn Værft & Flydedok A/S, 17, 32, 43, 44, 85, 142, 185
Frederiksstads Mekaniske Verksteder, 44
Freeport, 89, 98, 99, 103, 107, 113, 115
Freia, 17, 18, 25, 32
Freyfaxi, 85
Frigg Sydfyen, 167
Fujinagata Shipyard, 87
Fulgur, 145
Fusus,, 145
G.C. Amdrup, 25
Galati Shipyard, 233, 245
Gardner, James, 125
Garm, 53
Gazania, 85
Gdynia Stocnia i Komuni Paryski, 174
Gedser (I), 61, 66
Gedser (II), 103
George Brown & Co. (Marine) Ltd, 28
George Brown (Marine) Ltd, 135
Gerda Rarberg, 89
Gerore, 55
Gertie, 195
Geslin, Stéphane, 215, 249
Gitte Danielsen, 85
Golden Odyssey, 131, 159, 160
Gotaas-Larsen, 119
Gothenburg–Frederikshavn Linjen, 32
Gotland (I), 66
Gotland (II), 111, 113, 181
Gotland (III), 190, 191, 195

Gotland (IV), 214
Gotlandia, 66
Gotlandsbolaget, 64
Govan Shipbuilders, 185
Grand Manan V, 191
Grenaa, 22, 35, 46, 59, 61, 109
Grenaa-Hundested Færgefart, 22, 35, 46, 59
Grieg, Halfdan, 55
Grimaldi Group, 237
Grung, Geir, 121
Guanabara, 243
Guanzhou Shipyard, 214
Guglielmo Marconi, 153
Gustav Vasa (I), 72, 77
Gustav Vasa (II), 107, 211
Gute, 144
H.M. Wrangell A/S, 35
Hagen, Jens C., 110
Hallen, Martin, 119
Hamlet, 84, 89
Hammer, Mogens, 82, 121
Hammershus, 21, 28
Hanjin Heavy Industries, 189
Hans Hedtoft, 44
Hans Mærsk, 43
Hans Priess, 85
Hansa Stahl & Schiffbau, 46, 47
Hanseatische Werft, 44
Hansen, Knud E., 7, 8, 13, 17, 18, 21, 25, 28, 36, 37, 43, 47, 55
Hapag-Lloyd Shipyard, 149
Hardanger Sunnhorlandske Dampskipsselskap, 36
Hardangerfjord, 36
Hardingen, 36
Harland & Wolff, 149, 152
Harry Borthen & Co., 44
Hartvig Mærsk, 43
Haugesunds Mekaniske Verksted, 54, 87, 145
Hawea, 97, 138
Heering Line, 87
Heering Lotte, 87
Heering Susan, 87
Heering, Peter, 87
Helen Sif, 195
Hellenic Seaways, 223
Hellenic Shipyards, 223
Hellenic Spirit, 217
Helsingborgs Varv, 53, 85
Helsingør Jernskibs og Maskinbyggeri, 7, 13, 25
Helsingør Skibsværft, 28, 36, 110, 131, 137, 179, 185
Henriette Mærsk, 43
Henriksen, Per, 142
Herald of Free Enterprise, 191
Hermes, 206
Hillah, 59
Hinckley, Steedman, 125
Hitachi, 54, 142, 145
Hoi Kung, 35
Holiday, 155, 156
Holland Jachtbouw, 243
Home Lines, 122
Homeric, 156
Horn, Klaus, 197
Howaldtswerke Deutsche Werft, 49, 195, 204
Hudong Zhonghua Shipyard, 237
Hundested, 61
Hurtigruten, 127, 181, 233
Husumer Schiffswerft, 47, 84, 85, 115
Hvalfangerselskapet Antarctic A/S, 32
Hvide Sande Shipyard, 216
HW Metalbau, 111
Hyundai Shipbuilding & Heavy Industry, 144, 145, 189, 195, 235
I.M. Skaugen & Co., 55, 119
Iberian Tankers Co., 32
Ibn Batouta, 67
IHC Verschure, 59, 91

Imperial Acadia, 85
Indian Reefer, 25
Indirka, 183
Industrie Navali Merchaniche Affine, 131
Inge Toft, 43, 156
Inge Wonsild, 215
Inger C., 195
Inger Højsgaard, 87
Innisfallen, 72
Iraqi Line, 87
Iraqi Maritime Transport Company, 53, 59, 89, 91
Iraqi Port Administration, 53, 90
Irish Continental Line, 109
Irish Ferries, 197
Irland, 85
Ischia Express, 17
Isefjord, 36
Ishikawajima Shipyard, 142
Island Venture, 122, 123
Isle of Innisfree, 197
Ivar Lauritzen, 189
IZAR Shipyard, 211
J. Lauritzen A/S, 22, 25, 44, 189, 214
J.J. Sietas, 114, 138, 243
Jadewerft, 85
Jadrolinija, 66
Jahre Line, 47, 49, 54, 79, 82
Jahre, Anders, 47
Jamal, 183
Janegaz, 85
Jansson, Bengt Olof, 195
Jansson, Kaj, 114
Javaj, 183
Jens Kofoed (I), 61, 75, 84
Jens Kofoed (II), 172
Jens Rand, 85
Jensen, Gunner, 55
Jensen, Jørgen, 46
Jensen, L. Harboe, 44
Johan Gerrards Rederi, 55
Jørgen Lauritzen, 189
Joseph and Clara Smallwood, 179, 211
Juelsminde–Kalundborg Linien, 59, 85
Julle, 59, 61, 66
Jydsk Færgefart, 110
K/S Bulkship A/S, 85
K/S Nordline A/S, 98
Kaldnes Mekaniske Verksted, 32, 55, 67, 185
Kalkavan Shipyard, 195
Kalle, 59, 61, 66
Kalle III, 109
Källström, Ragnar, 80
Kanstrup, Jesper, 183
Kappel, Jens J., 145
Karras, John C., 149
Karstensens Skibsværft, 243
Kassim, 54
Katherine Sif, 195
Katzourakis, Michael, 131, 159
Kattegat (I), 45, 46, 59, 98
Kattegat (II), 110
Kekkonius, Erik, 80
Kenitha, 85
Ketty Danielsen, 85
Khawla, 145
Kherson Shipyard, 89
Kilgas Champion, 195
Kinshasa, 87
Kirsten Sif, 195
Kirvi, 85
Kjærgaard, Hans, 89, 90, 91, 92, 111, 127, 131, 138, 145, 149, 152, 153, 155, 156, 159, 160, 172, 180, 185, 190, 195
Kleven, 85
Kloster, Knut, 81, 82, 91, 92, 97, 98, 126, 149, 151, 152, 153, 155, 159, 199
Knud E. Hansen A/S, 7, 13, 14, 21, 25, 28, 32, 33, 36, 37, 38, 40,

43, 44, 45, 46, 47, 49, 51, 53, 54, 55, 58, 59, 61, 64, 66, 67, 72, 75, 77, 79, 80, 81, 82, 84, 87, 89, 90, 91, 92, 97, 98, 99, 103, 107, 109, 111, 114, 115, 119, 122, 123, 125, 126, 127, 131, 135, 137, 138, 140, 142, 144, 145, 148, 149, 151, 152, 153, 155, 156, 159, 160, 167, 172, 178, 179, 180, 181, 183, 185, 189, 190, 191, 195, 197, 199, 206, 211, 214, 215, 216, 217, 219, 223, 225
Knud Lauritzen, 189
Knutsen, Knut, 21
København, 81, 82, 84
Københavns Flydedok & Skibsværft, 13
Kong Olav V, 167
Kongedybet, 28, 32
Kongelige Grønlandske Handel, 44
Kongsholm, 44
Koningin Juliana, 84, 89
Kørbing, J.A., 21
Korsør, 14
Kraakerø, 72
Kremer & Sohn, 54, 72
Kristiansand Dampskipsselskap, 36, 75, 77, 84
Kristiansands Mekaniske Verksteder, 36, 44, 55, 85, 137
Kristiansen, John, 142
Kriti I, 206
Kriti II, 206
Krögerswerft, 84
Kronprins Carl Gustav, 72
Kronprins Frederik, 172
Kronprins Harald, 49, 51, 54
Kronprins Olav, 21, 22, 25, 35
Kronprinsessan Ingrid, 32, 66
Kungsholm, 72, 122
Kurki, 85
Kvaerner Masa Yards, 204
La Bonita, 85
Laakso, Vuokko, 121
Laivateollisuus Oy, 85, 89
Lalonde, François, 98
Lalonde, Pierre, 98
Langeland III, 185, 189
Langeland To, 167
Langenberg, Hans, 145
Langesunds Mekaniske Verksteder, 44, 66, 72, 75
Larsen, Niels Georg, 249
Larvik-Frederikshavn Fergen, 47, 59, 84, 114, 137, 138, 142, 167, 177
Lasse, 61
Lasse II, 110
Laura Danielsen, 85
Laurentian Forest, 135, 137
Lauritz Kloster Rederi, 81
Lauritzen, Ivar, 22
Lauritzen, Knud, 22
Leif Ericson, 172
Leivur Ossursson, 44
Leonora Christina, 225
Levander, Kai, 155, 156
Leviathan, 14
Liburnija, 66
Lignes Maritimes du Detroit (Limadet), 67
Linblad Explorer, 245
Linda Clausen, 25, 126
Linda Scarlett, 47, 66
Lindblad Explorer, 99
Lindholmens Varv, 79, 81
Lindstøls Skips og Båtbyggeri, 82, 115, 181
Linjebuss, 45, 47, 66, 84
Lion, 89
Lion Ferry AB, 67, 72, 80, 107, 109
Lissos, 190
Lloyd Werft, 152, 217, 219
Loesch, Henning, 215

Loewy, Raymond, 25
Lohals, 82
Lokki, 85
Lone Krogh, 85
Lonni, 85
Lorentzen, Øivind, 44, 122, 123
Lübecker Flenderwerke, 81, 115, 145
Lucy Maud Montgomery, 172
Lund, Thorkil, 21, 28
Lütken, Herluf, 33, 40, 55
Lysland, 55
Mabella, 35
Machinefabriek en Scheepswerf van P. Smit Jr, 125
Madsen, Erik, 33, 55
Madsen, Gunnar Toft, 28, 33, 55, 92
Maersk Delft, 217
Maersk Dover, 217
Maersk Dunkerque, 217
Mærsk Euro Primo, 195
Mærsk Euro Quarto, 195
Mærsk Euro Quinto, 195
Mærsk Euro Tertio, 195
Mærsk Lima, 195
Malmö, 84
Maren Mols, 61
Margit Brøvig, 35
Marianne Wonsild, 215
Marine Atlantic, 179, 211
Marinens Hovedverft, 44, 46, 55
Marsk Stig, 22, 36
Marstal, 82
Marstal Skibsværft, 89
Martin Jansen Werft, 82
Massalia, 98, 195
Matthews, Victor, 131
Mayflower Energy, 223
McGoff, John P., 153, 155
Mercandia Rederi, 92, 142, 185
Mercandian Arrow, 185
Mercandian Carrier II, 142
Mercandian Continent, 185
Mercandian Exporter II, 142
Mercandian Giant, 185
Mercandian Globe, 185
Mercandian Merchant II, 142
Mercandian Ocean, 185
Mercandian Sea II, 185
Mercandian Sun II, 185
Mercandian Supplier II, 142
Mercandian Trader II, 142
Mercandian Transporter II, 142
Mercandian Universe, 185
Mercandinan Importer III, 142
Mercantic, 85
Mette Mols, 61
Mette Pan, 85
Meyer Werft, 54, 84, 110, 156, 159
Midnatsol, 181
Mignon, 135
Mikkel Mols, 61
Mineral Ougree, 55
Minoan Lines, 199, 206
Mitsubishi Heavy Industries, 156, 197
Mobil Engineer, 145
Mobil Navigator, 145
Mobil Tankers Co., 145
Mogens Græsborg, 85
Molindris & Associates, 223
Møller, Erik, 47, 54, 87, 145
Moltzau, Ragnar, 37, 61, 82, 103, 109, 115, 140, 181, 215
Morten Mols, 61
Moss Verft & Dokk A/S, 35, 85
MPI Resolution, 223
Mundogas Brasilia, 44
Munster, 72
Nakskov Skibsværft, 25, 172
Nanfri, 55
Narvik, 181
National Shipping Company of Saudi Arabia, 7, 235
Nauta Ship Repair, 243
Nedlloyd, 185
Nelly Mærsk, 43

Neue Flensburger Schiffbau, 211
New Suzuran, 206
New Yukari, 206
Niels Mærsk, 43
Nielsen, Harry, 53
Nielsen, Steen, 152, 180, 199
Niestern Kerstolt, 87
Nighashi Nihon Ferry, 206
Nili, 82
Nils Dacke (I), 107, 115
Nils Dacke (II), 199
Nils Holgersson, 199
Nilsson, Eric D., 66, 110
Nilsson, Finn, 127
Nippon Yusen Kaisha, 156
Nora, 25
Norasia Line, 195, 214
Norasia Adria, 195
Norasia Fribourg, 195
Norasia Hong Kong, 195
Norasia Kiel, 195
Norasia Melita, 195
Norasia Shanghai, 195
Norasia Singa, 195
Norbella, 55
Nordbornholm, 22
Nordby, 58
Nordia, 53
Nordic Prince, 121, 122
Normandiet, 87
Norröna (I), 211
Norröna (II), 211
Norsea, 185
Norske Københavnlinje, 81, 82
Norsun, 185
North East Shipbuilders, 181
Norway, 92, 149, 151, 184
Norwegian Caribbean Line, 82, 92, 97, 98, 110, 119, 121, 126, 127, 149, 151, 152, 155, 159
Nuka Ittuk, 185
Nyborg, 14
Nystads Varv AB, 99
Oceanic, 122, 126
Odd Berg Rederi, 35
Odessa, 99
Odfjell Rederi, 85
Odin Sydfyen, 167
Øernes Dampskibsselskab, 115
Ofelia, 84
Ofotens Dampskipsselskap, 181
Ölanningen, 66
Olau Britannia, 225
Olavur Halgi, 44
Olesen, Ole, 91, 92, 160, 190, 206, 249
Olofsson, Helge, 72
Olsson, Sten A., 59, 72, 75, 110, 138, 166
Olympia Explorer, 211
Olympia Voyager, 211
Olympic Champion, 217
Olympic Voyager, 211
Orenstein & Koppel und Lübecker Machinenbau, 61, 67, 81, 91, 98
Øresund, 46, 77
Øresundsbolaget, 46, 84, 107
Øresundsvarvet, 66, 67, 177, 181
Orlogsværftet, 14, 84, 179
Ormen, 89
Ørskov Skibsværft, 44, 45, 85, 89, 185, 195, 197
Oskarshams Varv, 32
Østberg, Christian, 44
Østbornholm, 22
Østbornholm Dampskibsselskab, 22
Österreichische Shiffswerften AG, 58, 138
Østersøen, 32
Overseas National Airways, 125
P&O, 97, 123, 126, 138, 144, 156, 159, 185, 197, 199
P. Høivolds Mekaniske Verksteder, 82
Pacific Clipper, 32
Pacific Orca, 223

Panagopoulos, Alexander, 199, 204
Panagopoulos, Pericles, 131, 156, 199, 223
Patria, 145
Patricia, 81
Pelmatic, 195, 214
Peter Pan, 199
Peter Wessel (I), 18, 21, 25, 32, 35, 47
Peter Wessel (II), 84, 114
Peter Wessel (III), 84, 114, 115, 167
Petersen, Franklin, 160, 185, 195
Phoenix World City, 152
Pimpernel, 85
Polaris, 99
Polarland, 55
Pollux, 145
Port Line, 149
Port Melbourne, 149
Port Sydney, 149
Port Weller Dockyard, 85, 135
Poseidon, 72
Post & Telegrafvæsnet, 53, 58
Poula Sinding, 85
Povl Anker, 172
Pride of Burgundy, 199
Pride of York, 185
Primula, 45, 46, 66
Prince of Fundy, 109
Prince of Scandinavia, 197
Prince of Wales, 215
Princess, 155
Princess Anne, 25
Princess Cruises, 123, 156
Princess of Scandinavia, 197
Prins Bertil, 67, 72, 172
Prins Filip, 191
Prins Joachim, 172
Prins Oberon, 107
Prins Richard, 197
Prinses Beatrix, 172
Prinses Paola, 190
Prinsessan Birgitta, 225
Prinsessan Christina, 111, 225
Prinsessan Margaretha, 77
Prinsesse Anne-Marie, 46
Prinsesse Benedikte, 197
Prinsesse Elisabeth, 46
Prinsesse Margrethe, 167
Prinsesse Ragnhild, 49
Prip, Niels, 195
Probo Bani, 189
Pulpships AB, 53
Pulptrader, 53
Pusnæs Mekaniske Verksted, 35, 36, 44
Qidissiyat Al Saddam, 160
Queen Elizabeth, 215
Queen Elizabeth 2, 125, 127
Queen of Esquimalt, 172
Queen of Prince Rupert, 67
Queen of Saanich, 172
Queen of Vancouver, 172
Queen of Westminster, 172
Raffles Shipping, 189
Ralf, Eva, 80
Ras Mærsk, 43
Rasmussen, Poul Erik, 36, 37, 38, 59, 144, 145, 156
Ratona Sopa, 195
Råwall, Sven Erik, 166
Rederi A/S Alpha, 35, 110
Rederi AB Atlanta, 85
Rederi AB Clipper, 32
Rederi AB Gotland, 64, 66, 107, 110, 111, 113, 144, 177, 190, 206
Rederi AB Nordö, 64, 66, 142, 144
Rederi AB Oceanfart, 85
Rederi AB Rex, 80
Rederi Ab Sally, 177
Rederi Clipperfart A/S, 40
Rederiet Tønseth, 55
Regie voor Maritiem Transport, 191
Regula, 84
Remontova Shipyard, 215

Rickmers Werft, 166
Ripley, Don, 82
Robert Mærsk, 43
Robin Hood, 199
Rogan, Tony, 82
Rogne, Dag, 32, 33, 55, 59, 66, 72, 75, 77, 80, 81, 82, 84, 85, 92, 107, 110, 114, 115, 135, 140, 142, 144, 166, 167
Rolandwerft, 54, 61
Rolf Wiglans Rederi A/S, 55
Rolwi, 55
Romeo, 85
Romø Mærsk, 43
Rønland, 89
Rotna, 28
Rotterdam Drydock Company, 125
Royal Caribbean, 119, 121, 122, 127, 131, 152, 159, 199, 215
Royal Cruise Line, 131, 156, 159, 199
Royal Odyssey, 156, 159
Royal Olympic Cruises, 211
Royal Princess, 155, 156, 159
Royal Viking Line, 127
Rubicon, 85
Rumalia, 90
Saga, 79, 81
Saga Cruises, 233
Saga Sapphire, 233
Saint Patrick, 109
Salén, Christer, 114
Salénrederiena, 114
Samothraki, 189
Sampe, Astrid, 79
Samsung Heavy Industries, 185, 223
San Sha 1 Hao, 233
Sankt Ibb, 14
Saqqit Ittuk, 195
Sarfaq Ittuk, 195
Sarpik Ittuk, 195
Sarpsborg Mekaniske Verksted, 28
Scandinavia (I), 142
Scandinavia (DFDS), 178, 179, 211
Scandinavia (II), 145
Scandinavian Star, 195
Scandinavian World Cruises, 178
Scandlines, 197
Scania, 75, 84
Scheepswerf Hoogezand, 85, 167
Scheepswerf Kerstholt, 85
Scheepswerf Ferus Smith, 87
Schichau Seebeckwerft, 199
Schiedam Scheepswerf, 47
Schiffahrts-Gesellschaft 'Jade', 59
Schiffbau-Gesellschaft Unterweser, 64, 103, 109, 131
Scottish Ship Management, 55, 87, 89
Sea Goddess I, 160
Sea Goddess II, 160
Sea Venture, 122, 123, 131, 190
Sea Venture Cruises, 190
Seatruck Ferries, 216
Seaward, 126
Sekwang Heavy Industries, 215
Selandia, 7
Sessanlinjen, 75, 77, 111
SF Line, 114
Shalom, 156
Shanhaiguan Shipyard, 223
Shin Nihonkai Ferry, 206
Silja Line, 111, 114
Siljarederiet, 51, 53, 61, 85
Siluna Ace, 215
Simara Ace, 215
Sisu, 85
Sjælland, 14
Skaarup, Ole, 145
Skagen, 36
Skagerak, 75, 77, 84
Skála Skibsvaerft, 89
Skandia, 51, 53, 61
Skandinavisk Linjetrafik, 46, 47, 66, 110
Skåne (I), 77

Skåne (II), 197
Skausund, 55
Skib A/S Widan, 85
Skrydstrup, Morten, 59, 185, 195
Skyward, 98, 99, 107, 121, 126, 184
Smyril, 211
Smyril Line, 211
SNCF, 77, 98
Sneland, 89
Snowman, 85
Società Esercizio Cantieri, 214
Sollys, 55
Sölvesborg Varv, 85
Sønderho, 53
Song of Norway, 121, 122
Sorvali, Heikki, 121
Sotka, 85
Southward, 126, 184
Spencer, Robert, 249
Spero, 80
Spirit of British Columbia, 191
Spirit of London, 126
Spirit of Vancouver Island, 191
Spitzbergen, 233
St George, 84
Stamboulelis, Costis, 159, 199, 223
Star Line Corporation, 153
Star of Detroit, 153, 155
Starward, 89, 97, 98, 99, 107, 110, 121, 126, 184
Stella, 85
Sten A. Olsson, 67, 72
Stena Atlantica, 166
Stena Baltica, 72, 75
Stena Britannica (I), 75
Stena Britannica (III), 216, 217
Stena Carrier, 214
Stena Constructor, 181
Stena Danica (I), 72, 75, 84, 172
Stena Danica (II), 103, 107, 110
Stena Danica (III), 110, 114, 167, 172
Stena Danica (IV), 174, 219
Stena Forecaster, 214
Stena Forerunner, 214
Stena Foreteller, 214
Stena Germanica (I), 75, 82, 98, 107
Stena Germanica (II), 177
Stena Inspector, 181
Stena Jutlandica (I), 110, 114, 167
Stena Jutlandica (II),172
Stena Line, 58, 59, 72, 75, 103, 110, 138, 144, 145, 172, 177, 191, 216, 219
Stena Nautica, 166
Stena Nordica (I), 72, 75, 84
Stena Nordica (II), 166
Stena Normandica, 181
Stena Olympica, 113
Stena Piper, 181
Stena Protector, 181
Stena Ro-Ro, 211, 214, 245
Stena Scandinavica (I), 113, 177
Stena Scandinavica (II), 217
Stena Seaspread, 181
Stena Seawell, 181
Stena Superfast VII, 219
Stena Superfast VIII, 219
Stena Supplier, 181
Stena Tender, 138
Stena Timer, 140
Stena Topper, 140
Stena Wellservicer, 181
Stensnæs, 40
Stephan, Edwin, 119
Stockholms Rederi AB Svea, 36, 45, 47, 49, 51, 53, 66, 67, 75, 77, 79, 81, 85, 107, 137
Stocznia im Lenina, 174
Stoomvaart Maatschappij Zeeland, 82, 172
Stord Verft, 36, 44
Storebælt, 22
Strandfaraskip Landsins, 211, 233
Studio de Jorio, 153
STX, 225

Suarez, Javier, 249
Suilven, 110
Sun Viking, 121, 122, 127
Sundbuss Baronen, 103
Sundbuss Erasmus, 115
Sundbuss Henrik, 37
Sundbuss Henrik II, 82
Sundbuss Jeppe, 37, 115
Sundbuss Magdelone, 115
Sundbuss Pernille, 37, 181
Sundbuss Pernille II, 82
Sunflower Tsukuba, 217
Sunward, 81, 82
Sunward Car Ferries, 81, 82
Sunward II, 126
Superfast, 199, 204, 206, 219
Superfast I, 199, 204
Superfast II, 199
Superfast III, 204
Superfast IV, 204
Superfast V, 204
Superfast VI, 204
Superfast VII, 204, 219
Superfast VIII, 219
Superfast X, 204
Superfast XI, 204
Superfast XII, 204
Svarer, Jørgen, 47
Svea, 79, 80, 81
Svea Drott, 67
Svea Jarl, 49, 51, 53
Svea Scarlett, 110
Svealand, 137, 138
Svendborg Skibsværft, 25, 32, 99, 145, 167, 185
Svenningsen, Hans, 28
Swan, Hunter & Wigham Richardson, 99, 149
Swedish Lloyd, 77, 79, 81, 82, 115
Swedish State Railway, 72, 77
SweFerry, 197
Swire Group, 223
Sydfyn, 82
Sydfynske Dampskibsselskab, 82, 167
T. Mariotti, 153
Taikoo Dockyard & Engineering Company, 97
Tavi, 85
Taygetos, 190
Technip, 225
Teddy, 28, 135
Temple Inn, 89
Terje Viken, 110
Terpet, Holger, 58, 156, 159, 177, 179, 185, 199, 204, 211, 223
Th. Brøvig Rederi, 35
Thea Danielsen, 85
Thor Sydfyen, 167
Thoresen Car Ferries, 67, 92
Thoresen, Otto, 59, 66, 67
Thorviks Rederi A/S, 55
Three Quays, 156
Tiira, 85
Tikkoo, Ravi, 152
Tillberg, Robert, 72, 75, 107, 122
Tina Scarlett, 46
Tine Gaj, 89
Tobitrader, 85
Tonto, 55
Tor Anglia, 81
Tor Britannia (I), 115, 185, 197
Tor Britannia (II), 214
Tor Hollandia, 81
Tor Line, 80, 81, 82, 114, 115
Tor Scandinavia, 115, 185, 197
Tor Selandia, 214
Tor Suecia, 214
Torben Mærsk, 43
Torm Helene, 189
Torm Herdis, 189
Törnquist, Åke, 80
TransNjord, 243
Trans-Oil AB, 80, 114

Trave Line, 67, 137
Travemünde, 61, 66
Troms Fylkes Dampskipsselskap, 181
Trondheims Mekaniske Verksted, 47, 181
Tronoen, 44
Tropicale, 155, 156
Tropicana, 190, 191
Trosvik Verksted A/S, 92
TSL Valiant, 195
Ulla Danielsen, 87
Ulla Skagbo, 44
Union Melbourne, 138
Union Steamship Company, 97, 138
United Axel, 190
United Tankers, 190
Uraniborg, 216
Ursula, 84
Usterud-Svendsen, Leif, 99
Valdemar Skogland A/S, 55
Valençay, 77
Valhall, 55
Valmet Oy, 43, 156
Van der Giessen, 185, 197
Varuna, 189
Venus, 13, 14, 28, 127
Verolme Scheepswerf Heusden, 172
Vesteralen, 181
Vesteralens Dampskibsselskap, 181
Vestland, 87
Vickers Ltd, 99
Victoria, 32
Viking I, 67
Viking II, 67
Viking III, 67
Viking IV, 92, 97
Viking Line, 110, 113, 114, 138
Viking Saga, 178
Viking Sally, 195
Viking Song, 178
Vikla, 85
Villandry, 77, 98
Virginia Ferry Corporation, 25
Visby (I), 66, 75, 84
Visby (II), 111, 113, 181
Visby (III), 177, 214
Vistafjord, 99
von der Lippe, Anton, 32
Wallenius, Olof, 135
Wanaka, 97, 138
Wandborg, Tage, 36, 37, 38, 40, 44, 45, 46, 49, 51, 54, 55, 58, 59, 61, 66, 72, 75, 79, 81, 82, 84, 85, 87, 97, 98, 99, 107, 110, 111, 113, 121, 122, 125, 126, 127, 131, 149, 151, 152, 156, 159, 160, 167, 177
Wappen Von Hamburg, 61
Warneke, Horst, 111
Wärtsilä Oy, 51, 119, 121, 127, 155, 156, 160, 178, 183, 204, 206, 211, 235, 245
Wasa Star, 177
Werft Nobiskrug, 67, 107, 109, 138
Westermøen Slipp, 37, 85, 87
Wikander, Lars, 115
Wilhelmsen, Anders, 119, 121
Wilhelmshaven, 61, 72
Wilstar, 121
Wilton-Fijenoord, 167
Wind Ambition, 225
Wind Perfection, 225
Wind Solution, 225
Wollesen Petersen, Finn, 214, 215, 217, 249
Wonsild & Søn, 215
Yardimci Shipyard, 195
Yarrows Shipyard, 191
Yran, Petter, 152, 215
Zaandamsche Scheepsbouw, 85
Zaanlandse Scheepsbouw, 66
Zenobia, 144